GREGORIVS

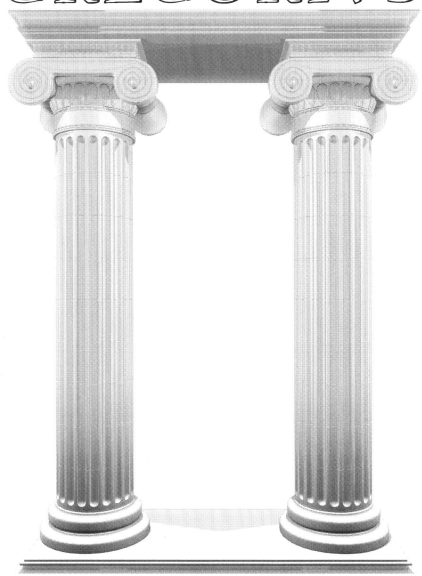

GREGORIVS PVBLISHING LLC Portland Oregon USA

To **Captain Robert B. Hock,**

the gallant and loyal comrade in the field,
the faithful and constant friend
during the dark days of my prison life,

the daring companion of my escape

and the three hundred mile tramp through the Confederacy,
who,
when I became too feeble to go farther,
so generously took out his purse
and gave me the largest half of its contents,

this book is gratefully dedicated

by the author.

In and Out of Rebel Prisons

By

Lieut. Alonzo Cooper,

12th N.Y. Cavalry

GREGORIVS Publishing LLC

GREGORIVS

GREGORIVS Publishing LLC
PO Box 230921
Portland OR 97281-0921

GREGORIVS@GREGORIVS.COM

WWW.GREGORIVS.COM

ISBN-10: 1452804230
ISBN-13: 9781452804231

Table of Contents

Table of Contents

Table of Contents

Table of Contents

Table of Contents

Author's Preface

Many books have been written upon prison life in the South, but should every survivor of Andersonville, Macon, Savannah, Charleston, Florence, Salisbury, Danville, Libby and Belle Island write their personal experiences in those rebel slaughter houses, it would still require the testimony of the sixty-five thousand whose bones are covered with Southern soil to complete the tale.

Being an officer, I suffered but little in comparison with what was endured by the rank and file, our numbers being less, our quarters were more endurable and our facilities for cleanliness much greater. Besides, we were more apt to have money and valuables, which would, in some degree, provide for our most urgent needs.

In giving my own personal experiences, I shall endeavor to write of the prison pens in which were confined only officers, just as I found them — "Nothing extenuate, nor set down aught in malice."

Being blessed with the happy faculty of looking upon the bright side of life, and possessing a hopeful disposition, unaccustomed to give way to despondency, I also write upon the bright side of my subject. The reader who expects to find in this book a volume of sickening details of the horrors of starvation and suffering endured by those whose misfortune it was to be confined in Andersonville, under that inhuman monster Wirz — the mention of whose name causes a shudder — will be disappointed. Having kept a complete diary of events during my ten months' imprisonment, I am able to give a reliable account of what came under my personal observation. I have often heard it said, even here in the North, that our men who were prisoners, were cared for as well as the limited means of the Confederacy would admit; but the falsity of this is seen when you remember that Andersonville is situated in a densely wooded country, and that much of the suffering endured was for the want of fuel with which to cook their scanty rations, and for the want of shelter, which they would have cheerfully constructed had the opportunity been afforded them. The evidence all goes to show that instead of trying to save the lives or alleviate the sufferings of those whom the fortunes of war had thrown into their hands, they practiced a systematic course of starvation and cruelty, that in this nineteenth century, seems scarcely believable. In this scheme, the arch traitor, Jeff. Davis, was most heartily assisted by the infamous Winder and his cowardly assistants, Wirz, Dick Turner, Tabb and others, whose timid hearts unfitted them for service in the field, but just qualified them for acts of atrocity and cruelty, such as were inflicted upon the loyal sons of the North who were in their power. Prison life, at best, to one who has been educated beneath the flag of freedom, is a trial hard to be endured; but when accompanied with indignities, insults and tortures, such as were inflicted upon the occupants of those prison hells of the South, it becomes simply unbearable.

Lieut. Alonzo Cooper

Chapter I.

Description of Plymouth, N. C.

Plymouth, in 1863-4, was a small town, situate on the Roanoke river, about six miles from where the waters of that stream enters the Albermarle Sound.

The river at Plymouth is nearly a quarter of a mile wide, and with a sufficient depth of water to float the largest draught gunboats. The shore next the town was supplied with a wharf for landing steamers that navigate the river; but the gunboats, of which there were quite a number stationed there, were usually anchored in the middle of the stream. The town was enclosed with earthworks, with the exception of about two hundred yards on the left next the river which was rather low and marshy, and covered with quite a thick growth of alders and other bushes. On the extreme right, on the bank of the river, was Battery Worth; a small earthwork, just large enough to work a two hundred pound Parrot gun, with which it was supplied, and accommodate twenty or thirty men to handle and support it. This was surrounded with a deep ditch; but on the side next the town it was protected only with a low breastwork with a wooden slat door, and a person could jump across the ditch and step over into the redoubt.

Extending south from this small earthwork ran a line of breastworks to the south-west corner of the town, when it turned at right angles, making a continuous line of works nearly two miles in length, completely surrounding the place, with the exception of the short space next the river on our extreme left, as before stated.

In the south center stood Fort Williams, a strong work; and some distance from the line of works on the right center was Fort Wessels, a small redoubt.

On the left of Fort Williams on the works facing east, were Comphor and Coneby redoubts, one each side of what was called the Columbia road. On each side of Fort Williams, which faced south, were sally ports, on what was called the Washington road and the middle road.

In our front, to the south, was an open field for a thousand or twelve hundred yards, the farther part of which was partially covered with the brush and stumps of the newly cleared field, and beyond this was woods. About a mile up the river, on what was called War Neck, as a protection to our extreme right, was Fort Gray, a work of considerable strength, garrisoned by the 96th New York.

Such is a brief description of Plymouth as it appeared in April, 1864.

Brig. Gen. W. H. Wessels was in command of the post, and Lieut. Commander Flusser was in command of the fleet of gun-boats, which consisted of the Miama, a large wooden double-ender, the Southfield, an old New York ferryboat under command of Capt. French, the Whitehead, Capt. Barrett, the Bombshell, and a small supply boat called the Dolly, with one or two other boats whose names I do not now remember.

These were all wooden boats, but were supplied with a good armament of heavy metal, and their commander, W. H. Flusser, was as gallant an officer as ever trod the quarter deck, and thoroughly determined to sink the rebel ram Albemarle, which had been built near Richmond, and was daily expected to come down the river, and attempt the destruction of our fleet, or sink every boat under his command. Being very intimately acquainted with Lieut. Commander Flusser, and knowing his plans, having been instrumental with the detachment of cavalry stationed there, in getting much valuable information in regard to the progress of the building and intentions of this ram, I can speak by card of his preparations for its destruction, when it should make its appearance.

Gen. Wessel's brigade consisted of two companies of the 12th N. Y. Cavalry, A and F, 85 men; two companies, H and G, of the 2d Massachusetts H. A., garrisoning the fort and redoubts; the 16th Connecticut, the 101st and 103d Pennsylvania, the 85th New York Infantry, and the 24th New York Independent Battery, Capt. Cady. There was also a company of North Carolina colored troops, Capt. Eastmond, and two companies of loyal North Carolinians, making in all about two thousand troops.

Chapter II.

the battle of Plymouth — the cavalry pickets driven in — Hoke appears

in our front with eight thousand men — a magnificent artillery duel —

four days hard fighting — sinking of the Southfield and defeat of the fleet

by the ram Albemarle.

On Sunday morning, April 17th, 1864, the consolidated morning report showed eighteen hundred and fifty men for duty. The day was warm and bright, and the men were scattered about the town with no thought of approaching danger. The cavalry had scouted the day before, a distance of twelve or fifteen miles, and found no signs of the enemy, but about 4 p. m., the cavalry pickets on the Washington road were driven in, and the Corporal, named Geo. Wilcox, came tearing through the company quarters of the 85th New York down to cavalry headquarters, with the nose bag still on his horse, which he had not had time to exchange for his bridle, swinging his hat and shouting: "The Rebs are coming! the Rebs are coming!"

By the absence of Capt. Roach, of Company A, and the sickness of Capt. Hock, of Company F, I was in command of the detachment of cavalry, and at once ordered a bugler who happened to be standing near, to sound boots and saddles; sent Lieutenant Russel, who was mounted, having just rode up, to headquarters, to notify General Wessels that our pickets had been driven in and ask for orders for the cavalry. He returned just as I had formed the two companies into line with orders to make a reconnaissance on the Washington road, and, without getting into a fight, ascertain, as near as I could, the strength of the enemy in our front.

I ascertained by a careful reconnaissance that Maj. Gen. Hoke was in front with about eight thousand troops. In this reconnaissance I lost one man, "Amos Fancher," killed, and one, "Lieut. Russell," severely wounded. Hoke formed his line and threw out his skirmishers, but made no further demonstrations that night, a few shells from Fort Williams having the effect of checking any further movement.

At 11 o'clock that night, Gen. Wessels sent the steamer Massasoit, carrying the women and other non-combatants, and the wounded, to Newbern. Among the women were Mrs. George H. Hastings, Mrs. Dr. Frick, Mrs. Capt. Hock, Mrs.

Bell, Mrs. and Miss Freeman and Mrs. A. Cooper (who had been with me from the 7th of February), and others. Preparations were made for a stout resistance by Gen. Wessels, who was a gallant officer. He established a strong skirmish line nearly two miles in length along our entire front and had everything in readiness to repel any attack that might be made; but the night passed without any further demonstration.

Early on the morning of the 18th there was slight skirmishing commenced along our entire front, and a bombardment was commenced upon Fort Gray, which was our extreme right and about one and one-half miles up the river.

In this bombardment the gunboat Bombshell, which had been sent to the assistance of the fort, was so crippled that she sank immediately upon reaching the wharf.

The attack on Fort Gray was repulsed, and our skirmish line in front maintained its position all day. At 5:30 p. m. I received orders to take the two companies of cavalry, dismounted, up to the breastworks near Fort Williams.

Fortunately I was mounted at the time, and rode up to the front, where, sitting on my horse, I had a splendid view of the battle that ensued.

We had just arrived at the breastworks when the skirmishing became brisk, our boys pushing the enemy's skirmishers back some distance, when suddenly, as if by magic, a line of battle over a mile in length seemed to spring up out of the ground and charged our skirmish line, driving them back towards the works. As they fell back, firing as they retired, Fort Williams opened with her entire armament, which, in a moment, was joined in by Comphor and Coneby redoubts, Fort Wessels, Cady's Independent Battery and the entire fleet of gunboats in the river.

Hoke opened on the town with forty-two pieces of artillery; Wessels replied with just about the same number of pieces, but of heavier caliber. From 6 until 8.30 p. m. was kept up a most terrific cannonade, which presented a spectacle awfully grand and magnificent. The gunboats, which were supplied with an armament of very heavy guns, sending immense shell shrieking and bursting over our heads as they were hurled into the lines of the enemy, the forts on our right and left keeping up an incessant roar, a stream of fire belching from the hot throats of Hoke's forty-two pieces in our front, the comet-like trail of fire from his shells as they hurried on their mission of death towards us, the rattle of grape and canister as they were hurled against the wooden buildings in our rear, or the woodwork of the forts and earthworks along the line, the loud bray of an immense number of mules, with which Hoke's artillery was supplied, the groans and shrieks of the wounded, combined to give me such a picture of "grim visaged war" as I had never before beheld.

Several assaults were made on our works, which were repulsed with heavy loss to the enemy. The heaviest fighting occurred on our right centre, where were stationed the 85th New York; but to quote from the gallant Phil. Kearny — "There was illegant fighting all along the line." A fearful assault was made on Fort Wessels, which was isolated from the line of works, and was a quarter of a mile distant on our right. This small fort or redoubt was defended by Lieut. H. Lee Clark, with part of a company of the 2d Massachusetts Heavy Artillery. It was protected by a deep ditch, twelve feet wide, with an abattis of pine limbs outside, with a draw bridge, which, when raised, formed a door to the entrance. It mounted four or five guns and was well supplied with hand grenades from one-half to two pounds. A number of determined assaults were made upon this work, and in one about sixty of the enemy got inside the abattis and surrounded the ditches; but Lieut. Clark used the hand grenades so effectually, the boys tossing them over with such precision, and at the same time keeping up such a succession of explosions at the sallyport, that they all surrendered, laid down their arms and were taken inside. Thus Lieut. Clark had twice the number of prisoners he had men under his command.

The small garrison of this fort were finally overcome by vastly superior numbers, but not until the enemy had lost in killed over triple the number of its brave defenders. The capture of this small redoubt was all they had gained in two day's persistent fighting, and then only after a fearful loss in killed and wounded. At 8.30 in the evening Hoke withdrew, having been defeated at every point with the exception of the capture of this small redoubt. Our loss was insignificant, as we were behind good works. During the engagement I was struck on the leg by a bullet out of a spherical case shot, but as my pants and drawers were inside of a heavy cavalry boot leg, and owing to the fact that the force of the ball was nearly spent, it only made a black and blue spot on the side of my leg. We lay at the breastworks all night, but no further demonstrations were made in our front that night. Before daylight the next morning, however, we were aroused by a shot from the two hundred pound Parrot gun in Battery Worth, and soon the gunboats opened their batteries and a terrific cannonading on the river apprised us of the fact that the long expected ram Albemarle had come down and encountered our fleet. Within twenty minutes all was again still, and we anxiously awaited the dawn to learn what had been the result. When the dawn finally came we were both mortified and surprised to find that there was no fleet in sight and that the powerful iron-clad ram Albemarle had full possession of the river, cutting off both our retreat and re-enforcements.

Chapter III.

a description of the battle between the Albemarle and our gun boats —

death of captain Flusser — captain French cuts loose from the sinking

Southfield and runs away.

With the reader's permission I will stop here to narrate the struggle between our gun boats and this ram, as it was detailed to me while a prisoner, by one of the crew of the Southfield, which, if correct, shows how the death of one brave officer and the cowardice and incompetency of another, served to make prisoners of two thousand brave men, and by the fall of Plymouth supply the Confederacy with an immense amount of artillery, ammunition and supplies of all kinds, of which they stood greatly in need.

Lieut. Commander Flusser, as I have said, was one of the most gallant and efficient Commanders in the U. S. naval service, and was fully resolved to either sink that ram or sink every gunboat under his command. As I have before stated, the Miama was a large double-ender, and she was also a very high boat, being a double-decker as well. This was Flusser's flagship, and she and the Southfield, which as I said, was an old New York ferry boat, with wales reaching ten or twelve feet over the water, were fastened together fore and aft with heavy cables, and lay out in the channel with steam up and lights out, intending to let the ram drop in between them and then push her ashore, or sink her. It was three a. m., when the ram passed battery Worth, where a two hundred pound Parrot gun, all shotted and waiting her appearance, was located. But when the ram passed battery Worth, she was so low in the water and came down so still, and the night was so very dark, that the lookout at battery Worth failed to see her until she had passed the work, although the gunboat Whitehead, Capt. Barret, dropped down just ahead of her, having been stationed up the river on picket, and notified Lieutenant Hoppins, who was in command of battery Worth, of the approach of the ram. Only one shot was fired at her, and this after she had passed the redoubt, but as she had got by, the aim of the gun was inaccurate, so she passed on uninjured.

She ran between the Miama and Southfield, striking the latter with her horn on the forward quarter, just at the water line. The bow of the ram had passed under the forward cable and her horn was, of course, under the wide spreading wales of the Southfield. This boat was now rapidly sinking, while both she and the Miama were all the time sending solid shot in quick succession against her iron-clad deck and sides. The ram was trying to disengage her horn from the fast settling Southfield, which was drawing her down with her as she settled, making it every minute more difficult for her to extricate herself. The water was pouring into the forward ports of the iron monster, when unfortunately Capt. Flusser was struck in the breast by a piece of a shell, that had by some mistake been placed in one of his guns, and exploded as it struck the ram at short range, killing him instantly.

As soon as Capt. French, who was in command of the Southfield, learned of his death, he jumped aboard the Miama, calling his crew to follow him, but they bravely staid by their ship. He then ordered the cables cut loose and steamed away down into the Sound, thus leaving the ram in a position to extricate herself from the Southfield, as she could not do while held down by the cable. If French had, instead of cutting the cables, just put on steam, he could have run the ram on the shore stern foremost, as Flusser had intended to do, and for which purpose he had the boats lashed together. Extricating herself from the Southfield, from whose guns she was continually receiving solid shot, she opened her batteries upon her and soon sent her to the bottom, picking up and making prisoners of the crew. These were very bitter in their denunciation of Capt. French, whose cowardice alone, they said, saved the ram from being run ashore and captured, as it would have been had Flusser lived.

Chapter IV.

our retreat cut off — a perilous reconnaissance by the cavalry — cavalry sent to capture a boat's crew — fleeing north carolinians — walking back into prison rather than to skulk a fight — firing the two hundred pounder at the ram — squelching a rebel sharp-shooter — a furious attack and fearful slaughter — a prisoner of war.

Being now in possession of the river, the Albemarle took her station about a mile below the town, just opposite our left, which, as I have said, was unprotected by works. This was the only weak point in our defense, and while our own fleet was in the river, they could effectually protect this; but now that they were replaced by the Albemarle, Hoke would have no trouble in getting through and gaining our rear. The greatest obstacle now to be overcome by the enemy, was the passage of a deep, wide creek and swamp, half a mile from the river, which was commanded by Comphor and Coneby redoubts.

At daylight of this, the 19th, we also discovered that the enemy had gained possession of Fort Wessels, the small works mentioned as being over a quarter of a mile on our right, and on a line with Fort Williams. This, taken with the fact that our retreat was cut off, made us feel a good deal as though we were prisoners.

At 6 a. m. Capt. Hodges, brigade-quartermaster on Gen. Wessel's staff, came to me and said the General had assigned me to a very delicate and dangerous duty, which was to take thirty picked men of my command, and pass between Hoke's right and the ram, and proceed to Stewart's Hill, which was on the river about one and a half miles below the ram, where he thought a boat's crew from the ram would land and attempt to communicate with Hoke. My duty was to capture this boat's crew, if possible. For a fourth of a mile we were compelled to ride in water up to our stirrups, and within eight hundred yards of the ram, which was in full sight. Anyone who has ever seen a troop of cavalry ford a stream, knows what a roar they make in the water, a noise that can be heard for nearly a mile. We could not expect to reach this place without attracting the attention of those on board the ram, and as we could not go faster than a walk, we would make a fine target for their shell, and we were in momentary expectation of having them exploding about our heads.

For some reason that I never could explain, we were allowed to reach our destination without being disturbed. Stewart's Hill, as it was called, was only a little pine knoll, containing about three acres, and is not over five feet higher than the river. After placing my men where they would not be seen, and cautioning a number of North Carolinians who had congregated there for safety, to keep out of sight, I took my station on the bank to watch for the boat.

I soon saw a boat crew put off the ram and start down the river, but they kept the north shore, which was a quarter of a mile away, and passed on down below me. Having thus failed to accomplish my mission, and knowing that marching back to Plymouth was equivalent to going into prison, I will say candidly that the temptation was great to patch up an old leaky boat I found there, or build a raft, and try to reach our gun boats in the Sound, only a little over five miles distant. But if I did, I would most likely be accused of sneaking out of a fight; for although I had no orders to return, I knew I was expected to do so, and we therefore mounted and retraced our steps back to Plymouth.

I found on my return, that Capt. Hodges had taken some men and attempted to get down the creek, but the boat was capsized and the Captain being unable to swim, was drowned. When I reported to General Wessels, he ordered me to take my men into battery Worth, which I did, spending the balance of the day and night in piling up bags of sand to strengthen our little redoubt; firing an occasional shot with our two hundred pound Parrot at the ram, which we struck many times during the day, but we could see by the aid of our field glasses, the immense projectiles glance off her heavily armored sides, like peas thrown against the round surface of a stove pipe. The projectiles were of such immense size that we could easily watch their course from the time they were twenty rods from the gun, without the aid of our glasses, and could trace their course the whole distance.

While we were busy as beavers, packing up sand bags, I noticed two or three times the zip of a minie ball past my ears, and watching the window of an old house about five hundred yards to our right, I discovered the cause. Taking a carbine from one of our men, I raised the sight for that distance, and placed it between two sand bags, and when a form appeared at the window again, took a good aim, and had the satisfaction of seeing the form suddenly disappear, and I think he received a detail for some other duty, for he did not return again to annoy us.

We worked during the whole night, expecting an attack on the right that night or the next morning, as the enemy were busy all day, throwing up an earthwork from Fort Wessels, which they had taken the night previous, running it parallel with our right towards the river. Instead of this, a furious attack was made early the next morning on our left, Hoke having, during the night thrown a pontoon across the deep, wide creek, in spite of Cady's light battery which was stationed there. Furious assaults were made on Comphor and Coneby redoubts, which were supported by the 16th Connecticut, and after two or three unsuccessful assaults, these works were carried, and the 16th Connecticut fell back towards Fort Williams, stubbornly contesting every foot of the ground; once or twice charging the advancing enemy, and driving them back, but overpowered by greatly superior numbers, they were driven under the protection of the fort, where rifle pits were hastily thrown up.

At the same time another column charged up along the river to Battery Worth, where I was stationed with thirty men of the 12th New York Cavalry, the ditches being filled with loyal North Carolinians. The ditches were so deep, however, that they were of no use, for the heads of the troops were at least three feet below the surface of the ground.

Cady fell back with his light battery as the enemy advanced, losing two pieces within two hundred yards of there doubt. These pieces were immediately turned upon our redoubt, which, as I have said, was unprotected on that side, this battery having been built solely for the use of the two hundred pound Parrot placed there for the destruction of the ram. These guns were trained on the slat door, and on the opposite side was the door of the magazine, which was well supplied with hand grenades, shell, and a large supply of powder. Should a shell come through the door and explode inside this magazine, it would blow us all into eternity.

The boys were using their carbines with terrible effect upon those serving the pieces; and although there were but thirty or forty of us, so rapid and accurate were the discharges, that for some time the enemy were prevented from using them upon us; but the heavy column of Confederates that had poured in on our left and gained the rear of our entire works, were closing in upon us along the river bank, which served them excellently as a protection; while they were within a few feet of the unprotected portion of our redoubt, so near were they, that after a council of the officers, a white flag was raised on a bayonet as a token of surrender, and it had scarcely appeared above the low earthwork, which was only about breast high, when half a dozen rebs stood upon it peering down curiously at us, whom they were surprised to find so few in number, having supposed from the rapidity and effectiveness of our firing, that there were at least a hundred of us.

When I found that a surrender was inevitable, I seized my pistol by the muzzle (a weapon that had been presented me before leaving home) and threw it far out into the river, rather than have it fall into the hands of the enemy. At the same time the Sergeant in charge of the big gun spiked it, by driving in a rat-tail file with a hammer and breaking it off close to the piece. We were at once asked to lay down our arms, and were marched under guard down to the left, receiving, as we went, a furious discharge of grape from Fort Williams, under the supposition that we were Confederates, Hoke's main column following along the line of works, taking them in detail until Fort Williams alone remained to Gen. Wessels; and this was completely surrounded, and hemmed in on all sides, while the sharpshooters of the enemy were stationed in the houses, where they could effectually prevent the men from serving the guns. Bravely did Wessels defend his stronghold, repelling all assaults until nearly noon, when he met Hoke under a flag of truce, to agree upon terms of the surrender, Wessels asking that he be allowed to march out with his colors, the officers retaining their side arms. This Hoke refused to grant, though complimenting Gen. Wessels on the gallant manner in which he had defended his works. He said that any further show of resistance would only result in an unnecessary sacrifice of life, and if Wessels still persisted in holding the works, and he was obliged to carry them by assault, he (Hoke) would not be responsible for what followed. This Gen. Wessels construed as a threat of a repetition of the Fort Pillow massacre, and saying, "You may go back and open fire," haughtily turned on his heel and returned to the fort. The men were well protected by heavy bomb-proofs, and only those who were serving the guns were exposed to the fire of the rebel sharpshooters, who occupied every available place on all sides, and were making fearful havoc among them.

Twice was the flag staff shot away and replaced, and so effectual was the fire of these sharpshooters, that it was almost certain death for anyone to approach a gun; when, after his nephew and aide-de-camp, Lieut. Foot, had received a very severe wound while trying to rally the men to the guns, the gallant old General reluctantly hauled down his flag, and Plymouth was once more in the hands of the enemy.

Hoke had won a victory after four days of hard fighting, but at what a fearful price. With eight thousand and veteran troops, and the assistance of the huge iron-clad ram Albemarle, he had made prisoners of nearly two thousand Union troops, after a loss of nearly or quite two thousand men in killed and wounded. In fact the Petersburg papers of the 27th acknowledged a loss of seventeen hundred in this battle.

Chapter V.

This attack commenced at half-past four, and at half-past six a. m. of April 20th, I was a prisoner. As we marched past Comphor redoubt to the Johnson farm, a mile to the south, we had an opportunity to witness the terrible slaughter the victory had cost the enemy.

Dead bodies of men and animals were strewn in every direction. Broken caissons and disabled cannon in front of these two redoubts showed plainly what a terrific struggle had been gone through with in their front.

The piteous cries for help of the suffering, the groans of the wounded that had not yet been removed (the ambulance corps not having yet been able to reach them) the roar of artillery and the rattle of musketry where the battle was still going on, the riding back and forth of mounted orderlies hurrying up re-enforcements, all served to make up a picture that I am unable to adequately describe.

The Johnsons, who were wealthy planters, had taken the oath of allegiance and claimed to be Union men, and were somewhat embarrassed at having us, with whom they had been on such friendly terms, brought to their farm as prisoners. They seemed to feel a sympathy for us, and one of them said to me, privately, that they were really in sympathy with the Union cause, but were obliged to be very careful of their conduct toward us while the Confederate troops were there, for their property, and even their lives, were at stake. I now believe they were honest. I do not wish to confound these Johnsons with one of the same name, who lived on the Washington road, near our vidette post. He pretended to be loyal, but we did not take any stock in him, and found after our capture that he was an open and exultant Secesh. While at the Johnson farm we could hear the crack, crack, crack of muskets, down in the swamp where the negroes had fled to escape capture, and were being hunted like squirrels or rabbits, I can think of no better comparison, and the Johnnies themselves laughingly said (when questioned about where they had been after their return), "They'd been out gunning for niggers."

After the surrender of Fort Williams we were marched back into Plymouth, where I received permission, on the pretext of getting some linen bandages for a wounded Confederate, to go into my quarters. I found half a dozen Johnnies in there hauling over my wardrobe and appropriating what they took a fancy to. I picked up my blanket, a cavalry jacket, a pair of new shoes and a satchel containing my papers, and tried hard to get a fellow to give up my dressing gown that I had received as a Christmas present a few months before, but he was so well suited with the bright colors and fit of the garment, that he could not be persuaded to give it up. Taking what I could carry, I went and delivered the linen bandages and fell into line with the rest, when we were all marched out on the Washington road, where we were joined by those who had been taken at Fort Gray and Fort Wessels. All the inhabitants of the town, with the exception of those who were known to be Secesh, were sent out to join us, men, women and children, white and black.

The negro soldiers who had surrendered, were drawn up in line at the breastwork, and shot down as they stood.

This I plainly saw from where we were held under guard, not over five hundred yards distance. There were but few who saw this piece of atrocity, but my attention was attracted to it and I watched the whole brutal transaction. When the company of rebs fired, every negro dropped at once, as one man.

General Hoke had the reputation of being a brave soldier, and with the exception of this cowardly murder, so far as I had the chance to observe him, seemed to be a gentleman. We were certainly treated by himself and those under him, with marked courtesy. Our gallant defense of Plymouth seemed to inspire them with a respect for us, and they accorded to us every privilege consistent with our position. For instance, we were drawn up in line — I mean the officers — and were told that they did not wish to subject us to the indignity of being searched for arms, but would ask us to give our word as gentlemen, to surrender everything that was contraband of war, and upon our so pledging ourselves, we were allowed to pass over what arms we had without further question. I was also allowed to send two of my sergeants who were wounded, Gleason Wellington and Sergt. Fisher, to the hospital. As I was near the spot where I lost a man in the commencement of the battle, I was allowed to take a squad to find his body and bring it into the camp and bury it, which I did, Chaplain Dixon, of the 16th

Connecticut, holding the service. This was Private Amos Fancher, the first man killed in the battle.

Chapter VI.

on the march — an eighteen mile march — treated to a drink of our own commissary at the end of the first days march — uniform good treatment by our captors — an attempt to escape frustrated — march to williamstown — the band at foster's mills treats us to "dixie" — kind hearted mrs. piffin gives us all the provisions she had cooked for dinner — hopes someone will do as much for her son (who is in the confederate army) — a ride in filthy cattle cars through charleston, savannah and macon — arrival at andersonville.

The next day, April 21, we left camp at 12 m., having been issued rations of some of the hard tack and coffee they had captured, and guarded by the 35th North Carolina, Colonel Jones, were marched about eighteen miles. We were well treated by officers and men, and so far as my own observation went, no insults or indignities were suffered by any. I marched all day at the head of the column, which I preferred to do, as it is much easier to march at the head than the rear, in dusty roads. As a specimen of Colonel Jones' treatment to me, I will state that at the end of the first days march, when we were halted to go into camp, he rode up to me and handing me a pint flask filled with captured commissary, told me to take a drink and pass it down the line as far as it would go, which I don't think was very far if all took as big a drink as I did. Being a cavalry officer and unused to marching, I was very tired with the long tramp and the last few days of hard service, and imagined I could see a look of envy on the faces of some of those farther down the line, as I held my breath on that bottle.

As we were making camp, Capt. Hock and myself went into the woods, on the opposite side of the road, ostensibly to gather some dry limbs with which to cook our coffee, but really in the hope of getting outside of the guard and sneaking off. We walked along, picking up sticks, and had as we supposed, got beyond the line, and were just discussing our chances, when we were ordered back into camp by one of the Johnnies who was still outside of us, so we took our wood and went into camp, cooked our coffee, rolled ourselves up in our blankets and slept as only tired soldiers can sleep.

Among those whom I had learned to rely upon as truly loyal and counted as my friends, were Captain Wynn, who lived near our vidette picket post, and a lawyer named Jones, who frequently visited me in my quarters. I also had a guide named Wynn, a relative of the captain, who had been with me on a good many expeditions, and another named Modlin, who had done me much service in giving information from outside our lines, and who had finally moved his family inside the lines for better protection. These two guides I furnished with our cavalry uniform and passed them as part of our detachment.

On our third day's march however, they were spotted as "Buffalos" by some of their North Carolina friends and concluded that the only way to save their necks was to escape, which they both did and reached our lines at Newburn.

The next day, April 22, we broke camp at 6 a. m., and marched to Williamstown, passing through Foster's Mills, which was surrounded with entrenchments and garrisoned with some North Carolina troops that we had often encountered in our frequent reconnaissances, their band treating us to "Dixie" as we passed. The next day we reached Hamilton, N. C., where we remained until ten o'clock Sunday morning. Col. Jones, who had thus far been in command, and who had treated us with marked kindness, often dismounting to give some weary Yankee a ride on his horse, here took his leave and turned us over to Lt. Col. Crowley, of the Holcomb Legion, who started us for Tarboro. It gives me great pleasure here to relate another instance of hospitality which I enjoyed, for up to this time we had received more acts of kindness than of rudeness.

We were out of rations and stopped for a few moment's rest in front of the plantation of Mrs. Piffin, and I received permission to go to the house and buy some provisions. This lady had just boiled a ham and baked some biscuit for the dinner, and upon learning of our not having had anything to eat that day, freely gave us all she had. I offered to remunerate her, but she would not take any pay, saying she had a son in the Confederate army and she was only doing by me, as she hoped someone would do by him should they see him in like circumstances. I sought out this lady after my return to Tarboro in 1865, and had the pleasure of a visit with that son, who was then home suffering from a wound, when I had the satisfaction of, in a measure, repaying her for her kindness to the Yankee stranger.

When we reached Tarboro we were a hungry and tired crowd. We camped on the east bank of Tar river opposite the town, where I prevailed upon the Sergeant to send a guard with me into the town to buy some provisions. I went to the hotel and bought nine sandwiches for ten dollars. The hotel was crowded with people from the surrounding country, who had come to town to see the Yankee prisoners, and I seemed an object of a good deal of curiosity dressed in the full uniform of a cavalry officer.

All were talking about the great victory that Hoke had gained in the capture of Plymouth. He had taken Plymouth and made prisoners of the garrison, but at what a fearful loss. A few more such victories would ruin the Confederacy! We remained at Tarboro until ten o'clock the next day, 26th, when we were crowded into cattle cars of the most filthy description, forty of us being placed in each car, besides two guards at each of the side doors. These cars had been used for the transportation of beef cattle and had not been cleansed in the least since thus used. It was, therefore, like lying in a cow stable. We now began to realize what short rations, or no rations, meant. I bought a pie when we arrived at Goldsboro, for which I paid five dollars. At this rate a millionaire could not long remain outside the poor house. At 5 a. m. on the 27th, we arrived at Wilmington, where we disembarked and crossed the river on the ferry. Rations of soft bread and spoiled bacon were here distributed, and we were again put on board the cars, which were even more filthy than those we had just left. We arrived at Florence at midnight, where we were allowed to disembark and remain until the morning of the 28th. Here our guard was again changed and the 19th Georgia took charge of us.

We passed through Charleston in the night, and reached Savannah at 3 p. m. the 29th. While we stopped at Savannah, a large crowd congregated to see the live Yankees. They all seemed pleased to see us, and some of our great political aspirants would feel proud of such an ovation as we received here, ladies waving their handkerchiefs and the men cheering us lustily, hurrahing and swinging their hats. One lady actually threw a kiss at me on the sly, and I believe she was in favor of the union — no pun. The next morning, April 30th, we passed through Macon, making a stop of two hours, then we started again, and at 4 o'clock we arrived at Andersonville.

Chapter VII.

Andersonville, one year before, had never been heard of a hundred miles away, but is now a place whose name is associated with all that is revolting, a place whose name is synonymous with suffering, hunger, starvation, despair and death. A place the recollection of which recalls, with a chill of horror, the most terrible scenes of anguish that were ever suffered or beheld. A place whose history can never be fully written. For were all the survivors of that Confederate Hell, presided over by that incarnate fiend, Wirz, capable of portraying the horrors they had endured there, it would still remain for the fifteen thousands, whose emaciated forms passed through its gates to their final rest, to write up the history of the torments through which they passed during so many days of agony and wretchedness, of suffering, despair and death, before the history would be complete and the "finis" affixed. Thank God I was not doomed to be a resident of this charnel house, where out of eighty-five of my brave comrades who belonged to our detachment of cavalry, and who were destined to suffer its blood-curdling horrors, only eighteen ever lived to relate the tales of fiendish cruelty to which they were obliged to submit.

On the plateau in front of the pen the officers and enlisted men were separated, as no officers were held in Andersonville, except a few who commanded colored troops, whose rank would not be recognized by such gentlemen (?) as Wirz and his aides. Though I had heard much of the hardships of Andersonville, I then had no idea what the real horrors were, and after being separated I called Sergeant Cunningham towards me, was talking to him about caring for them, and endeavoring to maintain discipline as far as he could, when a Dutchman, mounted on a white horse, rode up with a cocked revolver in his hand and ordered him, with a terrible oath, to "Git back dere in de ranks, and if you come oud again I blow your tam head off."

Having up to this time been treated with the respect supposed to be due an officer, I must say that I was not quite prepared for such a bombastic display of authority. The ludicrous gestures and evident bravado of the man (for I believed then, and do now, that he was a craven coward) only caused me to laugh as I told him that the place for men who were fond of shooting was at the front; that I called my Sergeant out of the ranks and was alone to blame for his leaving his place in the line. Knowing Sergeant Cosgrove (or Cunningham, as his right name was, he having, as he told me on leaving the service, enlisted under an assumed name), and having been with him in places that tried what kind of stuff men were made of, I could understand the look of contempt with which he quietly took his place again in the line.

After the enlisted men had been sent to the pen, the officers were conducted to a small church, or rather chapel, on the opposite side of the road, where we remained over night. We were not very closely guarded, and if there had been a probability of getting through I could have got away, for I went some distance alone to a house and bought some milk, and had a supper of hard tack and milk. The next morning I again went out and bought some beefsteak and milk for breakfast. This being Sunday, Chaplain Dixon held divine service in the little church, preaching from the text, "I have been young and now am old, yet have I not seen the righteous forsaken nor his seed begging bread." The service was held immediately after breakfast, and at ten o'clock we were on board the cars, again headed for Macon, where we arrived at 4 p. m. We were placed in Camp Oglethorp, a fair ground, and were furnished with shelter tents, no stockade having then been built there, and were furnished with rations of salt pork and corn bread. Here for the first time our rations were furnished in bulk, and we divided them ourselves. It was here that I first witnessed the amusing spectacle of a blindfolded man dividing rations.

The manner was this: The bacon would be cut into as many pieces as there were men in the mess, and as nearly equal as possible, then a man was blindfolded, and as the officer of the mess touched a piece of meat he would say, "Who shall have this?" and the blindfolded man would name one of the mess, and so on until all were served.

I was now out of money, but I had brought along an extra pair of shoes and quite a supply of extra clothing, so I sold my shoes to Captain Freeman for ten dollars Confederate money and two dollars in greenbacks, which was about as much more. I bought with this money six radishes for one dollar, a pound of rye coffee for three dollars, and a pound of sugar for ten dollars, so that all I had for my shoes was these three articles, which could be had to-day for ten cents, and six dollars of Confederate money which amounted to about one dollar in greenbacks.

Many ladies visited our camp, some coming out of mere curiosity and to see what the Yankee officers looked like, for in Macon, at this time, Yankee soldiers were not as common as they were when the war closed. The march through Georgia had then not been made and "Sherman's bummers" were not yet known.

Some seemed to openly sympathize with us, and brought us books and bouquets of beautiful flowers. One young lady — Maggie Langley — handed me a bouquet, in the centre of which I found concealed a note giving her address, and saying that if I should make my escape, to come to their house and they would conceal me until I could get away. Lieut. Fish, of the 2d Massachusetts Heavy Artillery, received a book from a couple of ladies named Richardson bearing a similar note on one of the fly leaves. Thus early we found that although we were held as prisoners by a hostile enemy, we were still in the midst of sympathizing friends.

Having so recently come from Plymouth, where we had been in garrison, we were dressed in our best uniforms, and being all officers, we, of course, presented a very creditable appearance. The Misses Richardson spoken of, said they were natives of New York State, and were heartily in sympathy with the North.

There was a stream that ran through the camp grounds, in which it was my daily habit to bathe. In fact, during all my prison life, I never neglected an opportunity to take a bath whenever I could get a chance to do so. To this I attribute, more than anything else, the good health I enjoyed during nearly all the time spent in Southern prisons.

I do not mean to say by this, that bathing would have saved the lives of all, or any great proportion of those who died in prison, but I do say that when the facilities of cleanliness were afforded us, there was a notable decrease in the mortality.

Hence the difference in the mortality of the officers' prisons and those of the enlisted men, where bathing was impossible. Had our men in Andersonville been placed in good, roomy, clean quarters, through which flowed a good stream of pure running water, thousands who now sleep in that densely populated city of the Union dead, would now be here to relate the sufferings and privations they endured. It was not altogether the insufficiency of food that killed off those true-hearted patriots, but the need of wholesome quarters, and the facilities for cleanliness as well. There is nothing so invigorating to the system as a daily bath in pure, cold water, and on the other hand there is nothing more debilitating, or conducive to disease and death, than crowded and filthy quarters, without the necessary sanitary conveniences to permit the enjoyment of this invigorating luxury.

On the 7th a fire broke out, and nearly all of the guards who were on duty at the time, went to town; when they returned they were drunk, and for a time it looked as though we would have to turn out and assist in their arrest. Guns and pistols were used, and the bullets came whizzing over our heads in the most reckless manner. This, of course, was very interesting for us, who were obliged to lie in our tents, surrounded with armed men, and take all the chances of a fight without being able to participate in it. The melee finally ended by four of the guards who were crazy drunk, being bucked and gagged to keep them quiet.

On the third day of May, twenty-nine officers were brought into camp, who had been taken at Chattanooga. This gave us some news from our western army, and for a day seemed to divert our minds. I see by a diary kept by me in prison, that on that day I paid ten dollars for a coffee pot, and three dollars for a cup, and on the 5th of May I bought one quart of strawberries for three dollars, and four dozen eggs for ten dollars. This was for our mess, which consisted of Captain R. B. Hock, 12th New York Cavalry, Captain Cady, 24th New York Independent Battery, and myself. I make this statement for fear someone who had kept track of my receipts and expenses, would think I was buying too much with the money received from the sale of that pair of shoes, and I will say here, although it may seem paradoxical, that although I had when I arrived at Macon, only one dollar in Greenbacks and a ten dollar North Carolina bill, still I spent while in prison, over ten thousand dollars in Confederate money, and got it all honestly too. And I wish to say here, that I had enough to eat nearly all the time I was a prisoner. We were always pleased to welcome new arrivals, for then we could get news from our armies that we could rely upon, and were cheered to hear by every *fresh fish* that came, that our bully boy Grant was pushing Lee back on to Richmond, and that Petersburgh was besieged. New arrivals were almost daily coming in, and we always crowded about them to hear the latest news from the front. It was noticeable that every one gave us something that was cheerful. Never while I was a prisoner did I hear any doubt expressed as to the ultimate result, either by those Union prisoners or the new arrivals. Naturally of a hopeful and cheerful disposition, and always looking upon the bright side of every question, I (to use a slang phrase) soon "tumbled to the situation," and tried to accommodate myself to the circumstances that surrounded me.

I found that in prison, as at home, there were some who were fitted for one thing and some for another. The same adaptability for different pursuits were found there as are found in our home everyday life. There were mechanics, tradesmen, artists and laborers. Some could take beef bones and out of them fashion all manner of beautiful trinkets, such as napkin rings, bibles, crochet needles, etc., others could make pencil sketches of the different scenes that were daily witnessed, portraits of prisoners, sketches of the different portions of the stockade and quarters. Others were better adapted to buying and selling, and still others could repair or make shoes. I remember seeing one pair of shoes made that I must describe. The sole was shaped out of a piece of pine board or plank, and the uppers were made out of an old pair of boot legs; a groove was made entirely around the sole, and the leather pegged on, so that the sole came out about half an inch each side, making a really artistic pair of shoes, and durable too, fastened together with wooden pegs whittled out by hand. I had a pair of slippers made out of the cape of my overcoat that were not only comfortable, but serviceable as well, and not at all bad looking. In this prison every trade was represented and nearly all were plied to some extent, sometimes for the purpose of gaining a living and sometimes to keep the mind occupied, and to make their quarters more comfortable.

As for myself, having up to the time of entering the service been a salesman, I found this to be my most profitable vocation. I sold on commission; I see by referring to a diary kept by me during my imprisonment, that on the 11th of May I sold a pair of gauntlets for one officer for twenty dollars and another pair for twenty-five dollars; also a hat for Lieutenant Hastings, 24th New York Independent Battery, for twenty dollars. By thus selling for others who could not sell such articles, or buying of them and selling to the Johnnies, I could make enough, with an occasional sale of some of my own surplus stock, to buy enough provisions to add to my drawn rations to make myself quite comfortable most of the time. I was always fond of a good meal, and I fear when I give a list of what I bought and the price I paid, the reader will think I had rather extravagant notions in this respect. For instance, one day I paid fifteen dollars for a beef shank and fifty-six dollars for a smoked ham, five dollars for a dozen eggs, and three seventy-five for a cabbage, and was offered peas in the pod at one dollar a quart, but I thought this would be rather too rich for my blood and postponed the purchase, hoping for a decline in the market. Now do not think that I ate all of this myself. There were three of us in the mess, and I did the buying and cooking for the party. The above purchase was only one of many, but will serve to show how much it cost us to live. When it is considered that five dollars in Confederate money was only equal to one dollar in greenbacks, and that a dollar greenback was only about forty cents in gold, it will be conceded that the price paid after all was not so very high, especially when it is remembered the scarcity of provisions at that time, May, 1864; for instance, the ham, for which I paid fifty-six dollars was only four dollars and fifty cents.

Chapter VIII.

moving into the stockade — skirmishing — mr. cashmeyer's sutler wagon — captain irsh bucked and gagged by order of tabb — captain tabb relieved — how we passed the time — the meetings — gambling houses — social and singing circles.

On the 17th of May the stockade was completed and we were moved inside, where we were joined by eight hundred other officers, who had been confined in Richmond, among whom were Brigadier Generals Wessels and Scammon. Twenty-one others, who had been confined in jail in the city of Macon, were also added to our number. Most of the Richmond prisoners had been there a long time and were out of money and nearly destitute of clothing. We had up to this time been comparatively free from vermin, having thus far been in an open field with only a guard around us and with some facilities for cleanliness. But contact with these old "salt cod," as they were called (we being designated as fresh fish), soon brought us to the daily skirmish line, and we thereafter found plenty to do to keep the graybacks in any kind of subjection. At first it was with a good deal of embarrassment and attempted concealment that this necessary duty was performed.

I shall never forget my first efforts in this new duty. All day I had been annoyed by something tickling my leg at a certain spot, and had tried all sorts of ways to rid myself of the annoyance, but though for a moment relieved, it would every time return to pester me. I more than half suspected the cause, but did not dare to let my companions see that there was anything the matter, lest they should drive me out of the tent and refuse to associate with me. I finally managed to be left alone in the tent, and quickly taking off my pants and drawers proceeded to investigate the affair. I was nervous and excited, fearing while I was prosecuting the investigation one or both of them might return and discover what I was doing. I felt like a culprit and blushed like a school girl at the sound of approaching footsteps. A sense of guiltiness took possession of me, and I felt as though I was committing some terrible crime. I know I should have fled most ignominiously had either of them come back, while I was thus employed, for such a thing had not been thought of as possible to us, and it would forever disgrace me to be the one who should bring such a filthy plague into our hitherto tidy and carefully-kept tent. It did not take long to solve the mystery, and to say that I was thoroughly disgusted and overcome to find my worst fears realized, in discovering two good, fat, healthy-looking graybacks under the seams of my drawers, would but faintly express the sensations I experienced.

After assuring myself that there were no more I hastily resumed my apparel, and tried to look as though nothing had occurred when my comrades again returned. But that guilty feeling would not forsake me, and I was really ashamed to look them in the face, and though I tried hard to appear natural, I thought they looked at me suspiciously.

"Conscience makes cowards of us all."

I know I was gloomy and dejected all the balance of the evening. This was noticed by my tent mates, but was attributed to a far different cause. They thought I was homesick, while the discovery had only made me sick at the stomach. It was not many weeks, however, before I could set down with my pipe in my mouth, in company with half a dozen others, and go through the same operations with the nonchalance that the same number of old ladies would gossip over their knitting work.

Before our prison life was over, it was no uncommon occurrence to receive a morning call from some old comrade, who would do as these old ladies used to do when they went a visiting, bring his knitting work along, and in passing one another's quarters such dialogues as this would frequently be heard: "Hello, Johnny! on the skirmish line, what luck?" "Oh I ain't doing much this morning, kind er drivin' in the pickets, git a stray shot now and then, but I keep annoying them so they don't get a chance to form."

It is astonishing how quickly we became accustomed to things of this sort. The Brigadier General, who in garrison or field seemed so reserved and dignified, was here on the level with the Lieutenant in the company. And while rank in prison, as in the field, was respected, and genius was honored, on the skirmish line all met on an equality. In other words rank was waived in the presence of a common enemy — and the officer who neglected to daily inspect his clothing, was unmindful both of his own comfort, and the respect of his comrades. Our facilities for washing and boiling our clothing was very limited, and nothing but boiling them would have any effect in exterminating these troublesome pests; soap was a scarce commodity, and kettles for heating water were difficult to obtain, so the only way to rid ourselves of vermin, was to strip off our woolen shirt, (white shirts were seldom seen in prison) set down and carefully scrutinize the seams, where they would be found hid away; for it is a singular fact, that although while the shirt was on we could feel them roaming around all over the body, no sooner was it doffed than with a celerity that is perfectly unaccountable, they would all be found securely hid away under the seams of the garment, where they would leave an innumerable number of eggs, which were soon to be hatched out and become almost full, grown by the next morning. Having thoroughly exterminated the living, and destroyed as many of the still inanimate as possible, we would resume our shirt, and removing our pants and drawers, repeat the operation on these garments, and would then be comfortable the balance of the day.

This duty was usually performed just after breakfast, while we were enjoying our pipes, and talking over plans for the day, and would occupy about an hour. After coming off of duty on the skirmish line, it would be about time to fall in for roll call, or more properly speaking, for count. We were made up into squads of ninety each, and one of our comrades chosen as commandant, who would, at a signal, fall in his squad in two ranks, when each squad would be counted to make sure that none had escaped. This counting was always done by a reb sergeant, who would be accompanied by an armed guard of twenty-five or thirty soldiers. When the count was completed, we would break ranks and separate, to pass the day as best suited each individual. Usually the first thing to be thought of was the purchases for the day, or as we would call it here at home, marketing. These purchases were generally made of a reb sutler named Cashmeyer, who was allowed to come into the enclosure, accompanied by a guard and attended by a negro, driving a mule hitched to a cart. The cart would be loaded with beef, bacon, potatoes, onions, cabbage, tobacco, cigars, soap, etc., which had been ordered the day previous. We also had two or three sutlers of our own number, who bought of the reb sutler in large quantities, and then retailed it out at a small profit, say about two hundred per cent, to those whose means were too limited to buy at wholesale.

Our mess, consisting of Capt. R. B. Hock, 12th New York Cavalry, Capt. Cady, 24th New York Independent Battery, and myself, was probably as well supplied with funds as any in the camp; and as I was caterer and cook, and unrestricted in my expenditures by Capt. Hock, who supplied most of the funds, our table was usually as well supplied as the scanty market would allow. I would send out by this reb sutler for fifty or seventy-five dollars' worth of provisions at a time, and by thus buying in large quantities, get the lowest rates. I have spoken about buying our provisions in large quantities — I mean by this a half peck of potatoes, a dozen eggs, a couple of loaves of soft bread, a whole ham which down there would weigh, perhaps, ten or twelve pounds, a quart of onions, etc. Now a small quantity as sold by our sutler inside would mean a couple of potatoes, an onion, a pint of corn meal, and half a pound of meat of some kind. This, in addition to the

rations we drew, would suffice for a day very well. We drew three or four days'
rations at a time. These rations consisted of two ounces of bacon, half a pint of
rice, a pint of corn meal, and a teaspoonful of salt a day per man; but when Capt.
W. Kemp Tabb took command of the prison camp he at once cut these down
one-third. Capt. Tabb took command the 18th of May, relieving Major Turner
(not Dick Turner), who was a gentleman and a soldier, and who seemed to try to
make our imprisonment as endurable as possible. On the other hand, Tabb was a
cowardly rascal, who seemed to delight in nothing so much as in adding to our
discomfort and annoyance.

He did not hesitate to plunder or rob the prisoners under his charge, and if
any one reposed confidence enough in him, to let him have anything of value to
sell for them, they were just out that amount. Captain Francis Irsh, of the 45th
New York, let Tabb take his watch and chain to see if he could sell it to some
jeweler for $400, and after having been put off on one excuse and another for
several days, threatened to report Tabb for swindling him, when he was bucked
and gagged for three hours, setting in the hot sun, as a punishment for his
offence. His watch and chain was subsequently returned, Tabb being afraid that
keeping it would get him into trouble. The next day, he having heard that I had a
good field glass, tried by soft talk about buying it, to get it into his possession, but
learning from one of my comrades that he was aware that I owned one, and was
trying to buy it, I took it apart and divided it up among half a dozen of my
friends, and when he came I told him I had disposed of it, which was true, for I
had done so most effectually. He succeeded, however, by pretending to wish to
buy, in inducing Doctor McPherson to show his, and when he got it into his
possession, claimed it as a contraband article, and confiscated it to himself. I find
in my diary of the same day (June second), this note: Captain Tabb was relieved
to-day by Captain Gibb, and started for Richmond. May he get shot.

He was well known to all to be an unprincipled coward, and on two different
occasions at least, he was most effectually snubbed. On one occasion it was by
Chaplain White, of the 5th Rhode Island H. A., who was an earnest Christian, and
in connection with Chaplain Dixon, 16th Connecticut, regularly held divine service
every Sunday, and prayer meetings once or twice during the week. In these
services it was his custom to pray for the President of the United States.

One Sunday morning Tabb came in at roll call, and notified the Chaplain that
he would not hereafter be allowed to offer prayer for the President. Chaplain
White told him that while he retained his power of speech, his prayers should be
dictated only by his conscience and his sense of duty. Chaplain Dixon opened the
service that morning and made in his prayer an eloquent appeal, not only for the
President of the United States, but for the success of our army, and for every

Union soldier, whether in hospital, in prison, or in the field, and was not interrupted or interfered with by Tabb, who could hear every word from his quarters.

On another occasion he told Col. Lagrange, who was in command of number nine squad, to which I belonged, that he should hold him responsible for any tunneling, or attempted escape of the men in his squad, who haughtily replied that he was not placed there as a spy or detective, and that he should not betray the secrets of his comrades, but would, to the utmost of his ability, render them any assistance they needed. This speech was cheered by the squad in the most hearty manner.

We always found that our treatment was fair whenever we were guarded by old soldiers who had seen service at the front; but when the *new issue*, who were a cowardly lot of home guards, were placed over us, there was no extremity of cruelty and meanness that they would not resort to, to render our condition more miserable and unbearable, even to shooting an officer who was quietly attending to his own business. A case of this kind occurred on the 11th of June, when Lieut. Gerson of the 45th New York Volunteers, who was returning from the sink about 8 o'clock in the evening, was shot and killed by one of the guards named Belger, of the 27th Georgia Battalion (Co. E). This was a brutal and deliberate murder, as the officer was not within ten feet of the dead line and was coming from it towards his quarters, besides the full moon was shining brightly, and the sentry could not have thought he was trying to escape. The truth is, he had told his girl when he left home, that he would shoot a Yankee before he returned, and was too cowardly to attempt to kill one who was armed. This fellow was promoted to a Sergeant and given thirty days' leave for his cowardly act. Of course, in a prison like Macon, where none but officers were confined, the indignities and abuses were less frequent and severe than in Andersonville, where the enlisted men were held. Officers of intelligence were less liable to submit tamely to these indignities than were the men, who had been schooled to obey orders, and could and did, command more respect; besides, there were less of us, and our prison was more roomy and better kept.

A certain number were detailed every morning from each squad, to thoroughly police the quarters, and keep them in a good, clean, healthy condition. Then, officers were usually possessed of more money and valuables than the enlisted men, and were better prepared to subsist themselves, when rations were cut down to starvation points. The wonder is not with me, that so many of our boys died in prison, but that any of them got out alive. When I saw officers reduced to skeletons, and driven to insanity by the treatment they received, and then think of the poor fellows whose sufferings were a thousand fold greater, the only wonder is that human nature could endure it all. But I started to tell how we passed the time.

After doing our marketing, which, by the way, was happily illustrated by a reb, who said he used to go to market with his money in his vest pocket, and carry a basket on his arm to bring home his purchases in; but now, he was obliged to take his money in the basket, and could almost carry home his purchases in his vest pocket.

We amused ourselves by reading, playing cards, chess, checkers, and other games, while those wishing exercise played cricket or practiced the saber exercise or fencing, to keep our muscles up, and perfect ourselves in the use of arms. Sabers and foils were whittled out of pine or ash sticks, with which we supplied ourselves. One German whose name I failed to take down, gave daily lessons in fencing, and he was not only an excellent teacher, but an expert swordsman. I have seen him allow three of his most advanced pupils come at him at once, and tell them to go at him as though they meant to kill him, and he would successfully defend himself against them all. One thing I distinctly remember was that he could not speak very plain English, and when he would give the order, "On guard en carte," in his quick way of speaking it, a person who did not know what he intended to say, thought he said "Cut-a-gut," and he was known in prison as "Old Cut-a-Gut" always after.

After we had exercised sufficiently we would lay down in the shade and read or sleep during the hottest portion of the day. A number of us formed a literary association, each subscribing toward the purchase of a library that a citizen of Macon had to sell. He said he had a library of about one hundred books, that he would sell for $500, as he was destitute and was obliged to part with them to buy provisions for his family. So twenty of us chipped in $25 apiece around and started a circulating library, appointed one of our number librarian, and in this way we were well supplied with reading matter for a long time.

I do not remember all, or any considerable number of the titles of these books, but what interested me most were some old Harper's magazines, in the reading of which I found days and weeks of profitable enjoyment. I do not think I ever fully appreciated until then, how much real comfort it was possible to extract from those old literary productions. Our reading was usually done during the hottest part of the day while lying in our quarters, when out of door exercise was too uncomfortable, and when we got tired of reading we would take a nap or go visiting to some of our friends in other portions of the camp, and there sit and talk over affairs, discussing the prospects of exchange, spinning yarns, cracking jokes, or singing old war songs to cheer each other up and pass away the time. Others would resort to the gambling tent, where there was always a game of cards going on; sometimes it was three card loo and sometimes poker; but they would sit there from early morning until dark and play for money, and, as is always the case, some would come away happy and some broke. But somehow or other the same gang would be there the next day, anxious to retrieve their broken fortunes of the previous day, or add to their gains. Men would there as here, sell the last button off their coat to raise money to continue the game, with a hope that luck would come their way. Thus, some who came into prison with enough to subsist them for quite a long time, would soon be obliged to live on the rations they drew, while others, who were nearly destitute when they came in, would live like fighting cocks. I could rehearse incidents of this kind that came under my personal observation, but as I could not do so without giving names, as the boys say, I won't give it away.

All sorts of games were played, some for money, and some for pastime. Cribbage, back gammon, euchre, seven up, and sometimes we would play poker for the beans we drew for our rations. When the bean ration was given out, each man would have perhaps a good tablespoonful, then five or six would sit down and play until one would have the whole, which would make him quite a respectable dinner, and the rest would have to go without. Thus it will be seen that our prison camp was a village, where all kinds of business was carried on, and all sorts of characters were to be found. We had our church, our prayer meetings, our social circles, our singing, our visiting, and our gambling houses, all in a space of four or five acres of ground.

We had some excellent singers, and were frequently entertained during the long evenings with solos, quartettes, and choruses, patriotic, sentimental and pathetic.

Among the patriotic songs oftenest heard, were "The Star Spangled Banner," "The Red, White and Blue," "The Sword of Bunker Hill," and "Rally 'Round the Flag;" but the one that touched a tender chord in every prisoner's heart, and that even the rebs used to call for, was this which I quote entire:

> In the prison pen I sit, thinking mother most of you,
> And the bright and happy home so far away,
> While the tears they fill my eyes, spite of all that I can do,
> Though I try to cheer my comrades and be gay.
>
> Chorus. — Tramp, tramp, tramp, the boys are marching,
> Cheer up, comrades, they will come,
> And beneath the starry flag, we shall breathe the air again,
> Of the freeland, in our own beloved home.

In the battle front we stood, when their fiercest charge was
    made,
And they swept us off, a hundred men or more,
But before we reached their lines, they were driven back
    dismayed,
And we heard the shout of victory o'er and o'er.

Chorus. — Tramp, tramp, etc.

So within the prison pen, we are waiting for the day,
That shall come and open wide the iron door,
And the hollow eye grows bright, and the poor heart almost gay,
As we think of seeing friends and home once more.
    Then there was another, the chorus of which I can only
remember, that the boys used to sing. The chorus was this:
    Hurrah, boys, hurrah! Shout glory and sing;
    For the rebels look sad and forsaken.
    Our glorious old eagle is still on the wing,
    And Vicksburg is taken, boys, taken.

Among the beautiful singers who were in the habit of entertaining us, I distinctly remember Capt. Palmer, who had a good voice, and to whose singing I was delighted to listen. I do not know to what regiment he belonged, but I do know that he afforded me a great amount of pleasure by his sweet songs.

Not being much of a singer myself, I nevertheless enjoy listening to others, and as I once heard a noted preacher say, it depends as much on a good listener as a good talker to have an enjoyable meeting, I thought that I contributed as much as anyone towards the entertainments.

Whenever there was any singing going on, there was always a good audience of appreciative listeners, and among eighteen hundred officers, I need not say there was plenty of talent to select from, and these evening entertainments were a source of great enjoyment to all, even though the same songs were sung over and over again by the same persons.

Chapter IX.

fresh fish — arrival of col. miller — death of lieut. wood, 82ⁿᵈ indiana — more fresh fish.

Upon the arrival of new prisoners at the gate of the stockade, there would be a cry raised throughout the camp, commencing near the entrance, and spreading rapidly to the farthest extremity of the enclosure, of "fresh fish! fresh fish!!" It was like the alarm of fire in a city, and quickly collected a crowd, and as the numbers increased, the din became more deafening, and to the new comer who did not know what it meant, perfectly appalling.

I have seen prisoners come in who looked perfectly bewildered as they gazed upon the mob of ragged, shoeless, hatless, unshaven, long-haired, howling beings who confronted them, looking more like escaped lunatics than officers; when someone back in the crowd would sing out, give the gentleman air, don't take his haversack, keep your hands out of his pocket, don't put that louse on him, why don't some of you fellows take the gentleman's baggage, and show him to his room, Johnny show the gentleman up to No. 13. I remember especially, the look of perfect bewilderment on the face of Col. Frank C. Miller, of the 147th New York, as he stood at the entrance of the enclosure, and the look of joyful relief as I called out, hello Frank, come over here, and he recognized an old and intimate friend. And he told me afterwards, that he never in his life was so pleased to see any one as he was to see me just at that moment, for, said he, I thought they were putting me into a lunatic asylum.

A stinging rebuke was given by, I think it was Gen. Schaler, who said to his escort, loud enough to be heard by all: "I thought I was going to be put in an officer's prison." This practice was mostly confined to the old Libby prisoners, who had, some of them, been confined for more than a year, and had, in a measure, become demoralized; for I do not believe there can be anything more demoralizing than the sufferings, privations, and hardships endured by our prisoners; and I wish to say right here, that to Chaplain Dixon, of the 16th Connecticut, and Chaplain White of the 5th R. I. Heavy Artillery, the officers owe a debt of gratitude for the faithfulness with which they performed their Christian duties. They were both earnest Christian workers, zealous in the cause of the Master, anxious for the eternal welfare of the souls of those who were placed in their keeping, and fearless in the discharge of the duties devolving upon them as ambassadors for Christ. While all did not profit by their earnest exhortations, there were few who were not benefitted by their presence and faithful counsels, and all held them in high respect and admiration for their Christian qualities. Speaking of Col. Miller's entrance into Macon, as soon as the crowd saw that he had found an old friend, they gave way and I escorted him to our quarters, where I went to work, and soon had the satisfaction of seeing him happy in the enjoyment of a good breakfast. I cooked a couple of eggs, with a small piece of bacon, and fried a few sliced potatoes, which, with a biscuit, made what we called an elegant meal. The Colonel was busy talking and eating when, looking up, he said, as he helped himself to the last egg and biscuit, "By George, Lon, they give you good rations here, don't they?"

"Good rations!" said I, "good rations! why, Frank how much do you think this breakfast cost?"

"Why, I don't know, I supposed you drew this for rations."

"Well," said I, "this meal cost just about eleven dollars. All the rations you draw for two days, wouldn't make such a meal as this."

Colonel Miller, who had been a near neighbor and associate of mine long before the war broke out, received a severe wound in the chest by a minie ball, at the Battle of the Wilderness, and was reported dead and was mourned as such by his family for a long time, but was rescued from the flames that broke out, after the battle, and taken a prisoner to Salisbury, and placed in the hospital there, whence he was removed when convalescent, to Macon. He soon found the Adjutant of his regiment, Lieutenant H. H. Lyman, who gave him a place in his quarters, and they afterwards remained together.

On the 23d of May, Lieutenant Wood, 82nd Indiana, died in the hospital, just outside the stockade, and was buried the next day at 1.30 p. m. Chaplain White being allowed to hold the funeral service, a number of us offered to give our parole to attend the funeral, but our request was denied. On the same day one hundred and eleven *fresh fish* were brought in, among whom were Brigadier Generals Seymour and Schaler. That night about ten o'clock a tremendous storm came up, which drowned out all who had not built themselves sheds, and the main building, where were quartered the general officers, etc., was crowded with those driven from their quarters by the drenching rain. This main building as it was called, was a large hall, that had been built for the display of goods during the fair, which had heretofore been held on these grounds, and was the only building in the stockade that was clapboarded and shingled, and with the exception of an old tumble down affair on the opposite side, east, was the only building in the enclosure when we took possession.

Having built myself a shelter on the first day I entered the stockade, I was all right; but those who had burrowed for shelter were driven out like rats from a flooded cellar, and were obliged to seek shelter in the large hall from the pitiless storm. There was not room for all, and those who could not crowd in there had to rough it out as best they could. On the 25th of May, I first met Adjutant H. H. Lyman, of the 147th New York, from whom I learned that Col. Miller was wounded and a prisoner.

About this time, they brought us in lumber, pine poles and nails, to build ourselves some sheds, and all went to work on the construction. I belonged to No. 9 squad, and on the 27th of May, our lumber and other materials were furnished, and we all went to work, and by night had our shed so nearly completed that we moved in, though it took us several days to get our bunks finished and everything comfortably arranged. It was amusing to see a squad of ninety men go to work to erect one of these sheds.

Out of the ninety, about thirty would do the work, and the rest would stand around and make suggestions. Among so many who should be equally interested, it was astonishing how many bosses there would be, who could tell how it ought to be done, but seemed indisposed to do it. Nothing was done to suit these Superintendents, but when their grumblings became too loud and boisterous, someone who was tugging away at the big end of one of these fifty feet pine poles, would rest it on his knees long enough to shout "Louder, old pudden head." This was a favorite epithet, used to quiet any one in camp who got too excited or eloquent on any subject, and I remember one Tennessee officer, Captain Hayes, who so objected to it that he was ready to fight any one who called him "old pudden head" — and I have seen him furiously searching for the man who had yelled this, while he was loudly proclaiming his sentiments on some subject, but it only caused him to be annoyed the more, for when it was seen how sensitive he was on this point, there were plenty to be found to thus pester him, while they dexterously avoided the blows, aimed at their heads with a stick he hurled after them. He was a large, powerful man, with a voice that could be heard from one end of the camp to the other, very excitable when talking, and could never understand a joke, but took everything in earnest, and nothing afforded the boys more pleasure than to get him boiling mad.

Chapter X.

manner of tunneling.

The manner of digging a tunnel was this: The place selected to commence a tunnel would usually be in some shed nearest the stockade. In these sheds we had built ourselves bunks, ten or twelve inches from the ground, which would usually be movable, and, after the camp had become quiet, one of these bunks would be removed and a well sunk five or six feet, first taking the precaution to carefully lay aside the dirt that was just shoveled off, because that would be dark and look old. Then a guard would be stationed to prevent anyone from seeing what was going on. Pickets would be thrown out, who, if any one approached, would enter into conversation with them, in a tone loud enough to be heard by the tuneless, and caution them to suspend operations until the danger was over, when the work would be resumed.

In a camp of eighteen hundred, with always some sick, there would be no time in the night when some were not going to or returning from the sinks; so that seeing anyone moving about camp in the night attracted no particular notice. One would dig and fill haversacks or bags, and another, with an overcoat on, would carry it concealed beneath that garment to some place that had been selected as a dumping ground and deposit it, returning to the shed by a roundabout way so as not to attract attention. After a well had been sunk about five feet, the tunnel proper would be started horizontally, in the direction desired, always keeping as accurate a measure of the distance tunneled as possible. When it came time to suspend operations for the night, boards that had been previously prepared, would be fitted in the well, two feet below the surface, and covered over with some of the earth that had been removed, always being careful to put the old dirt that had been preserved on top, thus giving the surface the same appearance as the rest of the ground; all would then be carefully swept over, and all traces of new or fresh earth removed. The bunk would then be replaced and everything resume the careless appearance of everyday life.

So cautiously would this work be carried on that officers sleeping only a few feet away would not be disturbed, and never suspect that anything unusual had been going on. Thus, night after night, would the work be prosecuted, the men spelling each other in digging and doing sentry duty, until, by careful measurement, it was ascertained that the tunnel had reached a sufficient distance beyond the stockade to insure an escape. No one in the prison, except those engaged in the work, would be let into the secret until the work was completed and the tunnel was to be opened. This secrecy was necessary to prevent a curious crowd from hanging around, which would attract the attention of the rebs, who, in blissful ignorance of any plot, would sing out: "Post number fo, twelve o'clock, and a-l-l's w-e-l-l. Post number six, twelve o'clock, and a-l-l's w-e-l-l!" When, perhaps, some wakeful wag of a Yankee prisoner would answer: "Post number fo, twelve o'clock, and the Confederacy has gone to h — l," in the same sing-song way the reb guard had just given it. Sometimes the Johnnies would take all of this good-naturedly, and at others would call out: "Here, you Yanks, if youens don't keep still I'll shoot in thar," which would have the effect of quieting them for a time.

On the 17th of May, we were moved into the stockade, and it was not long before we commenced prospecting to find an opening for an escape.

A tunnel was commenced almost immediately, but after working ten nights upon it, it was discovered and filled up. This did not discourage them, however; they must have something to occupy their time; and although we were busy all day building sheds, this did not prevent us from trying nights to find a way out of our confinement. When the first tunnel was discovered, that had just been started, all hands were fell into line, and a general search was made for tunnels, but none were discovered. On the next day, however, Captain Tabb succeeded in discovering another, and in an altercation with Maj. Pasco, of the 16th Connecticut, who was claiming that he had a right to escape whenever he could, slapped the Major in the face for asserting his rights. This was a cowardly act, for Tabb was not only armed, but surrounded by a guard, while, of course, Major Pasco was an unarmed prisoner. It made a fellow's blood boil to witness and suffer such indignities; but what could we do under such circumstances? To resist was certain death, while to submit was a mortification and humiliation that it was hard for a proud-spirited officer to submit to, in the presence of his comrades. All we could do was to hoot and hiss him from a safe distance, and chaff and exasperate him by sneering, deriding and laughing at him; so that although he was the king, and we the subjects, we managed to insert in the crown he wore, more thorns than laurels. On the second day after the discovery of this second tunnel, Tabb had a platform built on the northwest corner of the stockade, and another on the opposite side, upon each of which he mounted a twelve-pounder brass-piece.

Here was a good chance to have some fun, and as we watched the progress of the erection of the platforms and mounting of the guns, we indulged in all sorts of comments and criticisms. Someone would sing out, "Say, Captain, get a good, strong force behind that gun when you fire it, to catch it when it goes over;" "Say,

Johnny, that gun is like the Irishman's musket, there'll be more danger behind it than in front;" "Tabb, when you fire that gun, just stand plumb behind it, and we'll be satisfied;" "I'll let you shoot that gun at me for a dollar a shot, and take Confederate money, if you will pull the lanyard yourself." "How is it that Lee never found you out, and placed you in command of his engineer corps or artillery, instead of keeping such a genius here, guarding Yankee prisoners, with no chance of immortalizing yourself?" "Barnum would make a fortune out of you. Why, he paid five thousand dollars once for a fellow that wasn't half as big a humbug, and done well out of the speculation." "Oh! go soak your head." "Don't shoot, Tabb; we won't tunnel anymore." "We don't want to get away; we just dig a little once in a while for exercise." "You can't drive us out of the Confederacy with that gun; we have come to stay."

Such exasperating expressions were kept up from morning till night, for the two days they were at work erecting these guns on the frail platforms, to prevent tunneling. But these precautions did not for a moment interfere with our tunneling, and while we were thus pestering Tabb, others were busy preparing other avenues of escape. Two tunnels were started simultaneously, one commencing in an old building on the east side of the camp, and the other in what was called No. 7 Squad, which was on the opposite side of the stockade. The one on the east side was already to open, and the one on the west nearly ready, when they were both discovered and filled up. There was strong evidence of treachery in the discovery of these tunnels, as Captain Tabb went directly to both of them, and seemed to know just where to find them.

There was at this time in the prison, one Hartswell Silver, who claimed to be a Captain in the 16th Illinois Cavalry, but who was generally believed to be a spy, placed in there to detect our efforts at escape, and to him was attributed the disclosure of our plot. Had these two tunnels been completed, at least half of the officers would have escaped, and as the force guarding us was small at that time, there is no doubt but that the majority of us would have succeeded in getting away. In fact the evening before, two or three officers escaped, by crawling under the stockade, where the branch or stream entered the camp. They were fired upon by the guard, and one was brought back. The long roll was sounded and the whole force turned out in expectation of a general break. All officers were notified that any one leaving their quarters, even to go to the sink, would be fired upon by the guard. A great excitement prevailed among the rebs all night, which was aggravated by those in their bunks calling out every little while — "Corporal of the guard post number fo." "Dry up there will you." "Oh! give us a rest." "Louder old pudden head." "What's the matter with you." "Put him out." "Shoot him." "Lie down." "Tabb try your big gun on this fellow," and like expressions, making a perfect uproar in camp all night long. After a moment's silence, some fellow would imitate the plaintive caterwaling of a cat, another barking like a hound, and another would answer from away off with the deep bark of the mastiff, another would crow like a cock. Sleep was out of the question, you might as well try to quiet a barroom full of drunken politicians who had elected their favorite candidate as to keep those fellows still. Once in a while the guard would call out, "keep still there you Yanks or I'll shoot in there," when someone at a safe distance would sing out "Put him in the guard house." "Buck and gag him." "Stone the loafer," etc., and so it kept on during the whole night.

The next morning Tabb had two more field pieces planted in the woods to the south of our camp, and horsemen appeared with hounds to track and capture the fugitives, but for some reason they could not get on the right trail and only succeeded in treeing a coon. There were several other escapes about this time. One by Lieut. H. Lee Clark, 2d Massachusetts H. A., who sought out Miss Frankie Richardson, who made arrangements to help him out of the city, but this same Hartswell Silver, who was boarding there, betrayed him and he was brought back again. This Silver was paroled the day the tunnels were discovered and was never in camp afterwards, and it is just as well for him that he was not, for, as the boys said, Silver was at that time at a premium, and would have been higher, if he had put in an appearance. Lieut. Frost, 85th New York, also escaped in a reb uniform, as did several others, and Lieutenant Wilson of the regulars was sent out in the sutler's vegetable box. This Lieutenant Wilson was an Englishman, and I think belonged to the regular army.

Mr. Cashmeyer came in one afternoon, as was his daily custom, with his cart, driven by a negro. Upon the cart was a dry goods box, filled with potatoes, onions, cabbage, turnips, bacon, beef, eggs, &c., which he usually disposed of to the Yankee sutler and others whose means justified them in purchasing, in what we call large quantities. He stopped as usual, at the shanty of the camp sutler, and there sold out his load. While he was in the shanty settling up, the crowd as usual gathered around his cart, and this Lieut. Wilson clambered into the box on the cart, while the crowd stood about the door of the shanty, the negro driver all the time maintaining that stolid look of innocence, so peculiar to the race, as he (the Lieutenant) was covered with empty sacks, that had contained the vegetables. And when Mr. Cashmeyer mounted the seat beside the driver, and left the camp, he was as innocent of helping a Yankee to escape, as the innocent looking negro seemed to be. The negro drove directly to the barn and unharnessed the mule, and as it was nearly dark, went to his quarters. The Lieutenant finding himself alone clambered out of the box and started off. Taking the railroad, he walked about five miles, when, as he said, he met a man who looked very fierce and who asked him where he came from, and where he was going. And after giving an equivocal answer the man asked him if he was not a Yankee officer, which he was too scrupulous to deny, and gave himself up, and allowed himself to be brought back, although the man who brought him back was like himself unarmed. But as he said on his return, the man spoke so gruff like, and looked so stern, that he thought there was no use of remonstrating. We nicknamed him George Washington, and tried to find a little hatchet for him, as an emblem of his innocence and truthfulness. As he remained in prison for a long time thereafter however, I think he may have regretted before he was exchanged, the conscientious scruples that would not allow him to tell a lie, even for the sake of freeing himself from the jeers of his comrades, and the tortures of prison life, which he had to endure afterwards.

It was a long time before he heard the last about that daring attempt to escape and the heroic defense he made against that unarmed reb who had recaptured and brought him back, and the desperate and successful resistance he had made against the temptation to tell a lie.

There is not an officer living who witnessed it, but will remember the celebration we held on the 4th of July. I will here quote what I that day briefly wrote in my diary of this celebration.

The day dawned bright and beautiful. I was up before the sun and prepared breakfast for Captains Hock, Cady and myself, which consisted of corn bread and butter, fried eggs, fried potatoes and coffee.

Our thoughts, now more than ever, turned towards the loved ones at home, who we see in imagination, with cheerful faces and bright smiles, hailing another anniversary of the day upon which *our glorious republic was born*, and methinks I can sometimes detect a shade of sadness flitting over the joyous features of kind friends, as the memory of the loved and absent is briefly recalled.

As we were being fell in for roll call, an officer displayed a miniature flag bearing the stars and stripes, which was greeted with cheer after cheer, by eighteen hundred prisoners. All gathered around that little emblem of liberty, and while every heart seemed bursting with patriotic enthusiasm, a thousand voices joined in singing that old song, which never fails to fire the patriotic heart — *The Star Spangled Banner*. After roll call, the officers by a common impulse assembled in and about the main building, in the center of the camp, and the services were opened by singing "Rally 'Round the Flag," by the entire audience, after which Chaplain Dixon was called upon for prayer. He appealed in eloquent terms in behalf of our beloved but distracted country, for the success of our cause, for the President of the United States and all in authority, for universal freedom all over our land and the world, and for the speedy return of peace, when we could beat our swords into plow shares, and our spears into pruning hooks.

At the conclusion of the prayer, the entire congregation joined in singing "My Country 'Tis of Thee." Captain Henry Ives was then called for, and mounting the platform gave us a very eloquent and stirring address. He was followed by Lieut. Ogden, 1st Wisconsin Cavalry, Lieutenant Leigh, 132nd New York, Captain E. N. Lee, 5th Michigan Cavalry, Captain Kellog, Chaplain Whitney, Chaplain Dixon and Lieut. Col. Thorp, 1st New York dragoons. I have during my life participated in a great many Fourth of July celebrations, but I never before — and I believe every officer at that time in Macon will say the same for himself — really and truly appreciated what a genuine celebration of the day meant.

If a stranger had come into camp Oglethorp at 3 o'clock that afternoon, he would have thought every man in prison was drunk, so intense was the enthusiasm, and yet there had not been a drop of anything of an intoxicating nature, to be had at any price for two months. Officers were drunk with excitement. The sight of that little flag that had been presented to Captain Todd by his sweetheart and smuggled into prison, sewed up in the lining of his vest, when shown in the morning, had created a degree of patriotic excitement that could not be kept down, and when someone said that Gibbs was coming in with a guard to take that flag, and suggested that it be secreted, a thousand voices shouted — stand by the flag boys — no traitor's hand shall touch that flag — keep her swinging — there's not rebs enough in Macon to take that flag to-day, &c., — and I really and firmly believe that a terrible and bloody struggle would have ensued, had there been any attempt on the part of the authorities, to interfere with it or take it from us. I never saw men wrought up to such a pitch of excitement, and the rebs were afraid all day, that an attempt would be made to assault the stockade and break out. From nine o'clock in the morning until three in the afternoon, the celebration was kept up, with speaking and singing, when finally the rebel commandant sent in his officer of the day, who said we had been permitted to have a good celebration, and now he wished us to quietly adjourn which we did; giving three hearty cheers for the flag, three for Lincoln, and three for the cause. No officer who participated in this celebration can ever forget it while reason holds its sway.

Lieutenant Col. Thorp who had made a ringing speech, full of patriotic fire and enthusiastic confidence in the justice of our cause, and the ability of the Northern soldiers to maintain our national unity, restore the glorious old flag, with the stains of treason cleansed from its shining folds by the blood of loyal hearts, with not a star missing from its azure field, urged with the most impassioned eloquence, every officer in that prison pen to consecrate himself anew on this sacred day, to the cause of universal liberty, and the perpetuity of our national institutions, and pledge himself anew beneath that beautiful little emblem of freedom, to never sheathe his sword, until every traitor in all this broad land had kneeled beneath its tattered and blood-stained folds, and humbly craved the pardon of an outraged people, for their dastardly attempt to trail it in the filthy slough of Secession. I cannot pretend to give his words, and cannot fitly portray the fierce impetuosity, with which his scathing sentences were hurled like red hot shot into the ranks of treason. It was one of the most masterly efforts of patriotic eloquence I ever listened to, and when he had finished his address, which had been heartily applauded throughout, his hearers were wrought up to such a pitch of patriotic frenzy, that I really believe that had he at its close, called upon that unarmed crowd to follow him in an assault against the wooden stockade that surrounded us, that few would have been found to lag behind. He was at that time senior officer in the camp, and as such had been assigned by Col. Gibbs, the rebel commandant, to the command of the prison inside.

But shortly after this speech, a notice was posted on the side of the large building where this meeting had been held, removing him from the position, for making an inflammatory speech, and appointing another officer to the place. Col. Thorpe seemed to feel almost as much pride in this recognition of his effort at a Fourth of July speech, as in the applause he had received from his prison companions, or as he would had he been complimented on the field by his superior for a dashing cavalry charge, and the compliment was all the more appreciated because it had been paid to him so unconsciously by Col. Gibbs.

The stockade at Macon was built of inch pine boards, twelve feet long, put up endwise and made as tight as possible. On the outside of this fence, and about four feet from the top, was a platform for the sentry to walk on, where they could keep a lookout over the camp to see that we were not trying to escape. Upon this platform were posted sentinels at intervals of about thirty yards, with instructions to shoot any prisoner who touched or attempted to pass the *dead line*, which was a row of stakes, or sometimes a fence of light slats, such as a farmer would build to keep his chickens or ducks from roaming, and was about twenty-five feet from the stockade. The original object in establishing the dead line was a precaution against a sudden raid on the stockade, but it often afforded an excuse for some cowardly guard to shoot a Yankee prisoner, who inadvertently came near enough to place his hand against it. We were not allowed to hang our clothes on this fence to dry, and on no account could a prisoner pass it with impunity.

Chapter XI.

receiving and sending off the mail — attempts to smuggle through forbidden matter — samples of letters sent home — boxes of letters received — my feelings at not receiving any.

We were allowed to write home, and by putting on a Confederate postage stamp costing 10 cents each, were promised that our letters would be forwarded to our friends, provided there was nothing objectionable in them. We were obliged to leave them unsealed, so they could be examined by the postoffice department, and in order to ensure an examination they must be limited to fifty words. I wrote home a number of times, and my letters, as a general thing, came through all right. I wrote some that I did not expect they would forward, and was much surprised when I reached home to find they had been received all right, and in some cases published in the daily papers. I will give you a sample of one or two. The first was written to my cousin, H. M. Cooper, and read as follows:

> C. S. MILITARY PRISON,
> Macon, Ga., July 6, 1864.
> My Dear Hal: —
> Nearly four months have now elapsed since I took up my abode in this land of bacon and corn dodgers, and like the prodigal son, I often think of my father's house, where there is bread enough and to spare. I dream nightly of fatted calves, but awake daily to the sad reality that my veal cutlets have all been transformed into salt bacon, my wheaten loaves into corn dodgers, and my wine into bran coffee.
> I had purposed to visit the North during the summer months, but the many friends I have found here are so anxious to have me remain, that I find it impossible to tear myself away. But I expect the General[1] will soon be here, when I shall be obliged to say farewell to my Southern friends and with much

---

[1] General Exchange

reluctance leave their sunny clime for my cold, chilly, Northern home.

But their kindness and hospitality will ever be green in my memory and I shall improve every opportunity to show them the gratitude I feel for the hospitality they have actually *forced* me to accept.

This letter, as I have said, was sent through all right, whether it was because they did not read it or because they failed to discover the satire — perhaps it should like Nasby's have been labeled a joke — I never knew. The next was written in the same vein, after I had escaped and been recaptured. Both had been published in the daily papers here, at the time, but the last one I have thus far failed to find. It was written after my escape and recapture, and detailed how, rather than risk the scene that would be sure to ensue, should I announce my intention of departing to my friend, the Confederate Colonel, and fearing I might be overcome by such an affecting leavetaking, that I concluded to start at three o'clock in the morning, while he was still sleeping, and thus spare not only him, but myself, an interview that would certainly be embarrassing to one or both of us.

But that, after I had traveled three hundred miles, his couriers overtook me, and were so urgent in their appeals for me to return, that I could not deny them, and had concluded to stay and see a little more of this beautiful Southern country before my return. But just as soon as I could persuade my friends to consent to my departure, I should surely return, and would try and make my friends in the North a good long visit, at least, before making another journey.

My letters were generally received by my friends in due time, but although they were promptly answered I never received a line to tell me whether my wife, who left for Newbern on the night of the first day's fight, had got home or not, and when I was finally released, after nearly a year's confinement, I did not know whether she was living or dead until I telegraphed from Annapolis and received an answer. We resorted to all sorts of devices to get letters through to our friends in the North, that contained matter that we were aware the Confederate authorities would not permit. I once wrote a short note in ink on a page of foolscap, and then filled up the sheet with a long letter, written with soda, which would be invisible until heated. My short note was an acrostic, and taking the first word of each line and reading it down formed this sentence: "I write with soda."

But this letter never reached its destination. The reb authorities soon got onto these dodges, and were very careful in their examination of all correspondence of prisoners, and everything that looked at all suspicious was destroyed.

I only received one letter while I was in prison, and that was from Col. James W. Savage, of my regiment, which, for brevity and news, I think I never saw equaled. I have the letter yet, soiled, faded and worn, but quote it entire:

HEADQUARTERS 12TH N. Y. VOL. CAVALRY,
Camp Palmer, July 31st, 1864.
Dear Cooper: —
Russell is in a Northern hospital, nearly well; Maj. Clarkson is assistant inspector; Rocha temporarily in command of "I;" Ellison and Mahon have resigned; Maj. Gasper also, though his resignation has not been accepted. We have lost a few men in skirmishes since you were taken. Prewster and Rice, of D, and June, of G, are dead. You and Hock are constantly remembered by us all.
Signed, J. W. Savage, Col. 12th N. Y. V. Cavalry.
My regards. J. A. Judson, Capt. and A. A. Gen'l.

On the 14th of June the first box of letters were received in camp, and as the adjutant mounted a table and called off the names, eager hands were held out to receive a missive from home; and to show my feelings I quote from my diary of that date:

"I listened with bated breath to hear my name called, but the last letter was called off, and I was obliged to turn away disappointed, as were a good many others. It seems too bad that even this comfort must be denied me. I feel as though I was dead to the outer world, and only for hope, of which I always possessed a good share, I believe I should die.

"If I could only get a letter from home, and know that my wife had arrived safely and knew of my safety, I could better bear this imprisonment; but this uncertainty and suspense is enough to drive one *mad.*"

I quote this to show how blue it made us feel, after having waited so long, hoping that a mail would come, and then find that it contained nothing for us; it made us envious of those who had been more fortunate.

Not getting any letters, made us doubt whether the ones we had written home, had ever reached their destination. Here is a modest order I had sent in my last. Please send me two pounds of dried peaches, five of coffee, five of corn starch, ten of sugar, two of tea, one bar of castile soap, four cans condensed milk, one codfish, five of dried beef, one of cheese, two cotton shirts, two pair drawers, thread, etc. Oh, what visions of good living were mine, while I waited for the arrival of the box containing all of these good things, but that box never came. I was not starving, far from it, I had plenty to eat such as it was, and in this respect was much better off than the most of my comrades, but I so longed for something from home, something to remind me that I was remembered. It was the subject of my thoughts through the day, and of my dreams at night; and I used to have such vivid dreams of home, that after I had been paroled and returned, I have stood and looked around and pinched myself, to be sure that I was really out of prison, and not merely dreaming again, fearful lest I should wake up, as I so frequently had, to find myself still a prisoner.

I had so frequently had such vivid dreams of home, and as frequently awoke with such a feeling of despair and anguish, when I found I was still a prisoner, that even in my dreams, I would doubt the truth of what seemed so evident to me, and would look about for some familiar object, and say as I saw something I recognized, I know now that this cannot be a dream. The first place I would make for when I arrived at Oswego, in my dreams, was the old Fitzhugh House, which at that time was the first class house of the city, and order a dinner, determined to have a good square meal the first thing, even before visiting my family. These dreams had become so frequent, and seemed so real, and the reaction so great when I awoke to the consciousness that it was only a dream, that I could scarcely suppress a wail of despair, as the truth was forced upon me, that I was still in that rebel pen, surrounded by an armed guard, with no prospect of release, and little chance of escape, I can scarcely command language to fitly describe my feelings at such times.

On the 10th of June the following officers were called out, it was understood, to be sent to Charleston, to be placed under fire of our batteries on Morris Island: Generals Wessels, Seymour, Shaler, Scammon and Hickman; Colonels Grove, Hawkins, Harrison, Lehman, LaGrange, Lee, White, Bollinger, Brown, Dana, Fordella; Lieutenant Colonels Burnham, Baldwin, Bartholomew, Cook, Dickinson, Fellows, Fairbanks, Glenn, Hays, Hunter, Higginbotham, Joslyn, Mackin, Mills, Maxwell, Mahew, Moffit, Alcott, Postley, Rodgers, Hepford, Stuart, Swift, Taylor, Lascella, and Majors Beers, Baker, Bates, Clark, Carpenter, Crandall, Grant, Hall and Johnson. We were quite in hopes that these officers were to be exchanged. I again quote from my diary of this date: "Exchange stock in this market has been very dull, but is advancing a little to-day. I do not take any stock yet."

In a few days, forty-four fresh fish came in from Grant's army, which gave us nearly our full number again, and as every few days brought us fresh additions, we soon had considerable more than when they were sent away. These officers all brought us cheering news from the seat of war, and strengthened our confidence in the ultimate triumph of our cause, but could give us but little encouragement in regard to exchange. In fact those in the field seemed to be too actively engaged in breaking up the Confederacy, to give much thought to their comrades in prison, or what provisions were being made for their release.

Chapter XII.

the first division leaves camp oglethorp — plans for escape — their

destination, charleston — thirty union officers and four of the "reb" guard

are missing on their arrival at charleston — the story of the lieutenant in

charge of the train as told to maj. lyman — departure of the second division

— stopped at savannah, thus foiling our plans for escape.

A t roll call on the 27th of July, the first division was notified to be ready to move to Charleston that evening. The prison camp presented a lively appearance all that day, baking, washing, packing up and getting ready to move.

About six p. m. we bid them good bye, and went back to our now half deserted quarters, to await our turn.

Plans of escape between Savannah and Charleston were freely discussed, and an organized break was agreed upon, when they came to the point nearest our forces.

This organized plot fell through in some way, but not being aboard of this train, I only know what I learned afterwards about the failure. About thirty officers did escape, by sawing through the floor of the cars, and were not missed until the train arrived at Charleston.

The following account of the affair, told by Lieut. Rogers, of the Confederate army to Maj. H. H. Lyman, this summer, however, throws a little light on the subject.

Lieut. Rogers said: "I was very young at the time, though a Lieutenant in the Confederate service, and was detailed to transport the Yankee prisoners from Macon to Charleston. I was very particular to instruct my men to be very vigilant, as the prisoners they were guarding were no ordinary fellows, but were a shrewd, sharp lot of Yankee officers, and would need a heap of watching; for if there was any chance to escape, they would improve it, and they must be constantly on the alert to prevent any of them getting away. Savannah was passed without any trouble, the Yankees seeming to enjoy themselves, singing, laughing and joking, and they and the guard seemed to be on the best of terms. Charleston was reached, and I proceeded to turn over my prisoners and turn them into the jail yard. I had been congratulating myself upon the successful accomplishment of my mission, when, upon counting them into the jail yard, what was my horror to ascertain, that I was thirty-four Yankee officers, and four guards short.

Instead of going to headquarters and reporting the situation, I sat down upon the curbstone in front of the jail to collect my thoughts, and consider what I should do.

While I was sitting there brooding over the affair, and feeling about as blue as though I was myself a prisoner, a Captain rode up and inquired if I was Lieut. Rogers and was in command of the guard, that brought the Yankee prisoners from Macon. I told him I was, and he told me I was ordered to report to the General's headquarters under arrest. I went up to headquarters, not knowing whether I was to be shot or sent to prison, but concluded to make a clean breast of it, and tell all there was about it.

The General listened to my story, and after keeping me in suspense for what seemed to me to be a long time, released me from arrest, and told me to go back to Macon with the balance of my men, and be careful that I didn't lose any on my way back.

The Lieutenant continued, I never afterwards heard from either the prisoners or my men. I didn't care so much about the Yankee prisoners getting away, but would like to have got my guard back.

He did not know whether they were killed by the Yankee prisoners or had been induced by them to desert, the latter however, is the most probable, but as I have never heard from any of them since, I am equally in the dark concerning the affair, and, like the Lieutenant, can only guess at what took place.

The next day we were notified to be ready that evening, and that night we were counted out and placed on board the cars. Instead of taking us to Charleston, as we had been told they would, we were stopped at Savannah, and placed in the United States marine hospital yard, around which a stockade had been built, thus spoiling our plans of escape. "The best laid plans of mice and men aft gang aglee." This was a yard of about two acres, quite well shaded with live oak trees, some of which grew to enormous dimensions, one on the south side, spreading over nearly or quite a hundred feet of ground. Here we drew rations of fresh beef, the first in many months, and our rations were generally better than we had heretofore received. We were strictly guarded, but, with few exceptions, were well treated. Colonel Wayne, of the 1st Georgia Regulars, was in command, who designated Colonel F. C. Miller, 147th New York, as senior officer of the camp, and all communications were forwarded through him.

Of course almost the first thing to do when we had got fairly settled in a new prison, was to commence a tunnel. Two were started, and had progressed nearly to completion, when as in Macon, these were both discovered and filled up. Another was soon started in a different direction, and was already to open, which would have given egress to half the camp, when, by a most unfortunate accident, it was discovered on the morning preceding the night we were to make the break. We had reached within a few inches of the surface, and ten minutes' work would complete the opening, but it was so near daylight we thought we would be already that night, and get a good early start the next.

That morning, however, as the sentry was watching a cow cropping the grass just outside the camp, what was his surprise to see her suddenly break through and nearly disappear. Of course an investigation showed what had been done, and again had our toil been in vain — no, not in vain, for it had kept us employed, and diverted our minds from the misery of our situation.

While in Savannah, we built ourselves what is known as the old fashioned Dutch oven, in which we could bake our pomes. To the younger readers a description of this oven may be interesting. A flat stone was secured about two feet square, for the bottom, and around and over this stone was erected an oven of stone, brick and mortar, capable of holding about four good sized pomes. Wood was then split up fine, and a good rousing fire built, and kept up until the oven was thoroughly heated, when it would be filled to its capacity with pomes, the different messes taking turns to do their baking, and in half an hour after closing the oven up tight, they would be taken out nicely baked, and when properly made, afforded a very palatable meal. In order to have them light, we would mix up a quart or so of corn meal in cold water, and set in the sun to sour. The pome was then mixed in the same way, stirring in a little of this sour rising and adding a little soda. This sour meal was kept on hand, so as to have enough for three or four days ahead.

A corn dodger was made in the same way, but was made the size of a large biscuit, and was baked in a skillet with an iron cover, a fire being built both over and under the skillet, and when not made light by the use of this sour rising and soda, would make a dangerous missile to throw at a man or dog.

Having now served an apprenticeship of about four months as cook for the mess, I flattered myself that I was qualified to take charge of any first class restaurant as chief cook and bottle washer, and I would bring my corn pome on the table, with all the pride with which a young wife, would present her best efforts at cooking to a tea party. And when I had wheat flour, I would be just a little put out, if my biscuit did not receive the fulsome praise I thought they were entitled to. Our rations in Savannah, were more liberal than they had been during our captivity, and by buying such things as were not issued to us, we always had a little ahead.

Colonel Wayne issued an order after the discovery of this first tunnel, that in order to give a better chance for inspection, tents must be raised three and a half feet from the ground. This order was usually complied with, but some claiming that they had no lumber, neglected to do as directed, and the result was that a detail was sent in, and removed sixteen tents that had not yet been raised, causing much inconvenience and suffering to those former occupants, as that night a severe storm came up, and being without shelter, many were drenched to the skin. These tents were returned in a day or two however, by recommendation of the surgeon in charge. Platforms were built at different points, upon which were built fires at night, to better enable the guard to see what was going on inside. Around these fires we would gather and sing old army songs, which served to put a little spirit into us.

These fires, while they were not built for our comfort or convenience, really were both to us. They drove away the mosquitoes and purified and warmed the chill, night air, thus making it more comfortable sleeping than it would otherwise have been. On the 2d of August an order came for our two Chaplains and seven surgeons to be ready to leave for parole. It was a day both of joy and gloom. We had learned to love those two earnest Christian soldiers, who had been so faithful to us, and were sorry to part with them, though we rejoiced at their good fortune and fondly hoped that it might be our turn soon. Most of them took with them only what they were sure to need, and freely gave to their most intimate comrades all else that could be of any value to them. But to show the difference in the dispositions of people, I wish to refer to two cases as illustrations of distinct sides of human nature. Dr. Robert Rae had a fine case of surgical instruments, which, although valuable to him, even after he was free, he gave to Adjutant H. H. Lyman, 147th New York, telling him they could be sold for money enough to subsist him for some time.

The other case is that of Dr. Brets, who had a mattress and some other camp property, that would be of no earthly use to him and which he could not take with him, so he magnanimously consented to sell them to the highest bidder, which happened to be Captain Hock of my mess. This mattress was quite a comfort to us and we were glad to get it, even at the exorbitant price we were obliged to pay. We did not begrudge the generous Doctor the greenbacks we paid him, and hope he is still living to enjoy them, for to such a generous soul, a few dollars, more or less, must be a great source of comfort. If I could find out his address, I would donate him a copy of this volume, just to show my gratitude. Before leaving, the Chaplains had a rousing farewell meeting, and each delivered a brief but eloquent address, and amid hearty hand-shakings and fervent God bless you's, they took their way out of the camp. Only one officer escaped while we were at Savannah

— Captain Sampson, 2d Mass. H. A., and he was soon recaptured and brought back.

He escaped by crawling out through a hole under the high board fence and tried to reach the fort on the coast about six miles away, but the swamps were simply impassible, and after wandering about through water and mud nearly knee deep for two or three days, was obliged to abandon the attempt to reach the coast, and was arrested by a patrol, who accidentally run upon him while he was trying to extricate himself from the impassible swamp.

He said that at one time he was in sight of the fort, but the water deepened so fast as he approached the shore, that he was obliged to retrace his steps.

It was a source of some little comfort to us to be once more within hearing of the morning and evening guns of a Union fort, but surrounded as we were by the guard of a hostile enemy, how long a distance that six miles seemed.

While at Savannah we were also furnished kettles, in which to heat water for washing our clothes; and as we had no extra changes of clothing, some ludicrous scenes were witnessed while the washing and drying was going on.

Lieut. Abbot, while boiling his clothing, tied a blanket around his waist until they were dry enough to wear again, making him look like an old woman, and while thus employed was sketched by an artist named Dahl, and presented with his own picture.

On the 13th of September we were placed on board the cars and arrived at Charleston the same evening, where we were placed in the jail yard, to be knocked out by General Gilmore's batteries on Morris Island. This was without exception the most filthy, lousy, dirty place I ever saw. There were only fifty A tents for six hundred prisoners, and scarcely any wood with which to cook our rations. At Charleston occurred the first death by starvation that I had witnessed, the deceased being a member of my company.

Soon after we entered the jail yard Capt. Hock and myself were greeted by two skeletons, whom we never would have recognized had they not made themselves known to us. They were reduced to mere skin and bone, and neither could walk, being on the very verge of death from starvation. As soon as possible I made them some gruel and tried to nurse them back to life. We fed them sparingly through the evening and then left them a pot of food to eat during the night, being particular to caution them not to eat too much, Sergeant Sweet, who was the stronger of the two, promising to be careful of his comrade, who could not be depended upon to control his craving for food. In the night this poor fellow crawled near enough to reach the pot of food while the Sergeant was asleep and ate it all.

It was his last meal on earth, for his poor starved stomach was too weak to endure so much, and the next morning he was dead. The guard carried him outside the dead line, where he lay all day, festering in the sun, and would not let me approach near enough to spread a blanket over his dead form, to hide the sight from our gaze.

There were a number of negroes belonging to some Massachusetts regiment, confined in jail, but were not allowed to come down into the yard. They were beautiful singers, and entertained us almost every evening while we remained there. This, with one exception, was the only sound that gave us any pleasure.

We could hear the boom of Gilmore's guns on Morris Island, and watch the course of the shell he was every fifteen minutes tossing into the doomed city. Two or three times pieces of shell fell inside the yard, one piece cutting off a limb of the locust tree that was at the time affording me shade, while I was reading one of those old Harper's that I brought along.

The only escape made from the jail yard was by Lieut. H. Lee Clark, 2nd Mass. H. A., who bought a reb lieutenant's uniform, and walked out without a question. He was subsequently brought back, however. Upon his return to the jail yard he gave the following narrative of his escape:

As he passed out of the gate, the sentry seeing his uniform and insignia of rank, faced and came to a present arms, which he answered by a salute, and passed on. Being now free from the prison, he started off, but being a stranger in the city, he did not exactly know what direction to take.

He had wandered about for some time, trying to think of some plan to reach our lines, when his attention was attracted by two ladies who seemed to be watching his movements, from the stoop of a house that looked as though it was occupied by people in moderate circumstances. After passing and repassing the house two or three times, he concluded to try to get something to eat there, and for this purpose approached the ladies. They asked him into the house and set a lunch before him, and thinking he would be safer here than in the street, he concluded to stay as long as possible. He found the conversation of the ladies entertaining, and by cautiously drawing them out in conversation, he found them to be strongly tinctured with union sentiments. Finally after satisfying himself that it would be safe to do so, he told them who and what he was, and appealed to them for shelter and protection, until he could devise some plan for leaving the city.

This they cheerfully promised, and also agreed to assist him to the utmost of their ability. They kept him at their house two or three days, until they could exchange his officer's uniform for that of a private, and then procured him a pass, as their brother, to visit Sullivan's Island, which was opposite Morris Island, and at one place was only separated from it by about three hundred yards.

This Island was reached by steamer and was strongly fortified. The bay between there and Morris Island was full of torpedoes to prevent attack by water.

He roamed about the Island all day, trying to find some means of crossing, but could discover no boat, not even a plank that would sustain his weight.

He stayed on the Island all night and tried again the next day to find some means to get across the short belt of water to Morris Island. He could not swim, and not a board was to be found that would assist him in his extremity.

He was without food and was now taken ill, and was finally obliged to go back to Charleston, and give himself up, when he was placed in the hospital, and after his recovery, sent back to prison.

September 26th, we were told that if we would give our parole not to attempt to escape, good quarters would be furnished us, and as escape from here seemed impossible, we gladly accepted the proposition.

Upon giving our parole eighty of us were sent to a house on Broad Street, which looked out on the bay. It was a three story, white house, with wide piazzas facing the water, and just across the street were bath houses, that we were permitted to use whenever we pleased. Here for the first time since we were placed in the pen at Macon, we had the facilities for cleanliness so necessary to insure good health. Then in the evening we could sit out on the piazza, and, looking down the bay, see the flash of the guns five miles away, anon hearing sharp quick reports, and then watch the course of the shell by the trail of fire, as it pursued its course into the city, while we amused ourselves by singing and commenting upon the bombardment.

We were visited almost daily by the Sisters of Mercy — God bless these brave, noble women — who brought in delicacies for the sick, and tobacco for those that used it, which they gave freely to those without means to buy, or sold to those who were able to pay. They also traded Confederate money for our greenbacks, giving us better rates than we could get elsewhere. Then they would take the greenbacks to the reb prisoners on Morris Island, for they had free access through both lines in prosecuting their Christian duty, and they were worthy of the confidence of both governments, as they never acted the part of spy for either. Braving every danger, and only intent on doing service for the Master, and relieving suffering wherever they could find it. How many of our poor boys, who were brought there from Andersonville, and were suffering from disease and starvation, were soothed, nursed and comforted by those noble women. May God reward them for all their self sacrifice, all their tedious pilgrimages, from one camp to another, all their weary watching beside the squalid pallets of the wretched suffering heroes, despite the hurtling missiles of death, that were flying in every direction about the city; nothing daunted or deterred them from making their regular daily visits, though I know of one instance, (and it was probably only one of many,) where a shell struck and burst only a few feet in front of the carriage that was bringing them to our quarters.

They were frightened badly, and what woman would not be, but this did not deter them from making their daily visits to the sick and suffering soldiers of both armies, and doing all in their power to alleviate distress, feeding the hungry, and watching by the bedside of the dying, administering the consolation of Christian faith and hope to those who were passing away, their only reward the consciousness of a duty well performed. "Verily they shall have their reward."

On the 5th of October we were again on board a train, and this time our destination was Columbia, the capital of South Carolina. We were placed in box cars, with two guards at each door, some of the same men who had been guarding us while in Charleston, and with whom we had been on terms of intimacy, we having been allowed many privileges while on parole, and had not been under as strict surveillance as heretofore, being permitted to go in and out during the day, whenever we pleased, and had gained the confidence of our guardians to such an extent, that they did not think it necessary to watch us very closely. This we thought would be a good chance to escape. It was agreed between us that Captains Cady, Hock and Eastmond and Lieut. Masters should jump from the car, which was running only about ten or twelve miles an hour, and I was to go on to Columbia with our baggage, of which we had considerable, so that in case of recapture, they would not lose all of this, to us, valuable property, but would again be in condition to commence housekeeping. Cady and Masters sat in the door with their legs hanging out, and I sat beside the guard, and after dark got into conversation with him. I had a pine stick which I was whittling, and as he would frequently bring his gun to an order beside me, I managed to remove the cap from his gun, and insert this pine stick into the tube.

This I communicated to my comrades. I then went back, and, standing alongside of this verdant reb, soon had him in good humor by getting off some funny yarns, joking, laughing and keeping him amused by swapping lies with him, until he thought I was one of the jolliest Yanks he had ever seen. And I did feel jolly, for I had a dead sure thing on *him*. We finally got on such friendly terms that he asked me to hold his gun while he took off his shoe to see what in h — l it was hurt his foot so; some dog gone thing was pestering him awfully; he reckoned it was a dog gone peg sticking up thar. Now was their time, and if I only had his belt containing the caps and cartridges, it would have been my time, too. We were passing through a swampy piece of woods, and none of us knew how deep it was or how far to high ground; but Capt. Cady and Lieut. Masters took in the situation and jumped. To show myself worthy of the confidence he had reposed in me, I snapped the old musket, but that only served to drive the pine plug more securely into the tube, and by the time he had put on a new cap they were out of range, even if the gun had been discharged. He exploded the cap, however, in the direction of the fugitives, and then relieved himself by cursing the d — n old gun; but my zeal was duly recognized, and our friendship was more firmly cemented than ever, as I was so mad to think they would play such a scurvy trick, especially while I was on guard. It was not long before the frequent report of arms told us that others were making a "jump for life and liberty."

About one hundred and fifty jumped from the cars and escaped into the swamp that night, and amidst all the firing there was not one hurt that I ever heard of. After Cady and Masters jumped, the guard at the opposite door was so watchful that Hock and Eastman could not get a chance to escape.

Had I not promised to stay on board and take care of the baggage, I should have taken the gun and followed Cady and Masters, which I think would more than ever convince my reb friend that I was zealous in the performance of military duty. I could see from my position in the door, dark objects leaping from the car in front, followed by a streak of fire from the gun of one of the guards, showing that the caps had not all been replaced with pine plugs, though I was told afterwards that a number of caps had been removed. I think the safest way, however, to prevent a gun going off, is when you remove the cap, to insert a plug into the tube. We were a jolly crowd that night, that passed through the swampy country between Charleston and Columbia, for it was fun to see our comrades getting away, and witness the frantic efforts of the guard to prevent them. Officers were shouting to their men to shoot the d — n Yankees, and the guards were doing their level best to obey orders.

But they had been deceived by the apparent submissiveness of the Yankees, and as I heard the fellow say whose gun I had fixed, "I didn't think they would do such a dog gone trick on me, when I'd used them so well." He seemed to lose confidence in all but me, and was mad all through, to think that the fellows he had treated like gentlemen should thus abuse his confidence.

We could have easily captured the whole force and taken the train if we had made an organized effort. But the great trouble was to get officers to obey orders and follow instructions; all wanted to be bosses. I would rather go into action with one regiment of enlisted men than with a whole division of brigadiers.

This fact probably accounts for the rebs always keeping the officers and enlisted men in separate prisons.

We arrived at Columbia October 6ᵗʰ, about 4 p. m., and were at once turned into a field of about five acres, on a sort of side hill. We had not drawn any rations during the day, and having had no opportunity to cook the raw rations we brought from Charleston, or buy anything to eat on the road, we were half starved.

There had been no preparation made for our coming, and the bakers were obliged to fire up and bake bread to feed this unexpected addition to their customers. This, of course, took time, and to men with empty stomachs the hours seemed like days. Women come to the fence that surrounded our camp, with pies, cakes, biscuits and other provisions to sell, and done a thriving business while provisions lasted; but the stock was soon sold out, and yet only a few had been fed. They only had to come to the fence with what they had to sell, and it was bought at whatever price was placed upon it.

I had just bought some bread of one of these venders, when Lieutenant H. Lee Clark, 2d Massachusetts H. A., came up and asked a woman the price of a pie, which she told him was five dollars; he handed her the five dollars, and was reaching through the fence for the pie, when one of the guard that had been placed in the camp, gave him a bayonet thrust in the back, without a word of warning or an order to fall back. It was a terrible thrust and made a wound three-fourths of an inch wide and one and a half inches deep, near the spine. A number of us saw it and watched for this fellow to come on guard again that night, but fortunately for him and perhaps for us, he was relieved and did not again make his appearance. If he had, we had determined to settle him quietly with a stone. An old wooden freight house formed the west boundary of our camp, and under it was stored a quantity of bacon. A number of hams were fished out by means of a hook attached to a long pole, and some even crawled under it to get their rations. Finally about dark, rations of white bread, warm from the ovens, were served and this, with the stolen bacon, made us a good hearty supper.

About this time a terrible rain storm came up, accompanied by a cold northwest wind, which caused intense suffering to those who had no shelter; and as none had any except such as could be made with blankets, nearly all were all that night exposed to one of the worst storms I ever experienced. As was my custom on going into camp, the first thing I did was to gather some boards and improvise a tent from our blankets, using some for a floor on which to place our mattress. This afforded but slight protection from such a terrible storm of wind and rain as that night swept down upon us, but over one thousand of the twelve hundred officers were destitute of even this slight protection, and many were suffering from wounds and disease. To those it was a night of terrible suffering such as few ever experienced before or since. In such a drenching rain fires were impossible, and there was nothing for them to do but tramp all night long in the wind and rain, to keep from perishing. Yet above the howling tempest and amid the drenching rain, could be heard the cheering chorus, "Tramp, Tramp, Tramp, the Boys are Marching."

Water was running down the slope in torrents, forming miniature rivers as the storm progressed, cutting deep furrows in the soft clay soil, and covering the whole camp with water and mud nearly ankle deep. Few who passed that night of the 6th of October, 1864, in the prisoners' camp at Columbia, will ever forget it while they live.

The next day we were asked to again give our parole, in which case we would be placed in a beautiful grove about three miles out, where we would have all the facilities for cleanliness and comfort that we could desire. We rather thought we would first see this haven of bliss, and then decide for ourselves about the bargain.

We hung our wet blankets up to dry in the sun which had come out once more to cheer us, and made ourselves as comfortable as possible during the day, not knowing where we were to go next. About four o'clock, teams were brought up to the fence along the road, and we were ordered to load on our traps and get ready to move into camp. Not having much baggage, we were soon ready and the line was formed, and we were again on the march. We had not gone more than half a mile, when we passed the building where was manufactured the Confederate money with which to carry on this great *rebellion*.

The windows were illuminated with the bright faces of about a hundred young ladies, who were employed in this great printing house, and some of the boys failed to keep step as they cast furtive glances in the direction of the upper story windows, some even going so far as to give a salute that was made a good deal like throwing a kiss, while a few cheeky fellows, who seemed to have forgotten their manners during their long imprisonment, actually had the audacity to sing out: "Say, sis, chuck me down a roll of *Confed.* Got any new issue to spare? Give us a bundle; you can make more." But what surprised me most, the girls seemed to enjoy all this chaffing, and some of them actually attempted to get up a flirtation with the detested Yankee prisoners, waving handkerchiefs, throwing kisses, and making such remarks as: "Ain't he handsome? Oh! look at that fat fellow; ain't he a daisy," &c., keeping up a chatter loud enough for us to hear until the whole column had passed.

After a march of three miles, we turned into a ploughed field that was bounded on three sides by what new settlers in the back woods call a slashing. There was not a tent or shelter of any kind, and this was the place that we had been told would afford us every facility for cleanliness and comfort, and for which we had been asked to give our parole.

A guard was formed around this field and we were turned in like so many mules into a corral. For fear of losing our mattress and other camp equipages, if we loaded them on the cart, we fortunately decided to lug them, not knowing how much of a tramp we had to make, and although it was a hard lug, we were well repaid for our labor when we reached the camp, for while many lost things that were invaluable to them, in that they could not be replaced, we were ready to go to housekeeping at once, when we were ordered to break ranks.

Like squatters in a new country, each man was permitted to select his location, and I at once pre-empted a dry knoll, under the shade of a pine tree, as a suitable place to squat and, dumping our household goods there, proceeded at once to improvise a shelter and skirmish around for something for supper.

Again, thanks to Doctor Brets' generosity (?) our mattress, which we had tugged on our shoulders for three miles, came into play to make us a comfortable bed on the ground, and, after such a supper as we could pick up, and a good smoke, we curled up in our blankets and lay down to dream of home and sumptuous dinners. While we were thus comparatively comfortable that night, there were a thousand of our less fortunate comrades who spread their still damp blankets on the cold wet ground, and almost supperless, passed a night of sleepless misery. The next week I spent in building a brush tent. I received permission to take an axe and go outside the camp, under guard, and cut brush and limbs to build it with. I cut six posts and planted them firmly in the ground, putting poles across to make a ridge tent, and then thatched the steep roof with pine boughs, making it water proof. It required a good deal of labor to complete the quarters, but when done it was warm and comfortable. Having completed our quarters, and got everything snug, I made up my mind that I would like to move North.

Chapter XIII.

the escape — i turn over my tent and household effects to colonel miller and adjutant lyman — crawling across the guard line — our escape discovered and we fired upon — captains geere and eastmond recaptured — tramp, tramp, tramp.

There was one of the guard, who had come with us from Charleston, and to whom I had sold my watch, who had become quite attached to me, and had always been ready to do me a favor, when he could. From our frequent interviews, I had been led to believe that he was strongly tinctured with unionism, and thought perhaps he could be induced to give me a chance to escape, if he could do so without danger to himself. Finding him on guard the 12th of October, at the northwest corner of our camp, which was the best place on the line to cross, I wrote a note to him, offering him fifty dollars if he would let me and some of my comrades cross his beat that night.

Wrapping a small stone in this note, I sauntered along near where he was pacing his beat, and, watching my opportunity, when none of the other guard were looking, tossed the note to him and sat down under the shade of a small tree to await the result. It would be impossible to describe with what feelings of hope, doubt, anxiety, and fear I awaited the answer to this note, as he paced his beat carefully reading it.

If he consented, I was free; but if he refused and reported me to Captain Semple for attempting to bribe him, there was no telling what would be my punishment; for attempting to bribe a sentry on duty was no slight offense. The stake for which I was playing was a great one, and the hazard was equally great. It was liberty on the one hand, and perhaps death on the other. No wonder then that the moment was an anxious one.

After carefully reading it, he walked to the farther end of his beat and wrote on the back of the note, and wrapped a stone up in it, and, on his return, when opposite where I sat, after cautiously glancing around, tossed it back to me. This act satisfied me that my secret was safe, at least; but when I read his answer, my gratitude to this noble friend was greater than I could express. He wrote: "I do not want your money; but if you will come just as the moon goes down and throw a pebble at my feet I will leave my beat; but be very careful not to make any noise." With a joyful heart I hurried to my companions to tell them the good news.

That was a busy day for me. I bought some flour, sweet potatoes and meat, and commenced making biscuit, roasting sweet potatoes, and frying meat to fill our haversacks. This, with our slight conveniences for cooking, was no easy task. I made two dozen biscuits; and this, with our other provisions filled our haversacks, and together with our blankets, overcoats, etc., was about all we could carry. Having completed our preparations, I went to where Col. Miller and Lieut. H. H. Lyman had taken up their quarters, which consisted of a dry goods box with one end knocked out, and about half long enough to cover their bodies. They were both too ill to build a brush tent as I had done. I told them that I was going to take a walk the next morning, and asked them to move into my tent, and if I was brought back I would take it back, but if not, then it was theirs, together with the mattress, extra blankets, and cooking utensils.

We then lay down and took a good sleep and rest, waiting for the moon to set, which would be at three o'clock.

By that hour we had eaten our breakfast, picked up what we intended to carry, and cautiously, one by one, gathered under a tree, a few feet from the dead line, where, concealed in the shade, we could plainly see my friend pacing up and down his beat. When the moon had disappeared long enough so that it was quite dark, I tossed a pebble, which struck right at his feet, at which he said in a low tone, "all right" and walked away, and commenced talking to the other sentry.

This was our opportunity, and lying flat on the ground, we crawled across the guard line like so many snakes. There were seven of us, viz.: Captains Geere, Hock, Eastmond, Hays, and Cratty, and Lieutenant Winner and myself. Having all got across, we raised up and stole softly away. We had not gone far, however, before someone stumbled over some dry brush in the darkness, which made considerable noise and attracted the attention of one of the guard, who immediately sent a bullet in our direction and called out lustily: "Corporal of the guard, post number fo." This was followed by other shots; but they could only shoot in the direction of the noise, and if ever seven fellows made good time, we did for about half a mile, till we gained a small patch of woods. We did not stop here long, but getting our direction, we made for another and larger woods about three miles away.

We entered these woods just as it was getting light; and making our way far into its dark recesses, made our camp for the day. We could plainly hear the reveille in the prison camp, from where we lay that morning, and would not have been surprised to have heard the dogs on our trail that day. But the dogs had been kept pretty busy for the past few days, and were perhaps busy then, following some other track. We spread down our blankets and took a nap for an hour or two, and then after eating a light breakfast, commenced perfecting our plans for the future.

We each cut a good, stout hickory staff, and then agreed upon our manner of march. Captain Geere, who had escaped once before and been recaptured, was chosen leader, and we were to march in single file, about ten paces apart, Geere first, Eastmond next, myself third, and the others behind. If the leader saw any danger, he was to raise his hand as a signal for all to drop down; and if he wanted to consult, he would stop and wait for us to come up.

The moon was full, and shone brightly nearly all night; so that when we were in the open road, these signals could be plainly seen by the man next behind, who was to raise his hand, and so pass the signal back to the rear. About ten o'clock that night we started for the road, which we had reconnoitered and found during the day. We had nearly reached the road, when we heard a dog baying as though on a trail of some kind, and also heard the voices of men shouting to him. Making quite a long detour, we again approached the road, this time where the timber was sparse, and the greensward soft beneath our feet. Captain Geere had just reached the middle of the road, and Captain Eastmond was near the edge of the woods, when suddenly a large white dog, with a loud bay attacked Geere. I was near enough to see Geere swinging his stick in front of the dog to keep him off, and dropped flat down. I saw two armed men come up and silence the dog, but waited for no more, and stealthily glided away as fast as I could, back into the woods.

The greensward beneath my feet, the barking of the dog, and the loud talking of the men, prevented them from hearing me, and I assure you it was not long before I was out of their hearing, no matter how much noise I had made. I was all alone, and did not know in what direction I was running, I only knew I was getting away from the sound of that dog. I had run, I should judge, about a mile, when I again came to the road and crossed it. Soon getting into a swampy piece of ground, I climbed over fallen trees, plunged into mud holes, tore through brier bushes, and stumbled over stumps, and finally sat down, completely out of breath, to listen.

It was now about 11 o'clock, and there was not a sound to be heard. After listening some time I again started for the road, feeling that I must make the balance of the tramp alone. I soon found the road, and then put in some of the tallest walking I had ever done, knowing that every stride I made was a stride towards safety. I had walked about five miles, as near as I could judge, and had just come to the open country again, when from the fence beside the road just behind me, I heard my name spoken; and knowing that no one but my comrades would know my name, I at once halted and answered. It proved to be Captain Hock and Adjutant Winner, who had heard me coming and waited for me.

We pushed on rapidly, knowing that our safety depended on the distance we placed between ourselves and Columbia that night, and at daylight went into camp in a piece of woods about fifteen miles from Columbia. I did not take any blanket with me; but had a good overcoat, which we spread on the ground, and covering ourselves with the blankets of Hock and Winner, slept soundly until about ten o'clock, when we awoke and took our breakfast of two biscuits each, and spent the balance of the day in chatting, smoking, snoozing, etc. About half past nine that evening (the 14th) we started on again, proceeding cautiously in single file, but we did not make more than twelve miles that night, on account of being obliged to make a long detour two or three times, to flank some wagons that had camped beside the road, on their way to market at Columbia.

People going to market there are frequently eight or ten days on the road, camping like gypsies, wherever night overtakes them. They would build a fire beside the road, and cook their supper, picket their horses, and go to sleep in their covered wagons.

In these detours, we sometimes came across a few sweet potatoes, or some corn in the field, which we would gather to roast for our breakfast. In fact, after the third day, our biscuits were all gone, and we had nothing to eat except what we could thus find along the road. On the third night out, my legs began to pain me, and the next morning they were quite swollen and inflamed. This was Sunday, and we camped in a pine grove, near a clear brook; and after breakfast I took a good bath in the cold water, and felt quite refreshed after it. That night, just after we started, we found a guide board, and mounting Captain Hock's shoulders, I got near enough to read that we were thirty-four miles from Columbia, having averaged not quite twelve miles a night.

Being now out of provisions, much of our time was spent in looking for sweet potatoes along the road. Sometimes we would see a nice patch in front of some wayside house; but almost every house had a dog or two, and they ever seemed on the alert for tramps; and it was quite a risk to attempt to dig sweet potatoes with those dogs making such a racket, and we were often glad enough to get away without being detected, and even without the desired potatoes. How those dogs would bark! It seemed as though they would arouse the whole neighborhood with their eternal yelping. I took a solemn oath during that journey that if I ever lived to get free, I would thereafter shoot every dog I could find, and I pretty near kept that oath, too. We were not so much afraid of their biting us as we were that they would be followed by their masters with loaded guns; and often we would make a detour of a mile, rather than have attention attracted to us by those yelping curs.

The fifth night of our tramp was cloudy and dark, so much so that the little North Star, that had thus far been our guide, as well as the full moon that had lighted up our road, was completely hidden from our view, and we were left to grope our way as best we could. In the darkness we came to where the roads forked, and although there was a guide board, it was in vain that I tried by mounting Captain Hock's shoulders and lighting matches, to read the directions, to find which road led in the right direction.

After talking the matter over, and consulting our little map as well as we could by the aid of lighted matches, we took the road to the right, and although it may seem paradoxical, for this once right was wrong.

We traveled on this road two or three miles, when we were satisfied that we should have taken the other fork, but thinking we would come to a road soon that bore in the right direction, we kept plodding along in the darkness and finally in the rain, and when near daylight we went into camp, we only knew we were in the woods somewhere in South Carolina, but in what particular portion of that state we could not tell. Of one thing we were satisfied, and that was that we were tired out and half starved. We spread our blankets on the wet ground and, with the rain falling in our faces, slept as soundly as though our bed was one of down instead of the wet ground.

Awaking about 10 o'clock, I started out on a reconnaissance, and, after carefully skirmishing around for an hour, found that we were near the Saluda river, and that there was a ferry nearby, the river at this point being very wide. We did not wish to cross this river, and had tried hard to avoid it, but by taking the wrong road at the forks had run right onto it.

Instead of laying by this day, we started out to try to find a road that led in the right direction. We found some persimmons, which we gathered and ate to satisfy our hunger; but tramped all day in the rain until 4 o'clock in the afternoon before we found a road that seemed to run in the direction we wished to go. When we finally came to a road that seemed to point to the northwest, we pushed on rapidly for sixteen miles before halting, although we were hungry and tired; and when we finally came to another guide board, we found that we were only forty-four miles from Columbia. This was Tuesday, the 18th, and we had left Columbia the morning of the 14th, thus making an average of only eleven miles a day, or rather a night.

We had nothing to eat but raw corn, which we shelled from the cob, and munched as we walked. My legs had now became swollen and inflamed to such an extent that, had I been at home, I would not have thought I could walk a dozen blocks, still we marched sixteen miles that night, and the next morning we went into camp within the sound of passing cars. That night we started out again, but had not gone more than half a mile before we again came upon the river. This was discouraging for, as I have said, we did not wish to cross the river but to go in a parallel direction, and this road ended at a ferry.

There was nothing to do but go back and try to find a road that branched off from the one we were just traveling. The country through which we were passing was densely wooded, and the weather was cloudy and rainy, and, after tramping all day and all the next night, we finally went into camp again; but where we could not tell, except that it was in the woods. We had traveled hither and thither for thirty-six hours without anything to eat.

After resting and sleeping until about 11 o'clock in the forenoon, we started out again to find a road. We found a corn field in which some beans had been planted between the hills, and gathered the ears of corn and picked some of the beans, which we shelled and cooked in a tin plate that I had brought along. We were near a spring of water, and, by placing the tin plate on three stones and building a fire with twigs under it, we could, by frequently pouring in water from a tin cup, manage to keep them from burning until they were soft enough to eat. It took a good deal of time and patience to cook enough for three in this way; but by working faithfully all day, I cooked enough to make us think we had had quite a dinner.

During the day, Captain Hock in skirmishing around the woods came across four or five shoats and an old sow feeding on the nuts and persimmons, and tried by shelling corn to coax them near enough to knock one over to cook for rations; but they were so wild he could not get near enough to capture one. He worked a long time to gain their confidence; and they would come within a few feet, and then, with a loud snort, would scamper off into the woods again, patiently followed by the Captain. Finally, however, he was obliged to give up the chase, and the prospects of a good dinner vanished.

About four o'clock we found a road, and then completely tired out, we lay down and slept. It was nearly midnight when we started on, and then it was with difficulty that I could walk at all. My legs gave me such pain that it seemed as if they would break off at every step. They were swollen to three times their natural size and were so inflamed that I thought I would be obliged to give up. The agony I suffered that night can never be told, but I would not let my comrades halt for my sufferings, and they would not go on without me — God bless them! They would not desert me, but rather stay and share my fate, whatever it might be. I never can forget those two noble comrades, who so faithfully stood by me, when, by leaving me behind, as I begged of them to do, they, who were strong and hearty, could have made double the distance I could make in my enfeebled condition.

We soon found the railroad, and knowing that it would take us to Knoxville, where we were making for, we started along the track. Although my sufferings were almost unbearable, I trudged along uncomplainingly, for I would not impede their progress; and when, shortly after, we came in sight of a covered bridge, which we thought might be guarded, I volunteered to make a reconnaissance, for I thought it better for me to be re-taken than either of them.

Fortunately, there was no guard at the bridge, and we crossed. Captain Hock was obliged to crawl across on his hands and knees for fear of falling, as there was nothing but the ties and stringers to cross on and it made him dizzy to walk upright. After crossing this bridge, we came to a sweet potato patch and filled our haversacks so as to have a breakfast.

Just at daylight that morning, we met a negro going to work in a mill; but, as we were afraid to trust him, we did not speak except to say "good morning" as we passed. This was the first person, black or white, that we had met since our escape, and we had then been out six days. We went into a piece of woods nearby, and I cooked sweet potatoes in that tin plate nearly all day to satisfy our appetites.

We had our camp this day in a small thicket near a sweet potato field; and, knowing that we could lay in a good supply after dark, we cooked and ate all we wanted of our former supply. It kept me pretty busy cooking them in that tin plate, as I was obliged to slice them up and then keep adding water as it boiled away; but we managed to make out a good dinner, and then lay down and slept until nearly dark. We made our supper on some of the potatoes that I had roasted in the hot embers, so we had a variety that day, boiled sweet potatoes for dinner, and sweet potatoes roasted for supper. After supper we went into the field, and filled our haversacks for the next morning's breakfast. It was hard digging, as the soil was gravelly, and we had nothing but our fingers to dig with.

If anyone thinks that a peck of sweet potatoes is not heavy, let him try carrying a peck all night, and walk the railroad ties. This, the seventh night, we started out early, taking the railroad track, which would take us direct; but it was hard walking, and especially for me, as my legs were so swollen and lame. I had been obliged on account of my swollen feet and limbs to cut off the legs of my cavalry boots, and split down the vamp nearly to the toe, to make them more roomy and comfortable, for my stockingless feet.

I used to think during that tramp on the railroad, how much better walking it would be, if they would place the ties straight across the road bed, and at an equal distance apart, say about eighteen inches, instead of putting every third or fourth one on a bias. We *discussed* this thing pretty thoroughly during the time we were engaged as track-walkers between Columbia and Wallhalla, and came to the conclusion that a reform was necessary, in this regard.

We were continually obliged to take one or two short steps and then a long one, and if the reader does not believe that to be tiresome, let him try it for two or three hundred miles, and he will believe that I am right, and that I know something about how railroads ought to be built for foot passengers. At any rate, I was so completely used up by one o'clock that night that I tried to have my comrades go on and leave me to try to get some negro to take care of me until I was able to resume my journey. I told them that it was impossible for me to proceed; but they said they would go into camp there, and see what success I met with in finding shelter.

We went into a piece of woods near the railroad and in sight of the village of Greenwood, S. C., at one o'clock in the morning, and lay there all day, watching for some negro to come along the road, which here ran along the railroad. Towards night, I walked out to the railroad, and saw a negro coming along on horseback. I sat upon the fence with my blue overcoat on, and the following dialogue took place:

"Hello uncle!"

"Howde massa?"

"Uncle, did you ever see a Yankee?"

"No sah, I spects I never did."

"Well, now, take a good look at me and you'll see one."

"Is you a Yankee, massa?"

"Yes, I am a Yankee, and I want you to help me. You know we are going to make the darkies all free. We are your friends. I have been a prisoner at Columbia, and have escaped to get back North; but I am sick, and cannot go any farther until I get better. Now I would like to go home with you and have you take care of me until I am able to travel again, and I will pay you well for your trouble."

"Well massa, you see I would like to do it mighty well; but I live six miles back, and there's so many chiller bout dare, and all the house servants dey can't be trusted. Our oberseer he's a black man, but he do any ting massa say. I don't dare trust him, and if dey kotch me, dey'd hang me, sure. But ders a collored fellah up the road, 'Free Mitchell,' he'll keep you if you get dere."

After making inquiries how to find "Free Mitchell," and getting as definite directions as it was possible to obtain from a black, which was quite vague, I bid him "good bye," after enjoining the strictest secrecy, and receiving his most solemn promise not to say a word. I went back to my comrades, and reported what I had done, and proposed that as soon as it was dark we should hunt up this free negro, and try and get help.

Soon after dark, we all started and walked two miles to the little village of Greenwood. Thinking by the directions given, that we were nearing the house, Hock and Winner lay down in the corner of the fence to wait until I could find this place of refuge, and, if possible, bring them something to eat.

Chapter XIV.

assailed by a dog — scaring a negro — free mitchell — he dare not let me into his yard on account of a yankee schoolmaster who kept blood hounds — flanking the hounds — meeting captain alban — losing my former companions i start out with him.

I walked part way into town trying not to attract attention, when a large dog came bristling up, and acted as if he would like a piece of me; but his master, who was a negro, gruffly called him back, and just then coming to the railroad, I turned up the track and walked rapidly for half a mile to get out of the village. I soon came to the place where the road crossed the railroad, and thought I would wait until my companions came up. I had told them that if I was not back in an hour to go on and leave me; for, if nothing happened, I would be back within that time with something for them to eat; and if I was not back they might make up their minds that I was recaptured, or something had occurred to prevent me getting back.

When I parted from them, Captain Hock, with his usual thoughtfulness and generosity, took out his pocket book and divided the contents with me, saying I might need more than he would. I sat down in the shadow of a large pine tree that stood close to the road, and, after about half an hour, I heard someone approaching from the direction of the village; and thinking it might be my companions, I waited until a large negro came up. Just as he passed me, I stepped up behind him and touched him on the shoulder, at the same time saying, "hello!" I think that negro jumped two feet straight up, when I thus abruptly saluted him. As soon as he could speak, he said, "Golly, massa, how you skeered me!"

I asked him where he was going, and he said he "done got a pass from de massa to go see his wife, about two miles up de road."

"Well," said I, "then you go past Free Mitchell's, don't you?"

"No, not zacly; but I go right near."

"Well, Uncle," said I, "I am going to Free Mitchell's, and if you show me to his house, here is a dollar for you."

"All right, massa; but you walk behind aways, for if we meet any one, and dey see me wid a white man, dey'll take me back agin, sure."

So we started on, and after walking about two miles came to a small cabin in the woods. My guide went in and called out the owner, who proved to be an intelligent looking mulatto, and who said he was "Free Mitchell."

I told him who I was and who had directed me to him, and asked him if he could keep and feed me for a few days, telling him that I had plenty of money to pay for the trouble I should cause him. But he said he would not dare even to let me in his yard, for he was already suspected of secreting fugitives; and there was a Yankee schoolmaster living just beyond, who kept a pack of hounds, and hunted around his house every two or three days, and if he found any tracks leading into his yard they would hang him right quick. He advised me not to make any stops until I got safely beyond those hounds. He had nothing cooked up to give me a bite to eat, so I thought I would start on and get beyond those dogs, and try for some safer place.

About a mile beyond this cabin I saw a house back from the road, and a pack of hounds commenced a fearful baying before I was within a quarter of a mile of the premises. Knowing the keenness of scent possessed by those brutes, I made a detour of about half a mile, and got into a marshy piece of ground covered with alders. Through this I tramped some distance, half way to my knees in the soft mud, and tearing myself on the bushes, until I finally came out on the road again, out of hearing of the dogs. I soon came to a place where the road crossed the railroad again and, thinking that my comrades must come on one or the other of these, I sat down on a pile of ties beside the track to rest and wait for them.

It was now nearly midnight and the moon was shining bright, while all around was still as death. Just behind me on the railroad was quite a deep cut and, after waiting some time, I heard someone approaching from that direction, their steps on the railroad ties resounding on the still night air with a wonderful distinctness. Thinking it must be my comrades, as no one else would be likely to be out at that time of night, I sat still and waited for them to come up.

Suddenly, a large powerful looking man emerged from the shade of the cut, and was so near before I saw him, that I could not have escaped detection if I had tried. Thinking to have the first word, I raised up before he discovered me, and sung out:

"Hello!"

"Good evening," said he, very civilly.

"Where are you going?" I asked somewhat sternly.

He hesitated and stammered out, "to Greenville, sir."

"Do you live in Greenville?" I asked.

"No, sir," said he, "I live in — in Columbia," hesitatingly.

"You are a Yankee officer, I believe!" said I.

"Well, sir," said he, "there is no use in denying it, I am."

"So am I, old boy," exclaimed I, grasping his hand, "put it there."

If ever two fellows were pleased to find a friend when they had both expected to find an enemy, we two were, just then. The hearty hand shaking that followed showed that we were mutually pleased to find, that, instead of running onto an armed reb, we had run across an old comrade. We had been in prison together in Macon, Savannah, Charleston and Columbia, and still were strangers to each other. This officer proved to be Captain H. H. Alban, 21st Ohio Vols., who was taken prisoner at Chicamauga. He had two dressed chickens, and a quantity of corn bread, that he had just bought in Greenwood of a negro.

He gave me a good sized piece of corn bread, which I thought the sweetest morsel I had ever tasted, for I had not eaten anything all day, and was half starved.

I bought one of the chickens for ten dollars, Captain Alban excusing himself for taking the money, by saying that he had just paid the last dollar he possessed for those two chickens and corn bread, and when they were gone he would be obliged to forage or starve.

He urged me to go on with him, promising to carry my haversack and do all the buying, taking the risk of recapture, if I would furnish the money. I showed him my legs, and told him that I would only be a hindrance to him, and would wait there until my companions came up.

Finally, after talking the matter over, I agreed that if my comrades did not come within an hour, I should think they had got ahead of me, and would go on with him, for this night at least. We sat there and waited until about one o'clock, and, as they did not come, I started on with him, feeling like a new man after the good lunch and the rest. Captain Alban, who was a large, strong man, six feet high and in robust health, took my haversack. This lightened me up a good deal, and I was too plucky to let him think I could not keep up, and so I stubbed along, notwithstanding my swollen legs and feet, and that night we put in seventeen miles, after I met him, before we went into camp.

Chapter XV.

how to roast a chicken — a good square meal once more — on the tramp again — we meet a darkey who furnishes us supper and chickens from his master's hen coop — surprised by two white men while eating breakfast — passing through walhalla — avoiding some cavalry.

When we made camp on this, the twelfth day of my tramp, it was back of a plantation, in a large woods, near a spring. We always made our camp near good water, if possible. Here I showed the captain how to cook a chicken; and for the benefit of camping parties I give the receipt here, which, if followed, will, I assure them, afford as fine a dinner as can be made from a chicken.

Bending over a small sapling about two inches through at the butt, I fastened the top to the roots of a tree, and then trimmed off the branches. From the centre of the bow thus formed, I hung the chicken by means of a limb with a hook on the lower end, so that the chicken nearly reached the ground. Then building a fire in a circle around the fowl, with dry twigs and bark, as a blacksmith would to heat a wagon tire, I soon had a chicken as finely browned as ever was cooked in an oven. I salted it as it roasted and within an hour I ate the first satisfactory meal I had eaten in eleven days, roast chicken and corn bread, with a tin cup full of cold water. After a good sleep which lasted until nearly dark, I felt like a new man, and only for my swollen and inflamed feet and legs, would have felt fit to endure anything.

We started out at dark, having made a supper of the remains of the chicken and some corn bread, and, before daylight had made twenty miles, though my legs kept getting worse, if possible, and pained me so that at times I could scarcely keep from crying out in my agony.

Captain Alban would not leave me, and encouraged me to renewed efforts when I was almost fainting from pain.

It was Saturday night that I met Alban, and on Monday we ate the last of our chickens and corn bread, and with full stomachs, but empty haversacks, we started out at dark again. About nine o'clock, as we were going along through a piece of woods, we suddenly came upon a negro with a large wooden trunk on his head. He was frightened at first but after finding out that we were Yankees, he was about the most delighted darkey I ever saw. I told him I would give him twenty dollars if he would get me five chickens, and corn bread enough to eat with them. This he promised to do, and told us to wait there until he toted the trunk over to his old grannies, and when he came back he would whistle, to let us know it was him, and when we answered the whistle, he would take us to the house and give us some supper. He was soon back and we went with him to the edge of the woods, near the shanty, when he again left us to make sure that everything was all right. It was not long before we again heard the low, musical whistle, which I answered, and he came up with two other negroes and took us to a cabin, where a good fire was burning and an old black woman was cooking some bacon and corn bread, or hoe cake, as they call it. While auntie was getting our supper prepared, the three men went out to see about the chickens.

It was not long before they were back, and had five nice fat fowl, which they proceeded at once to dress for us, and by the time we had finished our supper, which we greatly relished, the fowl were ready, the feathers burned, and the floor carefully swept, so that every trace of the transaction was removed. I had a silver quarter in my pocket which I gave to aunty, and which she received with profuse expressions of joy and gratitude. We stayed with them until eleven o'clock, and although we only walked eleven miles after that, I was completely used up the next morning when we went into camp again. I cooked three of the chickens that day, and we eat one for dinner and one for supper.

That night we walked twenty miles on the railroad, crossing four long iron covered bridges, and went into camp in a large piece of woods some distance back from the railroad, as daylight again warned us to seek shelter.

About eight o'clock we made a fire and were roasting our last chicken, making our breakfast in the meantime, on the one left from the night before. I had laid aside my overcoat, and was therefore in the full dress of a cavalry lieutenant, shoulder straps and all, and we were chatting over our breakfast, when I heard the brush crackle close by, and looking up we saw two white men within a few rods of us; one dressed in the homespun usually worn by citizens in the south, and the other wearing the uniform of a Confederate soldier.

I just had time to say to Alban, they are unarmed and I can handle one if you can the other, when they came up to where we were sitting. They both seemed a little embarrassed, and the situation was slightly embarrassing to us.

After the usual salutation, the elder of the two said, somewhat apologetically: "We saw the smoke out here, and thought someone had built a fire while possum hunting last night, and was afraid it might get into our fence, which is just through yonder thicket."

We assured him that we would put the fire out carefully when we went away, which we would do as soon as our chicken was done. I was well aware that they must know we were Yankees, and feared that our tramp was over for the present, but anything was better than suspense, and rising to my feet I said to the old man who stood near me: "Well, sir, I suppose you know that we are Yankees; now, what do you propose to do with us?"

"Yes," said he, "I know you are Yankees, but you need have no fear of us, we are Union men."

"How is it, then, that this young man wears the Confederate uniform?"

"Well, sir, to save being conscripted and sent to the field, he joined a company of home guard, who are nearly all Union men, and by doing so is kept about here."

I well knew he was telling the truth, and I grasped his hand and shook it heartily, and while we all sat around the fire, I told them of our imprisonment and escape, and of our long tramp for freedom. They told us their names were John Addis and William Addis, father and son, and that they would do anything they could to assist us.

They went to the house and had some wheat biscuit baked, and some sweet potatoes roasted for us, the young man promising that if his mother would consent, he would go with us to our lines; but she was so fearful that he would be captured and shot as a deserter, that she would not listen to the proposition for a moment, but sent by him a hearty God-speed to us.

Mr. Addis directed us to his brother in Towns County, Georgia, and said that he had heard, that the Union forces were in that county a few days before, and it would be perfectly safe for us to travel in the day time, passing ourselves for Confederate soldiers on furloughs.

He said that at Walhalla, thirteen miles ahead, they were very vigilant, and at Tunnel Hill, (nineteen miles) there was a picket station, at a gap in the mountain, which it would be necessary for us to flank. He gave us the name of the captain of a company of youths who guarded this pass, which I carefully noted, and instructed us as well as he could, how to get around this gap. The young man went with us about two miles, to get us past the depot without being noticed, and then bade us good bye, saying that he would like to accompany us north if he could. We started on, feeling much encouraged, expecting to get beyond the picket at Tunnel Hill before daylight. But it soon commenced raining fearfully, and the walking was slippery, which made it intensely painful to my poor inflamed limbs, and chafed the skin off my stockingless feet, as they slipped up and down in legless boots.

I stood it as long as I could, but at twelve o'clock I was obliged to give up, and drenched to the skin, we lay down under a pine tree beside the road, and covering ourselves with a wet blanket, with my overcoat for a bed, and the rain beating in our faces, we slept the sound refreshing sleep of tired soldiers. We awoke just before daylight, wet, cold and stiff, and started on towards Walhalla, which was about a mile ahead. I thought the one street that passed through that little hamlet, was the longest I ever saw. It was daylight when we entered the town, and the early risers were stirring, but they were all negroes. We walked rapidly, but it seemed as though we would never get through the village and gain the woods beyond. And finally seeing some covered wagons just at the further edge of the town, with the owners cooking their breakfast, we concluded to make a flank movement to the right, as though we were going to work in the woods. We gained the woods in safety, and crossing the road, went in a considerable distance, and sat down on a fallen tree, ate our breakfast and rested for about an hour.

As it was still raining and very cloudy, we concluded to go on, and try and flank the picket post at Tunnel Hill before night, thinking they would not be as watchful during the day. We kept in sight of the road, and hearing some mounted men coming, we hid until they passed. We could plainly hear them talking, and concluded that it was the relief, going up to change the guard. Going on, we kept the road in sight, until we came to a plantation, which we thought best to go around, keeping in the edge of the woods that skirted it. It was a long detour, and when we tried to come out on the road again, we could not find it. There was a path in the woods, leading up quite a steep looking hill. It seemed to be well traveled, and thinking we could go over this hill and probably come out on the road, we followed this path in a circuitous way for nearly a mile, when we came to the top of a ridge, that seemed about ten rods wide, and densely covered with large timber. Looking down on either side, we could see through the clouds and fog, a valley of wooded land on one side, and clear land on the other. We walked along this ridge all day, and as the sun was completely obscured, we could not tell in what direction we were moving. We examined the moss on the trees, but sometimes it would be on one side, and then on the other. About five o'clock, our path led down the mountain, and in half an hour more, we were surprised to find, that although we had followed the path all day, we had come out just where we went up in the morning. We learned after, that this was Cheat mountain, and is a high ridge shaped like a bowl, with a valley in the center, and we had walked around the crest all day, making nearly ten miles. It was now about sundown, and reconnoitering in different directions, we finally found the road again, and laying down in some weeds, waited for darkness.

Chapter XVI.

back into walhalla — we run into a rebel picket in the dark and are taken in — a little judicious lying secures our release — overtaking some wagons going from market — chatting with a company of rebel cavalry.

tarting out again at dark, we walked on rapidly for about five miles, when we came to some covered wagons beside the road, and just after passing them, I said to Alban, "I believe this is Walhalla again." He thought it impossible; so said I, "we won't go far before we come to a carpenter shop, with a bench outside." Sure enough, we soon came to the carpenter shop that I had noticed as we passed hastily through the town that morning. Turning about we walked back, and soon found how we had made the mistake in the darkness. Near where these wagons were camped, there was a fork in the road; we had taken the right hand fork in the morning, and turned into the woods to the left of the road. The road we had found at night, was the other branch of the fork and turning to the left again, we had walked directly back to where we started from in the morning. It was now nine o'clock, and again taking the right hand road, we started back towards Tunnel Hill.

There were mile boards on this road, that told the distance, and as we had been told it was six miles to Tunnel Hill, we walked along briskly for nearly four miles, when all of a sudden there rang out clear and distinct that well known challenge: "Halt! Who comes there?"

The voice was not five rods ahead, and through the darkness we could discern the outline of the sentry, and just beyond a dim fire of dying embers.

"Soldiers!" was the prompt reply to the challenge by Captain Alban. "Have you got any showance?" (pass.) "Yes, sir," he answered. "Well, come in and let's see it." Alban was about twenty yards ahead of me, and as I had not yet spoken, I thought perhaps I might not have been seen, and as he approached the sentry, I crouched down, preparatory to sliding into the woods. But the guard saw me, and asked if that was another soldier behind, and upon being answered in the affirmative, told me to come in too. I said I didn't think he would allow us both to approach at once; that we never would at the front allow but one to approach at a time.

"Oh, we've got force enough to take care of both of youans," said he. So we walked in, and he took us up to the smoldering fire, where six or eight others were sitting and lying around, and speaking to someone whom he called Dock, told him to get up and look at our "showance." While Dock was crawling out, pulling on his boots, and rubbing his eyes, the guard asked what command we belonged to. We told them that we belonged to the 32d Georgia. (This was the regiment that was guarding Yankee prisoners at Columbia.) That we were stationed at Columbia, guarding Yankee prisoners; that we had just come to Walhalla by the train, and thought we would walk as far as Tunnel Hill, and stay there all night, and see the Captain, (giving his name,) who was an old friend of mine, that I had not seen since the war broke out, and I wanted to have a visit with him. That we were going to Towns County, Georgia, where my sister (giving a fictitious name), who was Alban's wife, lived; that I had a sick furlough for thirty days, and Alban had a pass for ten days, to go and see his wife. We mentioned two or three names that had been furnished us by Mr. Addis, and asked if they knew them.

By the time "Dock" was ready to examine our papers, we had got them thoroughly interested in us, and had so thoroughly impressed upon them the belief that we were all right, and then I showed them my legs which were so terribly inflamed, and told them that I was suffering from inflammatory rheumatism, — which was the nearest the truth of anything that I had yet told them — and groaned over the excruciating pain I was suffering. When I had fully impressed them with the truthfulness of my story, I took from my pocket an enlistment paper that I had, and produced it as my furlough. I told them that I bought that overcoat of a Yankee for five plugs of tobacco, and got the pants for two plugs; that you could buy anything of those Yankee prisoners for tobacco; They would sell the shirt off their back for tobacco. Finally "Dock" took my furlough, and as it was raining hard, and the fire would not burn, he got down on his knees beside it, and would blow up a little blaze, and try to make out the papers; but could only see that it was a printed and written document of some kind. At the same time I was groaning over my suffering legs, and rubbing them, and wishing I was at the captain's quarters, where I could rest and care for them. After "Dock" had tried in vain for sometime to make out my furlough, I said it was too bad to keep me there in the rain where I was sure to take cold in my legs; that the Captain could examine the papers in the morning, and see that they were all right. So he finally said, well I reckon you are all right, you can go ahead. If you want to go to Clayton it is the nearest way to take the left fork, but if you want to go to Tunnel Hill take the right. We passed on a few yards to the forks, and not wishing to let them see how anxious we were to get away, we stopped and discussed the question whether we would go on to Tunnel Hill, or turn towards Clayton.

We finally turned towards Clayton, as we had all the time intended, and when we got out of sight and hearing of the picket post, we just lay down and rolled and laughed. Up to the time that "Dock" told us we could go on, we had scarcely the slightest idea that they would not detect the fraud, and march us off under guard to headquarters. Sick and lame as I was, I could not restrain my laughter at this adventure, for hours after.

We hurried forward however, for fear the officer of the guard might be making his rounds, and learning of our passing the picket, follow us up to ascertain that we were all right. About one o'clock we halted, completely tired out with our almost incessant march of nearly forty-eight hours, in the mud and rain, with little to eat, and as wet as we were, we lay down in a thicket beside the road, and slept soundly until daylight. When we awoke, we were wet through and completely chilled, and started on to try and get warm. We soon came to a river which we were obliged to ford, the water being nearly up to our waist, but as we were already as wet as we could be, it did not make much difference whether we were in the water or on dry land.

We soon came upon some teams that were camped beside the road, being on their way back from Walhalla to Cherokee County, North Carolina. There were two rebel soldiers acting as guard for the teams, and the owner was a Doctor Washburn, formerly from Livingston County, N. Y., as he informed me. They were cooking their breakfast, but did not say anything about our taking breakfast with them. They, however, directed us to the house of a widow, a little farther on, where we could be accommodated. We stopped there, and she got us up a nice breakfast of corn bread, sweet potatoes and fried mutton, and I guess she thought by the way we eat that we had not had anything before in some days, and did not know when we would get anything again. This widow was quite bitter towards the Confederacy on account of her son having been conscripted, and she left alone, with no one to work her little farm or care for her children. She was too poor to hire the work done, and was obliged to do all that was done towards supporting herself and children; as her son's pay scarcely amounted to enough to keep him in tobacco, and left nothing towards the support of his mother and a family of small children. Having eaten and paid for our breakfast, we waited for the teams to come along, and then we concluded to travel with them, as it would give us the appearance of being all right, if we should meet any soldiers on the road.

We soon made ourselves at home in their company and I found Dr. Washburn a very kind-hearted gentleman, and I think that he more than half suspected our true characters, though he did not pretend to doubt that we were Confederate soldiers, belonging to the 32d Georgia. He offered to loan me all the money I needed, which, as he was a perfect stranger, seemed to me pretty good evidence that he knew I was an escaped prisoner and wanted to help me to get home. He inquired whether there were any prisoners at Columbia who were from Livingston County, N. Y., which he said was his native place; and I said I didn't know where any of them were from, except I had heard Captain Cady say that he was from Rochester, N. Y., but I did not know what part of the North that was. I was more than once on the point of revealing myself to him, and now believe that had I done so, he would have assisted me. We traveled in company with them two days, and it was quite a help, to me especially.

The teams were so heavily loaded that I could not ride much, but on down grades and at the different fords we came to, he asked me to get on and rest up a little, which offer I gladly accepted, crossing the Chatuga river on the back of one of the mules. Dr. Washburn had a Columbia paper, which gave the particulars of Sheridan's famous fight with Early in the Valley. When they went into camp the first night, Alban and I went into a barn nearby, and slept until morning. Having travelled until ten o'clock and forded three streams, we were very tired and slept soundly. The next day we started on ahead of them, but they overtook us before night; as they halted early, however, we kept on and were overtaken by a man on horseback who told us he lived about five miles further on, and if we got that far, we were welcome to stay overnight with him. We found his house about dark, and he gave us a good supper and a good drink of apple-jack, which he fished out from under the bed.

Alban would not drink any, and tried by winks and sly nudges, to keep me from accepting a second invitation, but I didn't take the hint worth a cent. Mr. King (for that was his name) was running an illicit distillery near where we first met him.

After we had taken two or three drinks, he became talkative, and I think my tongue was a little loose. He did not go a cent on the Confederacy, and thought the whole thing was about gone up; and he didn't care much how soon it collapsed. If he was in my place, he would not go back into the Confederate army and I told him that I did not intend to. Before we went to bed, we were on pretty good terms with one another and the world in general, with the exception of the Confederate government. He lived near the bank of the Teroria river, and before breakfast we went down to the river, and cold as it was that morning, stripped off and took a good bath. When we went back to the house, he again fished out the demijohn from under the bed, and we took a good one for an appetizer. Alban was fidgety and nervous, for fear my tongue would run away with me, but I was as jolly as a lord, and as wary as a member of Congress.

After a good breakfast, for which he would take no pay, we crossed the Teroria river and pushed on briskly. I felt just in humor for any adventure, and one soon presented itself.

We had not gone far when we saw a company of reb cavalry coming towards us from ahead. We sat down on a log beside the road and waited for them to come up, as there were no woods to slip into just there. When they came along I saluted the Captain and asked, "Whar youans going, Captain?" "Oh, just going up the road a piece," he answered, and passed on without questioning us.

One of the men at the rear of the column stopped long enough to ask us where we'uns were from, and I told him we had just come from the valley and had had some right smart fighting with Sheridan. I then hastily detailed the fight as I had read it in the Columbia paper. He seemed flattered with the fact that he had talked with two old soldiers who had been with Earley (for they were home guards), and rode briskly forward to overtake his comrades.

We soon came to Clayton, Georgia, and the court being in session, there was quite a crowd gathered about the court house. We were debating whether or not it would be safe to keep the road, which led directly past the court house, when a mounted officer, who had evidently found some applejack somewhere, came riding down to meet us, and when he learned from us that we belonged to the 32d Georgia, and had just come from Earley's army, wanted the latest news. We told him that we had had a right smart fight with Sheridan, and taken his camp, with all of the stores and a number of pieces of artillery, but that while the boys were plundering the camp, Sheridan had surprised us and cut us all up. Having filled him as chock full of news as he was of applejack, we told him we were going to Hiawassee, and asked the most direct road.

He directed us across a common, that would take us to the road leading to Hiawassee, that would not necessitate our passing the court house, and rode back to retail the news we had given him.

After passing Clayton two or three miles, we stopped at a farm house to get dinner. As we sat down at the table, the host introduced us to the sheriff of Rabun county. We chatted pleasantly with him during the meal, but felt greatly relieved when we were once more on the road.

The next day (Sunday) we struck the Hiawassee river, and fording it, we pushed on, and just about sundown, came to a house that seemed to promise good fare, and, representing ourselves to be Confederate soldiers on a furlough, asked for supper and lodging.

The gentleman, who had the appearance of a wealthy planter, hesitated, but when I told him we wished to pay for the accommodation, he said he reckoned they could keep us, and invited us in. The family consisted of the planter —

Major Carter — his wife, and one daughter, and a lady teacher, who seemed to be of Northern birth. After supper the conversation naturally turned on the war, and we discussed the situation freely, and finding that he was a rank reb, we were, of course, in favor of a vigorous prosecution of the war as long as there was a soldier left to fight or a dollar in the treasury. We got on swimmingly for a time. Major Carter was a man of intelligence, and was thoroughly posted on the situation, as well as the position of the two armies. In fact, I began to fear that he was too well posted to make it safe for me to attempt to tell too much of where I had served, and it soon became convenient for my inflamed legs to pain me so much that his good wife had one of the colored servants bring me some warm water out on the stoop to bathe them in.

This brought the conversation, which was getting a little too deep for me, to a close; and I asked to be shown to my room, after offering him a ten-dollar bill to take out for our supper and lodging. I told him we should probably wish to start before he was up and so preferred to pay that night. The fact was, I did not wish to meet him the next morning, after he had taken time to think over the matter, for I was quite sure his suspicions had been partially aroused. He would have taken two dollars, but could not change the ten, and I told him I would call on my way back and pay him.

Chapter XVII.

at major carters — my swollen limbs give me an excuse to cut off the conversation — rev. mr. burch gives us a hearty welcome and a good breakfast — passing a confederate soldier — recaptured — eccentric but loyal tom hubbard — taken back to fort emory.

Having partaken of a good hearty supper, we were given a room, and, for the first time in many months, I enjoyed the luxury of a good feather bed. Oh, how gratefully my poor tired limbs reveled in its downy recesses. It seemed almost too bad, to soil those snowy sheets with our dusty and travel stained clothing. Weary and tired as we were however, we soon forgot all our troubles, and were reveling in sweet dreams of home and loved ones.

We were awake bright and early next morning, and hastily dressing, we quietly left the house before any of the other inmates were awake.

This was Monday, the eighteenth day of our tramp, and we had passed through South Carolina and Georgia, and were near the extreme north-west corner of North Carolina.

We walked about two miles, when we came to the house of the Rev. Mr. Burch. He had been milking and was just going to the house with a pail of milk when we came up and asked if we could get some breakfast there. He gave us a hearty welcome to such fare as they could give us, and invited us into the house. We soon discovered that he was a strong Union man, and, although we did not reveal ourselves to him as Yankees, I believe he at least mistrusted we were. We learned from him that the Union forces had been at Murphy, and when we got across the river from there we would be in Tennessee, where we would be safe, as our forces held the ground there. We had told him that we did not intend to go back into the army, but intended to get inside the Union lines and stay there.

I being a member of the Independent Order of Odd Fellows, gave him some signs of that order, which he thought was a clumsily given Masonic sign, and, as he belonged to that fraternity, he tried to test me in the signs of that society. I told him I was not a Mason, but was an Odd Fellow, and he could trust me just as freely as though we both belonged to the same order. He said: "I do trust you, and believe you are all right, but when we express Union sentiments in this section of the country, you know, we do so with a halter around our necks. I have already said and done enough to hang me if it were known to the rebel authorities, and I know they would resort to any trick to trap me into saying or doing something that would convict me of treason to the Confederacy. But I will trust you, though I place my life in your hands by so doing, for God and my own conscience tell me that I am doing right."

He then gave us explicit directions about getting across the river, near Murphy, which was about twenty miles further. He said it would not do to cross the bridge at that place, as it was guarded night and day; but we could probably find boats above there that we could use in crossing. After breakfast he walked with us a short distance, and bidding us an affectionate good-bye and God speed, he turned back and we pursued our way.

About three miles further on we passed the little hamlet of Fort Emory, where I noticed a Confederate officer sitting on the stoop of the only store in the village. Passing by with a nod and a good morning, we were soon out of sight, and as we felt a little uneasy after this, we walked as rapidly as it was possible in my enfeebled condition.

The country through which we were passing now was mostly woods and sparsely settled. In fact, I think we did not pass but two or three houses in the next ten miles. At that distance from Fort Emory we came to a large house that looked as though it belonged to a well-to-do planter, and seeing the owner out near the road we stopped and asked if we could get some supper. We had as yet said nothing about paying, and he put on a long face when he told us that he had nothing cooked in the house. He was a miserly looking old seed, and thinking a little money might tempt him, I said that we were not particular what it was, but would pay him for any kind of a "snack," if he could manage to give us something that would stay our stomachs until we got to Murphy.

Mr. Harshaw — for that was his name — thought he might find something if we would wait awhile, till he could go into the house. While we were yet talking two mounted, armed men, came suddenly around a bend in the road, and galloped down to where we were standing, each with a drawn pistol, and a carbine slung over his shoulder. Dick Hancock the Sergeant, asked, to what command do you belong? 32d Georgia I answered. Where are you going? To Murphy to see my sister; giving him a fictitious name. Let me see your pass said he. I felt in my pocket and said, by golly Alban I left those passes in my haversack at Maj. Carters; and then turning to the Sergeant, I explained that we stayed at the Major's last night, and as we intended to go back to-morrow or the next day, we thought we would leave the haversack which was pretty heavy, and our passes were in the haversack.

You can consider yourselves under arrest, said the Sergeant; and told his companion, Tom Hubbard, to dismount and search us. Tom was a very excitable person, and had a habit of spitting about sixty times a minute. He first took a large Morocco pocketbook that I carried in the breast pocket of my coat, and looking over the papers, came across my recruiting authorization paper, which I had received from the Governor, authorizing me to recruit volunteers, for the service of the United States. Tom read this aloud, spitting between each sentence. He read along until he came to the clause above spoken of, when he stopped suddenly and said: "You are a Yankee officer, by thunder!" I laughed and said: "Well, a Yankee could not guess better than that."

"Well, you are, by jingo."

"Well, who said I wasn't?"

Tom got terribly excited, and spit faster than ever, as he said: "Well, by thunder, you are a Yankee."

I should have laughed if he had been going to shoot me, and I did laugh heartily at his excitement. This made him more excited still, and by the time he had finished reading the paper, he was so excited that I could easily have disarmed him, but the Sergeant sat there, with his pistol ready to shoot if we made any attempt to get away.

I then told them that we were Yankee officers, and that we had for six months suffered the horrors of prison life, that we had escaped from Columbia, and had walked three hundred miles to gain our liberty, and pulling up my pants I showed them my legs, which were swollen to three times their natural size, and very much inflamed, and asked if, after having tramped so far with such a pair of legs, I was not entitled to my liberty. The tears started into Tom's eyes, his mouth twitched convulsively, he spit with fearful rapidity, and he finally said in a choking voice, "By thunder, I am sorry I ever saw you."

If I had my way I would let you go, but if we did old Harshaw, who is a bitter Confederate, would report us and we would be shot. And Tom meant what he said; for as will appear further on, he was a Union man at heart. But the Sergeant was unmoved by our distress, and was only too proud to think he had captured two Yankee officers, to contemplate letting us go; so he ordered us to walk between them back to Fort Emory, ten miles. No Sergeant, I said, I am your prisoner, only because my legs gave out; and I shall never walk back. If you want me to go back to Fort Emory, you will have to carry me, for if I could have walked you would not have seen me. He insisted that I start on, but I told him plainly that I would not walk a step, that I had just about as leave he would shoot me right there as to take me back into prison.

Tom finally said, Dick, you take him up behind you, and I will take this big fellow up behind me, and we will get along much faster. To this proposition the Sergeant consented, and we both mounted and started back. If I could have had a chance to have said a dozen words to Alban before starting, without their seeing us, we would not have gone far; but the Sergeant and I rode ahead, followed by Tom and Alban, and if I had made a move to disarm my man, Tom would have been just in a position to have helped him. I was on the alert, thinking that perhaps Alban would pinion Tom's arms from behind, and give me a signal to do the same for the Sergeant, which I could have easily done.

If I had only known what was going on behind me that night, this narrative would have a different termination. But I did not know Tom Hubbard then, nor did I know how strongly he was attached to the old flag. I learned all this afterwards, and learned to appreciate him, for a true-hearted, loyal man, whose fidelity could always be relied upon, and whose sympathetic nature was as tender as a woman's. The circumstances which surrounded him, compelled him to assume an allegiance to the Confederacy that his loyal soul revolted at. And there is no man North or South that I would give more to see to-day than this same eccentric Tom Hubbard.

Chapter XVIII.

in prison again.

We arrived at the house of Captain Sanderson about ten o'clock that night, and were treated by him like gentlemen. Late as it was, after placing us in an out-house, in which was a weaver's loom, he brought us a good lunch, and gave us every possible privilege he could.

We were strictly guarded, but were made to feel our captivity as little as possible.

We were allowed to go down to a stream near the house the next day, and wash our clothes, which we had worn nearly a month, and the captain, in every way, treated us more like guests than prisoners.

Captain Sanderson was in command of a company of home guards, and had never seen active service. He was a well-to-do farmer, and most of his command were his neighbor's sons, who, like himself, did not care to go into the regular service, and most of them were strongly tinctured with Union sentiments. I don't think he was a very bitter Confederate himself.

The next afternoon, after having washed and dried our clothes and took a good bath in the stream nearby, we were started under guard for Franklin. We walked about three miles, when we stopped at the house of a Union man named Johnson, and whose son had joined Captain Sanderson's company of home guards to save conscription, and who was detailed as one of our guard.

They filled our haversacks with choice fruit, and Captain Lyons, of the 1st Georgia Regiment, whom we met there, loaned me a horse to ride. Our guard the first day was Lieutenant R. N. Leatherwood, Sergeant Dick Hancock, and D. J. Johnson. We found by talking to Mr. Johnson that he was a Union man, and that Captain Lyons, who had so kindly loaned me his horse, was one also, but they dare not show it. We only went three miles the first afternoon, and the next morning Tom Hubbard overtook us, leading a mule for me to ride, as I had only borrowed Captain Lyons's horse for the first afternoon. Tom Hubbard soon found an opportunity to tell me, that his brother and a Captain Tidwell were going to try to assist us to escape. This Captain Tidwell was in command of another company of home guards, and we had not gone far on this second day of our march, before he met us as if by chance, and we halted, and after chatting a few minutes, Tom asked him to ride along with us.

He had a canteen of applejack, and invited all hands to take a drink. This we all did, though Captain Alban and I drank very sparingly. The canteen was passed quite often, and though we all seemed jolly, I noticed that it held out pretty well, and concluded that they were all trying to get the rest drunk, without getting drunk themselves. What we wanted was, to get enough of this apple brandy down Lieutenant Leatherwood and Sergeant Dick Hancock, to affect them, and then make a break; but it did not work. They pretended to drink, but were as wary as ever, and were evidently onto our little game.

We were a noisy crowd that passed along that road through the woods that day, we sung, shouted, laughed and swaggered, but that canteen still held out. Finally as we were passing a spur of the Nantahala mountains, we saw some mules feeding upon the mountain to our left and rear, and as all were mounted except Captain Alban, it was suggested that the Lieutenant and Sergeant try to catch one of the mules for him, so we could get along a little faster.

The Sergeant gave Captain Tidwell his revolver, to guard us while he was gone, and they started up the mountain in pursuit of the mules. When they had got half way up, Captain Tidwell told us to run into the woods and up a ravine that separated the two spurs, and he would fire his revolver towards us, to make believe he was trying to shoot us, but would be careful not to hit either of us. We had never seen him until an hour previous, and of course did not know but this was only a dodge to give him an excuse for shooting a Yankee, but we took the risk, and started into the woods.

He shouted halt! halt!! and fired three shots in quick succession; the bullets sounded uncomfortably near our heads, but we kept on. My legs were stiff and cramped from riding, and I made very poor headway. I threw off my overcoat and haversack to lighten me, but it seemed as though I was in a nightmare; and though I strained every nerve to make the utmost speed, I seemed to be moving at a snail pace. Alban, who had been walking, and was strong and robust, outstripped me and was gaining at every step. I was perspiring at every pore, and my breath was short and hot, but still I did not seem to get ahead much. I was just thinking I would soon be out of sight, when I heard Lieutenant Leatherwood's voice close behind me, saying, hold on Lieutenant, I don't want to shoot you; and looking over my shoulder, saw him within five rods of me, with his revolver pointed at my head.

Seeing that any further effort at flight would only result in my getting the contents of that revolver, and not hankering after anything of that kind, as I was near enough dead already, I stopped and went quietly back, Alban, who was five or six rods ahead of me, doing likewise.

One of the bullets from Captain Tidwell's revolver had struck a rock near me, and a piece of the bullet hit me just under my right eye, thus saving his reputation as a marksman, and giving color to his intentions to shoot me.

As we slowly made our way back to the road, I picked up my traps that I had discarded in my flight, and laughingly told the boys that I only came back because it was so much more pleasant to ride than go on foot. Dick Hancock, the Sergeant, however, did not seem to relish the joke, and, demanding his revolver of Captain Tidwell, said he would shoot the d — d Yankees anyhow.

Captain Tidwell told him that he wouldn't shoot anyone who was a prisoner, that if there was any shooting going on, he would have a hand in. Dick swaggered considerable, but I finally told him that if he really wanted to shoot someone, he had better go to the front, where he would find lots of it to do. Said I, (for I was then satisfied that in case of a row the chances were in our favor) "I want you to understand now, that while I am a prisoner in your hands, I shall make every effort to escape; and it is your duty to keep me if you can, and if you shoot me while I am trying to get away, you will only be doing your duty; but while I am a secure prisoner, you have no more right to murder me than you have to murder anyone else."

You must watch me closely, for I give you fair warning, that I shall escape if I can. This talk seemed to exasperate him more than ever, and regaining his revolver, he swore that he would shoot the d — d Yankee any way. Said I, "Dick, if Captain Tidwell will let me take his revolver, I will step out here and shoot with you for a while, and see who is the best shot; for I had about as soon die here, as to be a prisoner much longer."

Lieutenant Leatherwood finally ordered him to put up his pistol or he would put him under arrest. He then subsided, but was grouty all the balance of the day. That evening we came to a school house in the woods, and concluded to stay there all night.

Gathering up some dry wood we soon had a roaring fire going in the large open fire place, and as we had been supplied with two days rations we ate our supper, and then lighting our pipes, enjoyed ourselves just as though we all belonged to the same army. I got even Dick Hancock in good humor, by telling stories, and with Captain Alban, who was a good singer, treating them to the "Red, White and Blue," the "Star Spangled Banner," and "Rally 'Round the Flag."

When we came to the line, "And we'll hurl the rebel crew from the land we love the best," they fairly made the woods ring with applause.

Before bed time, Dick Hancock came up to me and apologized for his rudeness to me that afternoon, saying, "You are a d — d good fellow, anyway, and I don't care a d — n how quick you get away after I turn you over to the guard at Franklin." I asked him to caution the boys against saying anything at Franklin about our attempted escape, and he promised to do so.

We laughed, sang, swapped funny stories, and cracked jokes until 10 o'clock, and a stranger going by would not have mistrusted that there were any heavy hearts in that crowd of boisterous soldiers.

At 10 o'clock the door was securely fastened, one of the guard spreading his blanket and lying down against it, and Dick and the Lieutenant took the precaution to have Alban and myself sleep between them.

About two o'clock the next morning, I awoke and asked to have a guard sent out of the house with me, and Captain Alban said he guessed he would go too.

I was in hopes the Lieutenant would send young Johnson with us, but Dick Hancock had not forgotten what transpired the day before, and said he would go along with the guard.

He was mistrustful of young Johnson, and rightfully so, for had we went out with him alone we would both have got into the woods and taken his gun along with us; and once in the woods in the night, it would have been next to impossible to find us again.

As it was we made no attempt to escape, but went back and slept until daylight. After breakfast that morning we again saddled up and started for Franklin, which place we reached about ten o'clock, and were then turned over to another guard, who were made up of some of the best citizens of that beautiful village. I have none but pleasant recollections of Franklin, and would like to visit the place again under the changed condition of things.

Chapter XIX.

Upon our arrival at Franklin we were taken to the jail, but before we were locked up, Doctor Moore, of the village, invited us to his house to dinner, and upon his agreeing to be responsible for our safe return, we were allowed to go with him unattended by any guard. Although no promise had been exacted from us not to escape, we would not have attempted to leave, had an outlet presented itself. We would have considered it a base betrayal of his confidence, as much so as the violation of a parole, to have taken advantage of so kind and generous a host. We were received at his house with all the cordiality of distinguished guests, and nothing was said or done, by any member of the family, that could be construed into a hint that we were other than welcome visitors.

Dr. Moore was an ardent supporter of the Confederacy, but was too much of a gentleman to allude to anything during our visit, that would be offensive to our ears. Books and papers were on the parlor table, photographs of the family and friends were shown us; a stereoscope was also on the table, supplied with views of scenes both in the North and South. I was looking at some of the views, when I, without knowing what it was, put one into the stereoscope and looking at it, almost imagined that I was in New York. It was a view of Broadway from the Battery up. Oh! how this picture reminded me of home. It seemed as though I could call a stage by raising my hand. I looked at it long and earnestly, so long that I almost forgot my surroundings, forgot everything, and was again among friends at home.

Altogether, we passed a very pleasant afternoon with the genial doctor and his interesting family.

As we were leaving, Mrs. Moore and a neighbor, Mrs. Siler, having noticed our stockingless feet, presented us each with a pair of nice, warm, woolen socks, that they had knitted for some member of their own family, and filling a basket with choice apples and potatoes, sent them with us to the jail, which was to be our quarters that night. Arriving at the jail, we found that the doctor, thoughtful of our comfort, had caused a fire to be built in the wide fireplace, the cheerful glow of which made our imprisonment more tolerable. These little acts of kindness left a green spot in our memory of prison life, that still remains as an oasis in the otherwise cheerless desert we passed through. When God makes up his rewards and punishments, I am sure he will say to the kind-hearted doctor and his family, "I was sick and in prison, and ye visited me."

The next day a Mr. Johnson was detailed as our guard, and instead of staying with us at the jail, he invited us to his house, where he kept us over night, giving us a good clean bed and a good supper and breakfast, and treating us as had Doctor Moore, more as guests than as prisoners.

The next day we were started for Ashville, N. C., with a guard, under Lieutenant Ammon. The Lieutenant, sympathizing with me in my enfeebled condition, furnished me with a mule to ride, and showed me every kindness possible.

One of our guard on this trip was Hon. Thomas S. Siler, ex-member of Assembly of Macon county. He was a very agreeable gentleman, who still had a strong attachment for the Union. He was intelligent and well posted on every subject, and my conversation with him during the march, seemed to lessen the tediousness of the journey.

We arrived at Ashville, N. C., on the 7th of November, and were crowded into an upper room in the jail, about twelve feet square, in which there were besides us, twenty-seven rebel deserters, two of them sick with the measles. I had not been able up to this time, to do anything for my swollen and inflamed legs, and they were in a most frightful condition, causing me intense pain and suffering, so much so that I was fearful of losing them entirely, as they had been neglected so long. A surgeon visited me in the jail, and recommended my removal to the hospital, but although I offered to give my parole for that purpose, Colonel Lowe, who was in command, refused to allow me to be sent there.

The room was so full, that it was impossible for all of us to lie down at once, and we were obliged to take turns standing up. Our water closet consisted of a wooden pail in one corner of the room, which was twice a day carried out and emptied by the guard; as we were none of us allowed to leave the room for any purpose. The intolerable stench from this pail, and the filthy slops around it, was enough to create an epidemic.

The atmosphere of the room was simply insufferable, and we were obliged to keep the windows raised, notwithstanding the cold weather, in order to get ventilation. We had one old stove in the room, but our supply of wood was quite insufficient to keep the temperature anything like comfortable, although the village was surrounded by good timber.

One intensely cold night our wood had given out, and so I took the large iron poker and commenced prying off the wainscoting of the room for fuel, and by morning I had completely stripped one side. That morning when the Sergeant came in he raised a great row about it, threatening to punish the one who had done it. I told him that I was the one, and that I had considered it a military necessity, and that if we were not furnished with wood, he would wake up some morning and find the old jail burned down. He said I should be reported and punished for destroying government property, but the only thing done was to give us thereafter a more liberal supply of fuel.

We occupied a front room in the north-west corner of the jail, and in the room back of us were twenty-nine more reb deserters and a large, powerful negro, who had been placed there by his master as a punishment for some alleged misdemeanor. There was only a board partition between the two rooms, and it was not long before I had established communication with our neighbors, by cutting a hole through the partition large enough to allow us to carry on conversation. Upon our entrance into the jail they had deprived us of our case knives that we had carried with us thus far, for fear we would cut our way out with them.

But I had a screw driver to a gun which they happened to overlook in their search. This I sharpened on the bricks on which the stove rested, and then commenced making an outlet for our escape. I took a strong cord, and lashed the screw driver to a round stick of stove wood, and at night removed one of the sick men, and commenced by punching across two boards in the floor just over the joist, to cut through the floor. It was hard work, but by spelling each other, we had the two boards completely loose before midnight. Upon removing the loose boards we found that there was a ceiling of the same thickness still between us and freedom. The floor and ceiling were both Norway pine, and very hard, and as we could not work with our short handled chisel we adopted another plan for that.

We took the large poker which I had used to tear off the wainscoting, and heating it red hot in the stove, commenced burning holes through the under ceiling. We had a pail of water for drinking, and when it blazed up too much, we would dash on a cup full of water. This was slow work, but just at daylight we had removed the last board and then carefully swept up all traces of our work, and placing the boards back in their place, carried the sick men back and laid them over them. Our windows were grated, and the room below was used as a store room and there were no grates at the windows there.

Once down in that room after dark, and we could easily make our escape. Everything went along smoothly that morning. The guard came in to bring our breakfast and empty our slop pail, without any suspicion that anything was wrong, but about ten o'clock the Sergeant came up with a guard, and commenced looking around as though in search of something.

I knew instinctively what was up, but as he had the stove removed and commenced poking around the brick platform without saying a word, I could not restrain my laughter, and asked him if he had lost something; saying that if he had, perhaps I might tell him where to find it. He did not seem to take kindly to my offer of assistance, nor feel in a mood to enjoy the pleasure his frantic efforts to find the lost treasure, appeared to afford me. In fact he seemed to take it as a piece of Yankee impertinence. After satisfying himself that there was nothing under the stove, he had us all take up our blankets and other traps, without deigning to tell us what it was all for.

We all cheerfully complied with his order except the two sick rebs, who were too weak to get up. After thoroughly searching every other part of the room, he had the two sick men removed, and there discovered the loose boards and seemed satisfied and pleased. Was that what you was looking for Sergeant? said I. If you had told me what you wanted I could have told you where to look when you first came up, and saved you all this trouble. You'ens Yanks think you are d — d cute, don't you? was all the reply I received. He left the guard in the room while he went and got a carpenter to repair the floor; He soon returned with a carpenter, and told him to nail them boards down securely. I told some of my associates, to keep him interested, by asking him how he discovered the hole, and I would fix the carpenter.

Carelessly lounging up to where he was working, I said in a tone that could not be heard by anyone else: "I can get those boards up easier if you break the nails off."

He replied in the same undertone: "I don't care a d — n how soon you get them up when I get away."

I watched him, and saw that he followed my suggestion, breaking the nails in two with the claw of his hammer, so that they only a little more than went through the flooring. After he had finished the Sergeant inspected the work, and judging from the number of nails that it was securely done, took his guard and went away.

It seems that the family who lived in the lower part of the jail, kept a barrel of corn in that room below us, from which they fed their chickens, and that barrel set right under the hole we had cut; and when the old woman went to get some corn for her chickens that morning, she found it covered with chips and cinders, and looking up to ascertain the cause, discovered the hole in the ceiling. She at once notified the Sergeant of the discovery, and the result was we had our trouble and work for nothing.

Captain Alban and myself were the only Yankee prisoners in the jail, and until our arrival there had been no attempt at escape, and to us therefore was attributed all of the attempts to break out.

While the reb deserters were willing to share with us all the benefits to be derived from a break, they were too shiftless and lazy to fully enter into our plans for an escape.

Chapter XX.

another attempt at escape discovered — a bold plot — lack of sand in the reb deserters — a brave negro — the flogging.

B eing satisfied that I could remove the flooring at any time within a few minutes, I told my fellow prisoners what I had said, and what I had seen done, and that when everything had become quiet, I would guarantee to get them out with ten minutes work. Some of the rebs were not satisfied, and insisted upon loosening the floor again at once, and despite all I could do, they persisted in doing so. The third night after was settled upon as the one to leave, as it promised to be dark and rainy, but just before night, the Sergeant took it into his head to try the floor, and procuring a long pole he went into the room below and punched at the loose boards, which immediately yielded, and then he brought in another carpenter, and personally superintended stopping up the aperture, which was done by spiking pieces of joist, against the floor joists, completely closing it up.

As I said, we had cut a hole through the partition, so that we could communicate with our neighbors in the next room. We made up a plot with them to seize the Sergeant when he came in at night to empty their slop pail, lock him in the room, take the keys and unlock our door, and we would all leave at once. We had bribed one of the guard to let us disarm him, and then we would be free to go out. When we got outside we would encounter another guard, but with one gun we could easily overpower and disarm him, and then trust to the two guns and our agility to gain the woods, which were close by.

It was all arranged that the large, powerful negro should seize the Sergeant from behind and hold him, while his companions secured his pistol and the keys. That night when the Sergeant came up, he brought one armed guard to the head of the stairs, and proceeded to unlock the door. As he entered, the negro, who stood behind the door, caught him from behind, securely pinioning his arms, and the keys and revolver were taken from him and all passed out except the negro, who was holding the Sergeant as securely as though he was in a vice.

When they had all got out the Sergeant was pushed into the cell and the door locked. The guard at the head of the stairs shouted, loud enough for the Sergeant to hear him: "Go back, or I'll shoot! go back!" all the time expecting they would rush up and disarm him; but the cowards, fearing he was in earnest, fell back and unlocked the door, released the Sergeant, and gave him back his pistol without unlocking the door to our room.

Not knowing that the prisoners in our room were in the plot, the Sergeant paid no attention to us, but calling the officer of the guard, told him what had occurred.

They took the negro out into the hall, and bringing up a plank, proceeded to lash him securely to it, with his face down, after having stripped him.

They then took a strap something like a tug to a single harness, and gave him one hundred lashes with it upon his bare back, the blood flowing at every blow.

We had cut slits in the door, and through them watched this brutal transaction. I watched the operation of binding him with some curiosity and a good deal of indignation, and was astonished to find such brutality among those who professed civilization. Unaccustomed to such scenes, I must say it was the most sickening transaction I ever witnessed.

The shrieks and groans of this poor fellow, was enough to send a chill of horror through the most hardened. He begged for mercy in the most piteous terms, and as the cruel strap laid open the quivering flesh, and the blood trickled down his body, I shouted indignantly to his inhuman persecutors, that the poor fellow was not to blame, half as much as the white men; that he was only carrying out the instructions of the cowardly whites, who had basely deserted him after promising to stand by him. I told them that the poor ignorant black's only fault had been, his confidence in the courage of his white associates, to as faithfully carry out their part of the program, as he had carried out his.

That if anyone should be punished it should be those whose lack of *sand* had got this poor fellow into a scrape and then like cowards basely deserted him. Finding that the infuriated monsters were bound to vent their spite upon this poor fellow, I turned away, and by holding my hands to my ears tried to shut out the sound of his pitiful cries for mercy. While reason remains to me I can never forget the scenes of that terrible night.

And to those inhuman monsters it seemed a pleasant pastime — such is the brutalizing effect of the system of human slavery. Once in a life-time is enough to witness such a revolting scene as this; I have witnessed one such, and I trust in God it may never be my misfortune to be obliged to witness another.

After this exhibition of fiendish cruelty, I am ready to believe that the system of human slavery was capable of developing total depravity into the hearts of slave holders. What man in the North could look on complacently and see such a cruel punishment inflicted? And yet the Southern whites seemed to look upon this brutality as a matter of course, and even before the preparations were made for the flogging, knew what would be the punishment inflicted upon the poor black, for his unsuccessful attempt to liberate his white skinned, and white livered comrades; and while they seemed to feel a sort of sympathy for their black skinned, but brave hearted comrade, they offered no remonstrance to his cruel tormentors, nor made a plea for mercy in his behalf.

When they seemed to become exhausted with their violent exercise, in swinging that cruel strap, they began to question the poor, fainting negro thus:

"What did you do it for, anyhow?"

"Oh, massa, dem white men dey told me to," moaned the poor fellow.

"Will you ever mind them fellows again?"

"No, massa; if you only let me go this time I'll never pay mo' 'tention to dem white trash dan I would to a fly," he said in a pleading voice.

He was not put back into the jail again, and what became of him we never learned. Our plan for escape had been well matured, and had it succeeded, as it would have done but for the weakening of the rebel deserters, there is scarcely a doubt but that we would have safely reached our lines, as these deserters were thoroughly acquainted with the country around Ashville and knew every turpentine path through the pine forests, and all of the mountain passes, as well as an old resident of Oswego knows the streets of the city.

Our plan was, to disarm the guard at the door, and then rush for the stack of arms belonging to the relief, who were not then on duty, and then fight our way through to Tennessee, where the loyal inhabitants of that state would join us in resisting recapture by the Confederates.

It was well understood by all, that once in Tennessee we were safe from molestation. This had been our objective point upon our escape from Columbia; and when we were unfortunately recaptured by Dick Hancock and Tom Hubbard, we were just intending, after getting something to eat at Mr. Harshaw's, to at once go into the woods, and not leave them again until we had gained the river, which was only about two miles ahead.

Once at the river we were to search for a boat of some kind with which to cross it, and failing to find one, to build a raft that would float us over to the Tennessee shore. But it was destined otherwise. We learned after our recapture, that the officer we had seen sitting upon the stoop of a store at Fort Emory, was a paroled prisoner of war who was suffering from a wound, and by having been a prisoner at the North, recognized us as Yankees, and informed Dick Hancock and Tom Hubbard, who thereupon mounted and followed us up.

They had about given up overhauling us when they arrived at Mr. Harshaw's, and said that if they had not found us there or learned by him that we were nearby, that they would not have followed us any further, as it was then almost dark and they had already followed us ten miles. They said that until they found that authorization paper upon me they did not believe that we were Yankees, but supposed we were deserters from the Confederate army, who were trying to make our escape into the Tennessee border.

Chapter XXI.

placed in an iron cage — breaking out and attempting to dig through a brick wall — an unexpected surprise.

The next morning, we were all marched into a room on the opposite side of the hall, and to the south side of the jail, and were placed in an iron cage, made of flat bars two inches wide, and half an inch thick, firmly riveted together, and as I told the Sergeant, although we could not wear diamonds, we could look through them. We were packed into this cage like sardines in a box, scarcely having room to move. There were iron benches along the sides for us to sit upon, but lying down was quite out of the question.

When all was quiet that night, we thought as we could not sleep we would try and get out.

The door was fastened with a round iron prop that fitted into a socket in the floor, and was fastened to the door by a padlock. This prop we wrenched from its fastenings by reaching out through the diamond in the door, and then with it broke the lock, and the iron door swung back, giving us free egress to the room. The cage was about twenty feet long and eight feet wide, with a partition in the centre. This cage set in the middle of the room, and was about six feet from the walls of the room on all sides. With the bar thus wrenched off, we at once attacked the brick wall, and while some detached the brick, others held a blanket underneath to prevent the falling brick and mortar from falling to the floor, as they would make a noise that would attract the attention of those beneath us. We had made an opening nearly halfway through the outer wall, which was large enough for a good sized man to pass out, when most unexpectedly two more prisoners were brought in, and our operations were discovered, and the attempt to escape was again frustrated.

A guard was then placed in the room, and as we could not sleep, we spent the night in singing "Rally 'Round the Flag," and other Union songs, and chaffing with the guard, who were nearly all, more or less, tinctured with Union sentiments, and only kept us from escaping, for fear of the consequence to themselves. Morning came and with it an order to get ready to go to Danville, Va.

I told the officer that I could not march on account of my inflamed legs, but he said that if I had got out of jail my legs would not have bothered me much, and he reckoned that it would do me good to take a walk anyway. And he would put us d — d Yanks where we wouldn't bother him anymore. So, after furnishing us with two days rations to last to Morgantown, they started four of us, Captain Alban, myself, and the two Union prisoners brought in the night before, whose names I do not now remember, under a guard consisting of a Lieutenant and four men, for a tramp over the mountains.

Our march over the mountains was a tedious one, interspersed now and then, however, with some amusing incident. We were in good humor with the guard, and laughed and joked along the road in a free and easy sort of way, and succeeded in making ourselves agreeable to them, gaining their confidence as much as we could, and after we had been marching half a day, a casual observer would have hardly distinguished the prisoners from the guard. We straggled along much the same as a dozen rebs would have done on a march by themselves.

On the afternoon of the first day's march, we came along to a hickory grove, where about a dozen black and gray squirrels were sporting about on the top branches, gathering nuts, and I asked one of the guard to let me take his gun a minute and I would get a couple of them for our supper. He was about handing the gun to me, when the Lieutenant stopped him by saying: "You d — d fool, do you know what you are carrying that gun for? That Yankee might miss the squirrel and shoot you."

I laughed, and said he must think I wasn't much of a shot. But he said he was afraid I was too good a shot to be handling one of their guns; anyway the squirrels were probably tame ones belonging to the house nearby, and his orders were not to disturb anything along the line of march. That night we stopped at an old farmer's and I thought that if we had a room with a window looking outside there might be a chance for escape, and asked to be given a room to sleep in that was well ventilated, as I always liked lots of fresh air in my room; but we were placed in a middle room upstairs, and a guard placed in the room with us all night.

The next morning, after a good hearty breakfast with the family, for which the Lieutenant gave the farmer a receipt, we started on again, and at noon we descended a mountain that was so steep that the road was made zig-zag to allow wagons to gain the summit; and as we came to the foot of the mountain we found a rude, log hut in which lived a hunter. We stopped there to get dinner, and were all at a loss to guess what kind of fresh meat we were eating, and in answer to my inquiry the host said: "That, Mister, is bar meat; I was up on the mounting one day last week, and came upon this varmint eatin' blackberries, and I fetched him home for winter. Don't be afeared; bar meat won't hurt ye more'n liftin' on a stick o' basswood."

That afternoon one of the most amusing incidents of the march occurred.

We came to a farm house, and the farmer being at home, we all sat down on a log he had hauled up to the front of the house, for cutting up into fire wood, for a chat with him and to rest a little. The farmer sat on one end of the log, the Lieutenant next, and the rest of us were strung along.

The fellow who sat next to me had an ear of corn, and there were quite a number of chickens picking around the wood pile. While the Lieutenant and farmer were talking, this fellow took out his iron ramrod and laid it against the log beside him, and then commenced shelling the corn and feeding the chickens. Watching the farmer, he would tap a chicken across the back of the neck with his ramrod, stuff him in the breast of his overcoat, and innocently go on shelling the corn for the other chickens.

In this way I saw him gobble three good fat chickens, when he told the Lieutenant he was going to walk on a piece. When we overtook him about eighty rods further on, he was sitting in the woods beside the road, picking the chickens he had stolen from the farmer. The Lieutenant called to him and said, sternly: "I thought I told you not to plunder while on the march." "Well," said he, with a comical drawl, "I don't allow no doggone chicken to come out and bite at me." That settled it; we had chicken for supper that night, and the Lieutenant seemed to relish the supper as much as any of us.

The next day we marched to Morgantown, and there took the cars for Danville, Va. We saw no opportunity to escape, for we were guarded very strictly, though at the same time we were treated with all the courtesy that could possibly be shown us, and I believe our guard would have defended us with force, against anyone who had attempted to molest us.

When we arrived at Salisbury, which was one of the most notorious rebel slaughter houses of the South, a place that vied with Andersonville in atrocities, cruelties, starvation and death. A place where thirteen thousand Union soldiers, became victims to the vindictiveness of their captors — no not their captors but their jailors — for the soldier, whether federal or confederate, who had the courage to risk his life in the field where prisoners were captured, possessed too great a sense of honor to treat with such heartless cruelty, those who so gallantly opposed them.

I say that when we arrived at Salisbury, we learned that there had been a desperate attempt made by the enlisted men confined there, to overpower the guard and make their escape that afternoon, and the artillery had opened on the prison pen with grape and canister, killing, and wounding, many of the Union prisoners confined there. Great excitement still prevailed when we arrived, and threats of shooting the d — d Yanks were freely indulged in by the "new issue," as the home guard were called.

But we were not molested; probably owing to the fact that we had a guard over us, of soldiers who were ready and willing to protect their prisoners from interference from outside parties.

We stayed in Salisbury until about eleven o'clock p. m., during which time the reb guard, and their lady friends, were parading around the depot where we were waiting for the train, singing, flirting, and talking about the Yankee prisoners.

While we were sitting on the depot platform waiting, we were smoking, and as the platform was filled with bales of cotton, we were, while apparently uninterested spectators of what was going on, emptying our pipes into the cotton bales.

We thus managed to set fire to a number of these bales of cotton, well knowing that after we were gone and the guard had retired, there would be apt to be a blaze; and the next day we heard that the depot at Salisbury was burned the night before, destroying a large amount of cotton stored there. On my arrival at Danville, I met Colonel W. C. Raulston, of the 24th New York Cavalry, with whom I was acquainted, and who introduced me to the members of his mess, Brigadier-General A. N. Duffie, Brigadier-General Hays, and Lieutenants Leydon and VanDerweed, who were all anxious to talk with me about the chances of escape. Knowing that I had had considerable experience in that line, they naturally concluded that I could give them some valuable points on how to escape, and how best to reach our lines after we had got out.

Well, we held a long and animated conference, in which I gave some of my own experience, in and out of rebel prisons, telling them of the hardships and exciting scenes through which I and my comrades had passed in trying to reach our lines, of the difficulties we had encountered, and the privations we had been obliged to endure. To get out of prison was not a difficult task for one or two, but a successful prison delivery was quite another thing to accomplish.

Two hundred officers, each having ideas of their own, were harder to control than five times that number of enlisted men, who had been disciplined to obey; and as no one had any authority to command, or control the actions, of his fellow officers, we lacked the greatest essential to success — organization. Various plans were suggested and discussed, but none which seemed to promise success, appeared to be practical just at that time. Almost daily conferences were held, but the prevailing opinion seemed to be, that an attempted general outbreak, without thorough organization, would prove disastrous, and only end in an unnecessary sacrifice of life, and almost certain failure.

Chapter XXII.

danville prison — a cold winter — double-quicking around the room to keep warm — excitement caused by the arrival of fresh troops — they stack arms in front of our prison — plans for escape.

D anville in 1864-5 was a town of considerable importance to the Confederacy, being the base of supplies for the Confederate army at Richmond and Petersburg. There were three or four military prisons there, in which were confined about two thousand enlisted men, captured from the Union forces, and four hundred officers. They were all confined in tobacco warehouses in different parts of the city, the officers being separate from the enlisted men.

The prison in which the officers were confined, was a three story tobacco warehouse, 40x100 feet, near the River Dan. The windows were securely grated with iron bars, and the whole building was rendered secure by heavy oaken doors.

The building faced the east, and a street ran in front and, also, one on the south side. In front, and on the south side, sentries were pacing up and down, night and day; and there were also two sentries stationed on the ground floor, inside, one along the south side, and the other across the west end.

The sinks used by the prisoners, were just outside the west end of the building, and were surrounded by a high board or plank fence. The second and third floors were occupied by the prisoners, and at the time I was there — the winter of 1864-5 — were each supplied with two large Peckham stoves, to furnish warmth to the building. On the ground floor where the guard was stationed, there was no stove; and during the winter, the cold air from below was anything but comfortable, as it found its way through the wide cracks in the floor, and came in contact with the thinly clad bodies, of those especially, who were sleeping on the second floor.

The winter of 1864-5, in Virginia, was extremely cold. The river that winter was frozen over solid enough to make a safe crossing on the ice; and the officers were frequently obliged to get in line and double quick around the room to keep from freezing. This could not be done unless all or a large proportion joined in the exercise; for if one or more attempted it while the rest were lying down, they would be obliged to step over the bodies of their recumbent comrades.

During the daytime, the ground floor was used for exercising, twenty being allowed down there at a time, and as there was plenty of room, it was no uncommon thing to see that number, or even more, down there at a time taking their exercise.

The rule of the prison was, that no one should approach within less than six feet of a sentry, or hold any conversation with them; and although there was no dead line in this prison, an imaginary line six feet from the sentry, was pretty generally observed. We were obliged to pass the sentry at the back end of the building, in going to and from the sink; but as he was continually pacing back and forth, it was his lookout that we did not come within the prescribed distance of him.

The prisons in which the enlisted men were confined were of the same description, or at least some of them were. Two or three of them were in sight of our front windows, one being just across the street.

Some of the enlisted men were detailed in the cook house, for which service they received extra rations.

This brief description of the Confederate prisons in Danville, is necessary, that the reader may more easily understand some of the incidents that follow.

In the last chapter I spoke of the conference between Col. W. C. Raulston, Gen. A. N. Duffie, and myself, as to the prospects of getting through to our lines if we should escape from prison. Many difficulties lay in the way of a general break being successful.

Danville at this time was guarded by quite a large force; and even should we be successful in getting out of prison, we would be obliged to overpower this armed force, and then make our way through the enemies' country in order to reach the Union lines; and on the march we would be liable to be intercepted by large bodies of Confederate troops. The nearest point at which we could reasonably expect to reach the Union forces, would be the Shenandoah Valley; and this would be to us a long, and difficult march, unless we could be well supplied with arms and rations before we started.

All this time however, a sharp lookout was kept up, for anything that looked like a favorable opportunity for a strike for freedom and home.

On the 9th of December, about sixteen days after my arrival, the opportunity seemed to present itself. On that day, a company of Confederate soldiers were drawn up in front of our prison, where they stacked arms. They were new comers, and of course at once attracted our attention.

Shut up as we were in a tobacco warehouse, with absolutely no knowledge of what was transpiring in the outside world, except such information as we could pick up from our guard, whose ignorance of passing events seemed almost as great as our own, the arrival of new troops was something to excite our curiosity, and give us something to think about.

Anything to excite our curiosity and relieve the monotony of the daily routine of prison life, acted upon us much the same as a band of music in the streets to-day affects the street idlers of the city. All who could do so, gathered at the windows to inspect the new comers, and speculate upon the occasion that brought them there. We judged them to be troops who had seen service, by their rough and ready appearance, and their well-worn and, in some cases, shabby uniforms.

Various were the speculations as to who they were, where they came from, and the reason of their appearance in Danville at this time. Had they come to relieve those who had thus far been our guards, and with whom we had became somewhat familiar?

Had they come to take us to Richmond to be exchanged? (This word exchange was ever uppermost in our thoughts while awake, and mingled in our dreams while sleeping.) Or had they been merely sent here, to more securely guard against any attempted outbreak?

All of these questions suggested themselves to our minds, and were freely discussed, while they were being formed into line in front of our prison, where they stacked arms.

Soon the order came, break ranks, and they dispersed without taking the precaution of leaving a guard over the stacks of arms. Soon there was a buzz of excitement throughout the building.

Longing eyes were directed towards those stacks of arms; if we could only get the door open upon some pretext, how easy it would be to gobble those forty guns, and the well filled cartridge boxes that hung from the bayonets, and before the old guard could be called out, overpower them, take their arms, capture Danville and be in the field once more. Groups assembled throughout the building, and excitedly discussed the chances of success or failure, if we should make the attempt. Some were for making an immediate sally down stairs, call the Sergeant of the guard, and as he opened the door to see what was wanted, seize him, fling wide open the door, make a rush for the arms, and let circumstances govern our actions afterwards. Others more cautious, counseled delay and a thoroughly organized attack.

A council of field officers was immediately called, and it was decided to make a perfect organization of the entire prison, having each arm of the service, Infantry, Cavalry and Artillery, in separate detachments, commanded by sets of officers of their own choosing, the whole to be under the command of Colonel W. C. Raulston, 24th New York Cavalry, Brig. General Duffie waiving his rank and being second in command.

This advice was finally accepted, and the work of organization was immediately commenced. Colonel Raulston was known to be a gallant Cavalry officer, whose coolness and courage could be relied upon, and whose military ability was well understood by all. Officers were chosen for the different detachments, the others all promising to cheerfully obey all orders, and perform all duties assigned them.

This necessarily occupied considerable time, and before the organization was completed, the guard, who were all unconscious of our plans, came out, took their arms and marched around to the shed on the north side of the building, that was used for the men's quarters, where they were out of sight, as there were no windows on that side of the building.

Thus the golden opportunity had been allowed to pass. The hour we had spent in perfecting our organization, and maturing our plans, while it was well employed, was the hour of our great opportunity, and had now gone, to be added to the many hours of great opportunities lost.

The work of organization went steadily forward however, hoping for another favorable opportunity to occur.

Chapter XXIII.

prison rules — starving in the midst of plenty — organizing for a break — trading with the guard — business in prison.

lthough the orders were very strict that the guard should hold no conversation with prisoners, and they were instructed to shoot anyone who attempted to approach them, their cupidity often led them to violate their instructions, which were equally well understood by us, and deterred many from attempting any familiarity. But there were those, who had tact and pluck enough to take all risks, to make a trade with them, of boots, rings, watches, and other valuables, for bacon, tobacco, flour, and other necessaries. In fact this had been my daily occupation, with the exception of the first week, since my arrival in Danville.

Buying gold pens, rings, watches, and everything of value, and selling them to the guard; and in return buying of them, provisions for myself, and to sell to my fellow prisoners, who had money, but did not wish to take the risk or trouble, to get up in the night and go down stairs to trade.

Most of the exchanges were made in the night, just after the eleven o'clock relief came on; although the bargains were usually made in the daytime.

Thirty men were allowed to go down stairs to the sinks at a time, and from fifteen to twenty, were allowed two or three times a day, to go out doors for the purpose of bringing water from the river, which was about forty rods from our prison, and get wood and coal, to supply the two large stoves on each floor, and do our cooking with.

I have been thus minute in my description, that the reader might better understand what follows. The four hundred officers were organized into eight companies, with full sets of officers for each, and the balance acting as privates. I belonged to the Cavalry detachment, and we were to mount ourselves as fast as we could get horses, as far as it was possible for us to do so, and act as the advance guard or vidette. There were, at this time, about eighteen hundred prisoners in Danville, scattered about in different buildings, and the plan agreed upon, if we succeeded in the break was, to seize all the arms we could, overpower the guards at the different prisons, release the enlisted men, capture and hold the town, take possession of the telegraph office (operators having been detailed who were experts in telegraphing), impress into the service all the horses we could find for the Artillery and Cavalry; supply ourselves with arms as far as possible, supply ourselves with rations and forage from the Confederate storehouses, form the enlisted men into companies, and march through as an army and join Sheridan in the Shenandoah Valley.

Danville was at this time, the depot of supplies for Lee's army at Richmond, and contained a large amount of Artillery and ammunition; besides having storehouses, well stocked with captured hard tack, so that there would be no lack of supplies for our army. We were therefore, actually dying of starvation in the midst of plenty. In going daily from the prison to the river for water, we passed a building 20x40 feet, two stories high, that was packed from bottom to top with captured U. S. hard tack, and others filled with bacon, and other provisions; and tried to get Colonel Smith, commanding the prisons, to give us rations of hard tack once or twice a week, but were told that this was held for the use of their troops in the field.

For fresh meat, we were supplied with the heads and lights of beeves, and for twenty-six days we did not even receive that; our only rations during this time, being a piece of corn bread, or johnny-cake, made from unbolted corn meal, four inches long, three wide, and two inches thick, for twenty-four hours.

This would not more than half satisfy an ordinary man for his breakfast, and a good feeder would then want a couple of eggs, a good sized potato and one or two cups of coffee for a full meal, and even a half-pound of beef steak would not be left to be thrown into the slops. While the rations we received would have been considered princely fare by our famished comrades at Andersonville and Salisbury, still it was just enough to keep us constantly hungry, and make us think what we would eat if we should ever get the chance to again sit down to a good square meal. Like the castaway upon the great ocean, with "Water, water, everywhere, and not a drop to drink," so we were dying of starvation in the midst of plenty. I say we, by that I mean the great majority of prisoners. As for myself, while in Danville, I only lived exclusively on the prison rations drawn for five days, and I thought I should die of starvation in that short time.

Then, as I have heretofore stated, I went *into business*, buying and selling jewelry, etc.

Now I suppose the reader would like to know where the capital came from with which to commence business; for goods must be bought before they are sold, and as I have before stated, I had sold even the buttons off my uniform, in order to supply myself with food to satisfy my hunger.

Well, I happened to be talking one day with Captain Albert Thomas, 24th New York Cavalry, who has now a studio in Syracuse, N. Y., and he showed me a gold pen and silver case, that he had been trying to sell, without success. He was entirely out of money, having some days before used the last cent of a one hundred dollar bill, which he had most ingeniously secreted upon his person, when stripped and searched at Libby prison, upon his entrance into that notorious rebel prison hell, presided over by the equally notorious Dick Turner. He said he had offered the whole thing for fifteen dollars in Confederate money, but said he, while some folks can sell any worthless article, I can never sell anything.

I told him to let me take it, and I would either return him his pencil or bring him fifteen dollars within half an hour. He gave me the pencil, and I went down stairs to interview the guard. It would not do to approach him and offer to sell, as he might assert his authority by trading me a Confederate bullet instead of scrip, and I was not hankering after rebel lead just then. So I walked up and down the floor near him, holding the pencil in my hand so that he could get a good view of it. After a while, looking around to assure himself that no Confederate officer was near, he asked in a low tone, "what d'ye ask for it?"

This gave me an opportunity to speak, and I answered as cautiously, "Twenty-five dollars." "Let me take it; I'll give it back in a minute." I walked up and handed it to him and stepped back, while he paced up and down examining it carefully. Finally counting out the amount, he beckoned me to come to him, and handed me the money. Of course, I was perfectly safe in allowing him to examine the pencil; for if he had refused to return or pay for it, I could have had him severely punished for disobedience of orders, in allowing a prisoner to approach and converse with him.

Within twenty minutes from the time I took the pen and case, I returned to Captain Thomas with the fifteen dollars, and had made ten dollars for myself. This ten dollars I immediately invested in a similar pencil, and immediately sold it to the same guard for thirty dollars. With this start, I succeeded in making enough to live upon, by buying of prisoners, and selling to the guard, and in return buying of the guard at night and selling to my comrades the next day.

Chapter XXIV.

Our organization being now perfected, and our plans matured, we lay down that night, and held whispered consultations about our proposed future operations. I have already stated that the prisoners occupied the second and third floors of the building; the stairs being located in the north-east corner, and at the foot of the lower flight, was a room about twelve feet square, with a door leading to the street. In this room we usually waited with pails, to be let out to bring water, wood and coal, for the supply of the prison.

The next day everything seemed quiet, and at nine o'clock, when we were fell in for count, nothing could be detected that would indicate that anything unusual was contemplated.

During the forenoon, I had a long talk with Colonel Raulston, and General Duffie, who both seemed to think that we had better be prepared, and hold ourselves in readiness to take advantage of any favorable circumstance that might occur, but that it was best for the present, to remain quiet, and bide our time. What was my surprise then, while sitting with the Colonel at dinner, to see a gunboat officer approach with his overcoat and traps all on, and say, Colonel we are waiting for you, sir. The Colonel replied, well, if that is all you are waiting for, you won't have long to wait; and leaving his half-eaten dinner, got up, put on his overcoat, and started down stairs.

About the same time, about a dozen or fifteen went down with pails, and entered the room that opened on the street.

Colonel Raulston approached the guard near the foot of the stairs, and was trying to trade boots with him, while General Duffie approached the one at the back end of the room, and began bantering him for a trade; the Colonel, and General, each wearing a pair of long riding boots, which was something the average reb seemed to have a great weakness for.

The men with the pails, asked the sentry with whom Colonel Raulston was talking, to call the Sergeant of guard and he called as usual — Sergeant of the guard post number fo. Then Colonel Raulston gave the signal — now — when simultaneously both he and the General, seized and floored their man.

Raulston placed his hand over his man's mouth, telling him to keep quiet and he would not be hurt, while Duffie held his man by the throat, to prevent him making any alarm. Lieutenant McGraw, 24th New York Cavalry, who had been assigned to the duty, took the guns away from the guard, and at the same time the officers from above commenced filing down the stairs. The Sergeant came to answer the call, but he must have heard the scuffle, for he only opened the door about two inches, when he slammed and locked it again, and immediately called out the guard to surround the building. Each officer had armed himself with a stick of stove wood, and all were packed up and in marching order.

An attempt was made with these clubs to batter down the door, but it was a heavy oak door, and would not yield to their blows. Satisfied that the attempt was a failure, General Duffie called out, "Too late, go back!"

Owing to the fact that there was by this time quite a crowd down there, and the stairs being only wide enough for two to go up abreast, it was some time before all could reach the top.

Colonel Raulston and myself were the last to go up, and I had just reached the landing, the Colonel who was three or four steps behind me, had stopped to look out of the window, when the report of a gun rang out from below, and he started suddenly, and hurrying past me, went up the next flight, to the place he occupied on the floor above.

Although shot through the bowels, and at so short a range, strange as it may seem, he did not fall or make any outcry; and it was not until sometime after, that I learned that he was wounded.

I subsequently learned by some of my comrades, that he went to the place where he slept, took off his overcoat, opened his clothing and examined the wound, saying as he lay down, "boys, I guess my goose is cooked."

Within a very few minutes, the guard led by the Colonel in command, filed up the stairs, where they found everything as quiet as though nothing had occurred.

Some were playing checkers, backgammon or cards, some reading scraps of newspapers, some washing dishes, and others smoking and talking; in fact, the whole building had on its every day appearance, and no one would have supposed that there had been the least disturbance.

It was really laughable to see the singular expression on the faces of the guard, as they looked around upon the peaceful looking room. I sat in my place just at the head of the stairs reading, and remember that one of the fellows who followed the Colonel up, had his gun cocked, and with a good deal of bluster, said, as he reached the landing: "Colonel, show me any d — n Yank you want shot," to which the Colonel replied, sternly, "Put up your gun, sir; I'll let you know when I want any shooting done." Colonel Smith, who was in command of the Confederate prisons at Danville, was a cool, brave man, and though strict in his prison regulations, was a humane gentleman who would not voluntarily inflict any unnecessary hardships upon those under his charge.

He and Col. Raulston had been great friends, and I believe they both belonged to the Masonic order, Col. Smith often visiting Col. Raulston, bringing him books to read, and showing him many courtesies which, though perfectly consistent with his position, showed him to be a gentleman of generous impulses. In fact, I heard Col. Raulston say that the most distasteful duty he had promised to perform, was to go to Col. Smith's office and secure him as a prisoner.

Guards were at once stationed about the rooms, and Colonel Smith proceeded up stairs where Raulston lay bleeding, and questioned him in regard to the affair.

This brave, unselfish officer, at once said, Colonel I am wholly responsible for all that has occurred; I am the instigator of the whole plot, and no one but me is to blame for what was attempted to be done, and I alone if any one, deserve the punishment for this attempted outbreak.

He was immediately removed to the hospital, where all that skillful surgery could accomplish was done to save his life, but the wound was of such a nature, that neither skillful surgery, nor tender nursing was of any avail, and on the 15th of December, he passed away — was mustered out. The shot that terminated his life, was fired by the guard he had disarmed, and the gun used, was the same one Raulston had taken from him, and had returned after the failure of the attempted outbreak.

We all felt deeply mortified at the failure of our plot, but our greatest sorrow was occasioned by the loss of so gallant and beloved an officer and comrade.

Lieut. Leyden and myself asked permission of Col. Smith to be allowed to go to the hospital and nurse him during his illness, offering to give our parole for that privilege. I urged, that as Col. Raulston and myself were both from the same place, and I was well acquainted with his family, it would be a source of some comfort to them, to know that his last moments were soothed by the presence of one of his comrades, who could receive from him his last message to loved ones far away.

Our request was not granted, but we were assured that he should have every attention shown him that was possible, and that all that medical skill and science could accomplish, would be done to save his life.

Lieutenant McGraw, who was recognized by the guard as the one who relieved them of their guns, while Colonel Raulston and General Duffie had them down on the floor, was placed in solitary confinement for a few days, and was then released without further punishment.

It was greatly feared that he would be shot for the prominent part he had taken in the affair, and I now believe that he would have been more severely punished, had not his dying Colonel interceded for him. There was one rather amusing episode in this tragic affair, that caused some merriment notwithstanding the fatal ending.

General Duffie was a Frenchman and did not speak very good English. While he had his man down, with his fingers firmly clutched in his throat, to prevent his giving the alarm, the man in his efforts to release himself from this uncomfortable position, made a gurgling noise, which some of us thought, might have caused the Sergeant to mistrust there was something wrong.

The General in trying to explain, said in his broken English: "I try to shut off ze wind, but ze more I chuck ze more he holly."

In a few days the affair blew over, and everything moved along as usual. I have said, that two or three times a day, from fifteen to twenty prisoners were allowed to pass out under guard, to carry water, wood and coal, for use in the building.

I was often with this squad, for I was willing to do the work for the sake of getting out, where I could get a breath of fresh air; besides I could sometimes get a chance to buy something, that I could not otherwise obtain. In going to the river for water, we passed an oven, where they baked the cones for casting shell over. This oven was large enough to hold two men, and the door was usually open.

Just before dark, we would go out to bring water for the night. Some would have one pail, and some two. In coming back, we would halt when the head of the column reached the oven, and sit our pails down to rest, and while someone in the rear would attract the attention of the guard, one man at the head would slip into the oven, and the man next to him would take up his pail, and his absence would not be noticed, as they never counted us on these occasions. When darkness came on, those who had thus escaped would quietly cross the river and walk away.

To prevent them missing the absent, a hole was cut through the floor of the upper room, and as soon as the Sergeant was through counting those on the lower floor, a number corresponding to those who had escaped, would be shoved up through this hole to be counted again on the upper floor; thus keeping our count all right. A crowd would always be around the hole up stairs, so that the Sergeant upon going up would not see what was going on.

One fellow had his blanket spread over this hole, and would be lying down there when the guard reached the room, so that it would have a natural appearance, and would not attract any more attention than any other part of the room. In this way some six or seven made their escape, and the count was kept all right, by sending a corresponding number up through the hole in the floor, and they were not missed for two or three weeks. In fact the only reason we had to believe that they had been missed at all was, that one day the reb Sergeant brought up his guard and counted us over a second time, and after figuring up the count, counted us over again, and seemed to still be unsatisfied, and repeated the count seven or eight times. Every time the count came out all right, which seemed to puzzle and perplex him terribly. He could not understand how it could be, that he still had his full number of prisoners, while he seemed to have positive evidence that half a dozen had escaped. His information was that several had escaped, but his figures told him that we were all there.

Every time he counted us and found us all present, his perplexity increased; for he seemed to have proven the falsity of the old saying, "that figures can't lie." He finally concluded to fall us in on both floors at once, and then he found he was short six or seven prisoners. This seemed to puzzle him worse than ever, and I don't believe he has up to this day found out, just how the thing was done. He certainly had not at the time we left Danville. After this there was no effort made to have the count overrun, and the use of that hole in the floor was abandoned.

All the time the different counts were going on, the officers, who of course understood perfectly well what all the fuss was about, were laughing and joking at the expense of the perplexed Sergeant, telling him that it seemed to be as much enjoyment to him to count Yankee prisoners, as it was for a miser to count his gold; asking all sorts of questions and offering all sorts of suggestions to tease and annoy him.

As he would call upon us to fall in again for count, someone would say, "well Sergeant what was the matter that time? Was there too many of us or not enough? What kind of an arithmetic did you study when you went to school? Let me figure that up for you. This is a new military rule you adopt, turning out the guard every time the Sergeant comes in." Others would say as they saw him coming up stairs again, "turn out the guard for the commanding officer!" "Turn out the guard for the officer of the day!" Others would attempt to beat the long roll on the floor, with sticks of stove wood, or try to whistle, "Boots and Saddles," or the assembly. In fact they all seemed to try to see how exasperating they could be.

The Sergeant, who by the way was a clever fellow, courteous and gentlemanly in his demeanor towards us, took all of this chaffing, with as good a grace as possible.

He tried hard to conceal his perplexity and the annoyance our joking caused him, and with a determined look that seemed to say, "I'll unravel this mystery if it takes all day," kept up the count until it came out as he wanted it to, or as he seemed to know it ought to come out.

Chapter XXV.

borrowing seven hundred dollars of a reb.

A long in January, 1865, I began to get short of money, and as the jewelry, watches, etc., were about played out, I was in danger of being obliged to suspend, for want of stock to sell from. Just at this time, the reb Sergeant came in one day and inquired if anyone had greenbacks, they wished to exchange for Confederate money.

He came to our mess, as it was the one most likely to be able to accommodate him, and said there was a gentleman outside who would give seven hundred dollars in Confederate for one hundred in greenbacks, or, if we had not the currency, a check on Riggs & Co.'s bank, of Washington, D. C., would be accepted, provided we would write a letter and give it to him, asking our friends at home to deposit the amount there, stating that we had drawn a check for one hundred dollars on that bank, to subsist ourselves while in prison.

I took seven hundred dollars of him and Lieutenant Leyden of my mess, took the same amount, just to accommodate him; and I wrote the required letter to my wife, while Leyden wrote one to his brother, in Rochester, N. Y. These checks and letters were given by him to General Hayes, who had been ordered to Richmond, as was supposed, for exchange; and who agreed to bring them through the lines, and forward the letters to their address, and deposit the checks with Riggs & Co. When I got all this money I was flush again; and distributed it around among my friends and comrades, ten dollars to one, and twenty to another, as their necessities seemed to warrant, keeping what I thought would do me until I got out, or could make another raise.

I laid in quite a stock of provisions for myself, and helped those of my friends who had no money, and needed something more than the rations they drew to live upon.

Colonel Smith had established a rule, that three officers could go every day, under a guard of two soldiers, to visit their friends in the hospital, a mile or so distant, by applying for permission by letter to him. Applications for this privilege would be filed, and permission granted when their turn came; it might be a week after the application was filed, before we could go. Lieutenant Leyden, myself and another, made our application, and waited for our turn, to take a walk of a couple of miles in the open air; for this was really all we wished to do. We were called out one day soon after, and with two guards over us, strolled over to the hospital, which was about a mile from where we were confined. We had a nice walk, and as we were returning, we asked the guard to take us into a saloon, where we could get a drink before we went back to prison.

The guard did not know whether they would be allowed to do this, but meeting an officer they asked him, if it would be right to go with us. Why of course, said he, take them wherever they want to go. They then took us into a little ten by twelve room, where there was a bar, and I asked all hands to have a drink. Applejack was the only beverage, so all five of us took that; and thinking as the Governor of North Carolina, has been quoted as saying to the Governor of South Carolina, that "it's a long time between drinks," I set 'em up again. The guards refused to drink a second time, probably fearing that it might incapacitate them from properly guarding us, so I only had eight drinks to pay for altogether. We were not given a bottle and glasses to help ourselves as is usual, but the bartender poured out a wine glass full for each. How much do you want I asked, pulling out a roll of Confederate; forty dollars was his reply. I handed him a fifty dollar bill and receiving my change, went on, stopping at two or three stores on the way back to make other purchases. We had a jolly time that night and whooped things up a little, for by the time we got back into prison, the applejack, which was old and powerful, began to work, and we were just in the proper frame of mind to make things look cheerful to us. I am afraid we were somewhat annoying to some of our comrades who wanted to sleep that night, and not having had any applejack could not appreciate the fun.

I shall never forget the Christmas dinner I ate in Danville prison in 1864, and I do not think any of the half dozen who dined with me that day, will ever forget it either. I bought a turkey weighing thirteen and three-fourths pounds for forty dollars, and took it over to the bake-shop to be roasted. The cooks were Union soldiers, who did the baking for the sake of getting better rations, and I got them to stuff the turkey with crusts of white bread, that they had baked for the rebs.

They brought it in nicely roasted, and I managed, by giving one of the guards ten dollars, to get a canteen of applejack, and I also bought a loaf of white bread, so that we had quite a civilized dinner. Six of us sat down together, viz: General Hayes, Captain Seeley, Captain Albert Thomas, Lieutenant Leyden, Lieutenant VanDerweed, and myself, "and we drank from the same canteen." Talk about starvation in Southern prisons! Why just see what a dinner six of us had that day; and all it cost was about seventy dollars. We could live like that nearly two weeks on a thousand dollars.

Of course every prisoner did not have the money to afford these luxuries, and were obliged to put up with the corn bread ration, served out by the rebel authorities; but the Confederate government "of course was not to blame if the poor boys starved, because they did not have money to buy all they wanted." There was plenty to eat, only our boys did not have the money to buy it with. I never asked Riggs & Co. whether they ever paid that check for seven hundred dollars or not, and have forgotten the name of the generous hearted reb who loaned it to me, but this I know, that I am still indebted to someone for my good fare for a month or two, during my last days in Danville. Now I have told you how I managed to get a living in Danville, and will tell how some others managed to get theirs.

I have spoken of Captain H. H. Alban, who was my companion during the latter part of my tramp through South Carolina, Georgia and North Carolina, and who was recaptured with me. The same opportunities were afforded him to make money enough to subsist himself, as were enjoyed by me, but he was not adapted to buying and selling. He earned money enough to get along, however, by hard labor.

He would go out with the water detail once in a while, and when he came back he would bring along on his shoulder a good straight stick of cord wood. Then with a case knife that he had made into a saw, he would cut it up into pieces about eight inches long, and with wooden wedges that he had whittled out, would split these up fine, say about half an inch thick, and tie them up into bundles for cooking rations with. These bundles would be about six inches in diameter and eight inches long, which he would sell for two dollars each.

By being economical, one of these bundles of hard wood splinters, (they were usually beach or maple) would last a person two or three days to cook his rations with.

Nearly all of the cooking was done in one quart tin pails or in tin plates.

Broken pieces of flat iron were sometimes used to build the fires upon, but most of the prisoners cooked on the stoves that were in the two rooms.

Some of the officers in the different prisons made beautiful trinkets out of beef bones, such as napkin rings, paper cutters, crochet needles, pen holders, imitations of books, etc., and sold them to their fellow-prisoners to take home with them as souvenirs of their prison life.

Some of these bone-workers were skilled artists, and could fashion anything out of a beef bone. I have seen as fine a piece of work of this kind, done with the rude tools that the mechanic had made himself, as I have ever seen made with the latest and most approved machinery. Carving of the most exquisite patterns, and in beautiful designs could be seen in one of these collections.

I remember of seeing one napkin-ring carved out in open work, connected with a continuous vine with beautiful clusters of grapes, the price of which was $100. I bought, and brought home with me, $35 worth of these trinkets.

A number of us belonging to five or six different messes bought a small cook stove for which we paid, I believe, a hundred or a hundred and fifty dollars. There were two griddle holes in it and a small oven in which one loaf of bread could be baked at a time. It was an old affair that here would not bring more than it would come to as old iron, but to us it was a great treasure. We arranged among ourselves to take turns cooking upon it, for instance one would have the first use of it one day, and then the next day he would be the last to use it, and so each in their turn would have the first chance to cook for one day.

Those who had the last chance would have a pretty late breakfast, dinner and supper, for it would take each one at least half an hour to get a meal. Those who had no means of cooking their rations, would come and beg the privilege of setting their tin cups on our stove to warm their coffee, which was usually made out of burnt rye or peas, and sometimes of scorched wheat bran.

Every morning the whole surface of the stove would be covered with these tin cups during the whole time the stove was in use; and even after the different messes had all got through it would be engaged by outside parties for nearly the whole day, each taking their turns in the order that their applications were made. Of course those who owned a share in the stove always took precedence if they wished to do any extra cooking or baking during the day. We often used to make griddle cakes for breakfast, either out of our corn bread rations soaked up in water with a little corn meal added, or mixed up with flour and water with sometimes an egg stirred in if we could afford it, but as eggs were twelve to fifteen dollars a dozen this expensive luxury was dispensed with most of the time.

The two large Peckham stoves for warming the room were always in use, the boys hanging their pails by hooked wires against the hot sides so that, especially in the morning, they would be completely encircled with these hanging pails, and there would always be a crowd waiting for the next chance. Some would hold their cups by the handle against the stove, changing hands whenever it became too hot, and others would stand, holding a pail out on a stick run through the bale.

Quarrels were frequent over their turns, for all were tenacious of their rights, and there, as here, some were always ready for a quarrel, and very jealous of their rights and watchful lest they were trespassed upon.

There were at least three artists in this Danville prison, viz: Captain Albert Thomas, who now has a studio in Syracuse, N. Y., Lieutenant VanDerweed and another, whose name I do not now remember; but almost every prisoner who was confined in Danville, will remember him as the officer who was once sent down the river from Richmond for exchange, but who, while passing Fort Fisher, was detected by the Confederate officer in charge, in making a sketch of that fortification, and return to prison. He was finally paroled with the rest of us, and we chaffed him considerable while we were going down the river, some of the boys teasing him to make them a sketch of the Reb iron-clads in the river, or of Fort Fisher.

Lieutenant VanDerweed made a number of sketches of prison scenes and some fine pencil sketches of officers. He also went outside to make pencil sketches of Confederate gentlemen and ladies, and while thus engaged, of course, lived well and enjoyed pleasant society.

Captain Albert Thomas was solicited to do the same, but said in his expressive way, that he would starve and see all the rebs in —— (he mentioned some warm climate) before he would make a picture of one of them. He made some excellent pencil sketches of different officers in the prison and among them one of Colonel W. C. Raulston, who met so sad a fate in the attempted outbreak on the Tenth of December, 1864, but this sketch unfortunately, was lost.

He also made a good one of myself, from which I have procured a cut for this volume, and which I highly prize.

There were also in Danville, as in other prisons where I was confined, sutlers who bought provisions of the Johnnies and sold to their comrades at a profit. They would buy two or three pounds of bacon of the Johnnies and cut it up into small pieces of about two ounces each, and sell these to their comrades, who either had not money enough to buy more, or were too fond of their own comfort to go down stairs at eleven o'clock at night to buy of the guard.

Chapter XXVI.

On the 17th of February we were ordered to get ready to leave for Richmond for exchange. The order was received with the most extravagant demonstrations of joy; officers who had heretofore been sedate and gloomy, throwing their arms around each other in the wildest excitement. Some laughed and shouted, some wept for joy, while others gave vent to their feelings by singing "Rally 'Round the Flag," "The Red, White and Blue," "The Star Spangled Banner," and other patriotic songs. All were jubilant, all were happy, and all were excited. With buoyant hearts and happy faces the preparations to move were made. Not having many possessions, everything was soon in readiness, and never was the order to fall in obeyed with greater alacrity, or with more cheerfulness, than was the order of the Reb Sergeant that morning at Danville.

Soon we were all comfortably (?) seated in the sweetly perfumed cattle cars, and were flying towards Richmond at the rate of twelve miles an hour. On to Richmond, was shouted by the jubilant prisoners, as we started from Danville.

The next day we were ushered into that notorious prison hell of the South, Libby prison, presided over by the equally notorious Dick Turner. While at Danville one officer was shot in the hand, by the guard, who fired at random through the window, because one of the officers accidentally spilled some water on the window sill, and it ran down upon him. Major D. Colden Ruggles, died in the hospital, and Lieutenants Baily, Quigley, Harris, Helm and Davis, escaped by means of the oven heretofore described. How many of the nearly two thousand enlisted men in Danville died, I have no means of knowing, but the mortality was not as great there as in Salisbury. Libby prison, and the treatment of federal prisoners there, has been so frequently described that I will not attempt a description.

I was there but a short time, but was told by those who had been there before, that Dick Turner seemed to be on his good behavior, and was evidently thinking of the day of reckoning.

We found Libby prison nearly filled with our enlisted men, whose emaciated forms told more plainly than words could possibly do, the terrible sufferings they had endured. They were confined in separate rooms from us, but we managed to pass them provisions through the openings in the partition, and also to converse with them. We were shown where and how the wonderful tunnel that secured freedom to quite a number of officers, and came near setting the whole prison at liberty, was started and where it ended. We were shown Castle Thunder, which at one time contained a number of prisoners, and where I believe Dr. Mary Walker, of Oswego, was at one time confined.

While at Richmond, General Hayes came in to see us, and said he was detailed to distribute the clothing to our men, which our government had sent for them, and as we would be home before he would, he gave us, Lieut. Leyden and myself, the letters and checks we had given to the old reb at Danville, in exchange for fourteen hundred dollars in Confederate money. And, shall I confess it, in a fit of absent-mindedness (?) I tore them up and threw them into the stove, thus saving the bother of taking them to Riggs & Co., at Washington. I have forgotten the old gentleman's name who so greatly befriended me by giving me such a liberal supply of money which, although worthless to him, served to supply myself and a number of my comrades, with the best the Confederacy afforded, for the balance of our stay in rebeldom.

Our stay in Richmond was of short duration, but we left it without regret.

On the twentieth of February, we were again ordered to "pack up," and this time for home. I cannot describe the wild tumult of joy with which the order was received. Many of the enlisted men, who with us occupied the building, though in a separate apartment, and to whom we had managed to smuggle some of our rations, were too weak to walk alone, and were obliged to walk between two of their comrades, who supported them to the boat and tenderly cared for them. Their emaciated forms and lusterless eyes, told a painful story of the starvation and suffering they had endured for the preservation of their country, and for their loyalty to the flag.

And yet there are those even here in the North, who grew rich through their sufferings, who begrudge them the beggarly pittance of a pension of a few dollars a month, to keep them from the poor house; when, by their heroic fortitude, and their indescribable sufferings, they made it possible for the bonds of the government to be worth a *hundred cents on the dollar in gold*; made it possible for these very men to be to-day enjoying the luxury of wealth in a happy and prosperous land; to be citizens of a country whose treasury is overflowing to such an extent that the President of the United States has deemed it necessary to cry out in alarm, that the country is in danger from a too plethoric treasury. These same heroic souls who twenty-five years ago, by their loyalty to the old flag, and whose patriotic devotion to the principles of universal freedom, led them to offer themselves upon the altar of their country, if they escaped a horrible death by starvation and are still living, are looked upon by many who profited so largely by their sacrifices, as beggars, because they ask to be remunerated for their shattered health, by a small pittance of ten or twelve dollars a month, to assist them in their old age and decrepitude.

On the morning of the 20th of February, 1865, the last ration of corn bread was issued, and I determined to preserve mine and bring it home to show to my friends. This I did, and have kept it ever since. It was twenty-three years old the 20th of February, 1888, and is still in a fair state of preservation, and on every anniversary of its issue to me, that old Libby prison ration and I have a little celebration, and revive old memories.

We were placed on board river steamers, which were skillfully piloted around the numerous torpedoes that had been sunk for the destruction of our gun-boats, should they attempt to assist in the capture of Richmond, and past the iron-clad monsters that were stationed all along for the protection of that rebel stronghold, and were conveyed to Varina landing, where, as we disembarked, we were met by an equal number of rebs who had been prisoners in our hands, and who returned on the same boats that took us down.

The contrast in the looks and appearances of these gray-backs and our poor boys, was painfully apparent. They were in robust health, full of life and vitality, and fit to at once take the field again, while our boys were scarcely able, many of them, to climb up the bank at the landing, without assistance. While they showed the effects of rest and plenty of wholesome food, our poor comrades showed equally the terrible effects of starvation and disease. They were in excellent condition to again at once go into active service, while we would need months of careful nursing, before any of us could again endure the hardships of camp life; and a large proportion, were forever broken in health, and would never again be able to perform the duties of a soldier.

We still had a march of six miles to make, before we reached the Union lines. Ambulances were in waiting, to convey those who were too feeble to endure the march, and the rest of us who had strength enough left, trudged along on foot.

Chapter XXVII.

The march from the landing to the headquarters of General John E. Mulford, was through a swampy piece of ground and the road was muddy, but, with freedom almost in sight, we tramped along cheerfully, with buoyant steps and hopeful hearts, singing snatches of army songs, though we were still inside the lines of the enemy. After a march of about five miles we passed the reb picket line, and about three hundred yards ahead, saw once more floating in the breeze, on a tall flag staff, the glorious old banner for whose defense we had suffered so long and so fearfully.

When the head of the column came under the shadow of "Old Glory," both our cheers and our old dilapidated hats went heavenward with all the velocity that we were able to impart to them. Some were too feeble to more than faintly whisper their greeting to the dear old flag they loved so dearly, while tears of joy attested the genuineness of their affection for that beautiful emblem of liberty, the sight of which had so long been denied them.

I never before realized how much I loved the dear old stars and stripes, or how much protection there was beneath its shining folds. How I longed to press it to my heart and lips. And not me alone, but of the nearly two thousand skeletons who that day saw it proudly waving high over their heads for the first time in many months; there were few indeed who would not have fervently kissed and caressed it had it been within their reach. As a mother's love goes out to her first born that has come to her amid suffering and pain, so that old flag seemed a thousand fold more beautiful and precious to us, for the sufferings and privations we had passed through in its defense.

Cheer after cheer went up as the straggling column passed along, feeble hands were waived, and feeble voices joined in the huzzahs, with which we celebrated our return to "God's country."

Arriving at General Mulford's headquarters, we were obliged to wait two or three hours for a boat to take us down the river. Once on board the steamer, our first thought was for a good square meal.

But, alas! a meal on board that steamer cost a dollar, and Confederate money was no good there.

A comrade whom I had befriended, however, invited me to take dinner with him, which invitation you may be sure I readily accepted; and for the first time in many months, sat down to a regular dinner of roast beef, Irish potatoes, bread and butter, and a genuine cup of coffee.

On the morning of Sunday, the 22d of February, we arrived at Annapolis. As the steamers were approaching the wharf, a band which had come down to welcome us, struck up "Home, Sweet Home." Involuntarily every officer took off his hat and bowed his head, as though receiving a benediction, so impressively solemn sounded that sweet, familiar tune just then.

Arriving at parole camp, the first person I met whom I knew, was Captain Eastmond, who escaped with me at Columbia, and who was recaptured the next night.

He told me that a few days after my escape, my name was called for special exchange, and he answered to my name, signed my name to the parole, and had been out nearly three months.

As soon as he reached General Mulford's headquarters he told him of the deception he had practiced, and the General told him it was all right and as soon as he could find out where I was he would send another special for me. But I, in blissful ignorance of what my friends were trying to accomplish in my behalf, was being shifted from one place to another, so that he did not get track of me again. The first thing I did upon my arrival at Annapolis, was to hunt up the store of the Ladies' Sanitary Commission, and get a complete outfit from head to foot, for which they would take no pay, and then getting a room in a hotel, I stripped off my lousy rags, and after taking a good bath, dressed myself in my new suit, throwing my old prison garments out of a window into an alley, thus effectually ridding myself from the annoying companions that had so persistently stuck by me during my imprisonment. I parted with them without a sigh, and have never to this day had a desire to renew their acquaintance.

I then applied for a twenty day's leave and wrote a long letter home, giving a brief synopsis of my experience in the prisons of rebeldom for the last ten months. This letter I directed to my wife, though I did not know whether she was dead or living, not having heard a word from her since parting with her at Plymouth, on the night of the first day's fight. After waiting a week I received my leave of absence, and at once started for home. I found that my letters had nearly all been received and promptly answered, but they were never delivered to me. I can never be made to believe but that our letters were purposely destroyed by order of General Winder, as a part of his plan to discourage and dishearten us, well knowing how much this would do towards undermining our health and destroying our lives.

I was home for days before I could feel fully assured that I was really out of prison; fearing all the time that it was only one of those vivid dreams that had so often come to me while there, and fearing lest I should awake and find myself still surrounded by stockades and rebel guards, often I would stop and pinch myself to see if I were really awake, and at home among friends.

Upon the expiration of my twenty days' leave, I returned to my regiment near Goldsboro, (having been exchanged) and was just in time to assist in taking in the North Carolina troops of Johnson's army, and seeing the conquered rebels lay down their arms, dejected and subdued, and seemingly heartily rejoiced, that the fearful struggle was finally at an end.

I reached Albany on my way back to Annapolis, on the 3rd day of April, and there first learned of the evacuation of Richmond. The first person I met whom I knew, as I disembarked from the cars near the Delavan House, was Hon. Elias Root, then Member of Assembly from Oswego Co. He saluted me with, "hello Cooper, you here and sober? Haven't you heard that Richmond has fallen? The orders are that any man found sober here after four o'clock will be arrested." This coming as it did from a staunch temperance man, and an active and consistent Christian, was a stunner; and I apologized by saying that I had just arrived in Albany and had not yet been able to comply with the order, but would attend to it immediately. I managed to avoid being arrested that day, for I had seen enough of prison life and did not care to be deprived of my liberty again so soon.

Proceeding to Washington and then back to Annapolis, and from there back to Newbern, via the Keretuck canal, I immediately joined my regiment at Mosley Hall, near Goldsboro, and reported for duty.

A few days after my return to headquarters we received the joyful news of the surrender of General Lee, at Appomattox, on the 9th of April. This news was received with great demonstrations of joy by everyone, and was celebrated with the wildest enthusiasm. About this time I was ordered to Camp Palmer, near Newbern, on some business, and saw an order posted, of which the following is substantially a copy:

Headquarters Department, &c.

General Orders, No. — .

The news having reached the headquarters of this department that General Lee surrendered the army of Virginia to General U. S. Grant on the 9th inst. at Appomattox Court House, the following order is promulgated.

1st. Any soldier found sober after four o'clock to-day will, if an enlisted man, be confined in the guard house, and if an officer, will be placed in arrest and charges preferred against him. By order of

Gen. Palmer.

[Signed.] A. A. Judson, Capt. & A. A. G.

I also found Capt. Judson at Camp Palmer to see that the order was properly enforced. I will only add that there were no arrests made under that order.

Upon joining my company I found Captain R. B. Hock, who had escaped with me at Columbia, and with whom I had parted from in the suburbs of Greenwood, S. C., when I started out to find the cabin of "Free Mitchell," and whom I had not seen or heard from since that time.

The meeting was a joyful one to both, and Captain Hock related to me the experience of himself and Lieut. Winner after we separated.

They took a route more to the east, and after walking about three hundred and fifty miles, which took them, I think, about twenty-one days altogether, they came out at Marysville, Tenn., where they struck the Union lines, and were, after resting a few days, sent on to Washington, and from there to join their respective regiments.

Captain Hock afterwards participated in the battle of Wise's Forks and was there again taken prisoner, but escaped the same night and walked through to Plymouth, N. C., the scene of the battle where we were both taken by General Hoke a year before.

Plymouth at this time was again in possession of the Union forces, and from there he again went to Newbern. He was subsequently made a prisoner again during another engagement near Goldsboro with Johnson's army, and again succeeded in making his escape, and after a long and tedious march once more reached his regiment.

When he came back this time the regiment was just out for dress parade, and Colonel J. W. Savage had him accompany him out in front of the line, where he introduced him to the command as the Greasy Captain.

Company F., Captain R. B. Hock, of which I was 1st Lieutenant, was for a time thereafter stationed at Kinston, N. C., and after taking the paroled men of Johnson's army, relieving them of their arms, but leaving them their "critters," we joined the regiment again and were encamped for a while at Goldsboro, and then marched to Tarboro, which place I had not visited before since I passed through there in April, 1864, a prisoner of war. Here I was placed in command of Company D, Captain Turner of that company having been detailed for duty in the Freedman's Bureau.

We remained in Tarboro until the middle or latter part of July, and while there I assisted in disinterring the remains of five of my comrades, of the 12th N. Y. Cavalry, who were killed in a charge near that place in July, 1863, and give them a Christian burial.

The following letter, which was written at the time and was published in the city papers, gives a brief description of the funerals:

Camp Near Tarboro, N. C., May 17, 1865.

Mr. Samuel Miller:

My Dear Sir — I have just returned from assisting in performing the last sad duties to the heroes who fell in the gallant charge near this place in July, 1863. I personally superintended the disinterment of the bodies, and readily recognized your brave boy by his hair, teeth, and the shape of his head. I also recognized the body of William Davis. Capt. Simeon Church was there, and recognized his twin brother, Capt. Cyrus Church, and others who were present recognized the others.

Six were buried in one grave, and all were in a perfectly nude state, the fiendish brutes having appropriated to their own use every article of wearing apparel. We had a coffin made for each one. When disinterred they were placed in coffins made of white wood, and their names written on the covers. The bodies were brought into camp, when the funeral procession was formed in the following order, viz: First, the regimental band; next, forty men mounted on white horses, with drawn sabers; next, the chaplain; next, the ambulance, with the bodies of Capt. Cyrus Church, and Sergt. John P. Miller and William Davis, with six officers acting as pall bearers by the side; next the officers of the regiment; next twelve men mounted on bay horses, with drawn sabers and commanded by a Sergeant; next the ambulance containing the bodies of S. Mulligan, H. Rood and David Carl, and in the rear the dismounted men of the regiment.

At 2 o'clock the procession moved with sabers reversed, the band playing a solemn dirge, and marched to a beautiful burying ground in the village, where the Episcopal burial service was read by Chaplain Palmer of our regiment. We are thankful that we have at last had the mournful privilege of giving a Christian burial to our fallen comrades.

Appropriate headboards were placed at the graves. The coffins were made small enough to be placed in other coffins for removal. I shall do all I can to send the remains of your son home, and if Captain Church sends his brother, I will send your son with him. I send you a lock of Johnny's hair, and some of the hair of Wm. Davis, which please give to his wife.

Deeply sympathizing with you and your family I remain,

Your obedient servant,

A. Cooper,

1st Lieutenant, Commanding D Troop, 12th N. Y. Cavalry.

From Tarboro the 12th Cavalry were moved to Raleigh, N. C., where we made up our returns and turned over our horses, and were then mustered out of the service.

From Raleigh we made the march to Petersburgh, and from there to City Point, where we took steamers for New York. We were sent to Hart's Island, where we were paid off and were soon at home again.

Chapter XXVIII.

more about charleston — exchange on the brain — more about macon — charleston jail yard more fully described — the old privy — the gallows or gibbet — terrible suffering for want of food and shelter — a fire and how gillman helped it along.

We remained in Charleston thirteen days, viz., from September 13th until the 26th, and it was thirteen days of intense suffering to many, and of great discomfort to all.

This jail yard itself was filthy to a fearful degree, and was enough to create an epidemic. An old privy occupied the south-west corner of the ground, the vault of which overflowed into the yard and emitted an effluvia that would be certain to create disease, even in an otherwise healthy locality. We petitioned to have this nuisance abated, and after a week or more, upon the recommendation of Dr. Todd, who was the attending physician, and who tried to do all within his power to render our situation more bearable, some men were sent in one night to tear down the old privy and clean out the vault.

This took all night and most of the next day, and during that time, Charleston jail yard was the most revolting place that civilized humanity ever occupied and lived.

As I have said, there were only fifty "A" tents to accommodate six hundred officers and, as not over two hundred and fifty could possibly be crowded into these, there were three hundred and fifty officers without shelter of any kind, and as the weather part of the time was rainy, the suffering among those was fearful and a frightful mortality must have ensued, had we been compelled to have remained there much longer. As it was, I have no doubt that the germs of disease were planted there that afterwards cropped out in some form, and perhaps in many cases resulted in broken constitutions, and even death.

Another prolific source of suffering was the lack of fuel with which to cook our scanty rations.

In our extremity we broke up the lumber of the old privy that had been torn down, and tried to cook with that; but as the pails we used to cook in were mostly without covers, and the old lumber was so thoroughly permeated with the filth it had so many years covered, that the rations thus cooked were too revolting to the stomach to be eaten.

The ground of the jail yard was a sandy loam, and the yard having been occupied by prisoners for a long time, was actually alive with vermin, with which we were soon supplied to an extent that was discouraging to those who had any ideas of cleanliness.

In the centre of the yard was a gallows, which had evidently been erected for a long time, and had probably done considerable service. This was a post about twenty-five feet high, with a horizontal arm extending out about eight feet; at the extreme end of this arm and also at the top of the post where the arm joined it, there were pulleys for a rope to run through. A weight at the end of the rope running down the posts, acted as a drop to elevate the body of the victim from the ground and lifted him towards the end of the extending arm. This gallows we cut down and used for fuel. Dr. Todd, as I have said was the prison physician, and was, I believe, a brother of Mrs. President Lincoln.

Reader, do you wonder that we were willing to give our parole not to escape, for the privilege of exchanging this loathsome and pest breeding jail yard, for good, healthy, clean quarters, where we could have all of the facilities for cleanliness, such as were offered to us?

About the 1st of October a fire broke out just after noon, about six or eight hundred yards to the north-east of where we were then confined, on Broad street, overlooking the bay.

As the alarm was sounded, we gathered upon the piazzas to watch its progress. We could see the firemen dragging their apparatus to the fire, and were watching their preparations to extinguish it, when suddenly, we heard the familiar boom of Gilmore's "Swamp Angel," and presently saw a shell explode among a group of firemen, who hastily scattered in every direction.

Shell after shell dropped into the burning building, or exploded among those who were endeavoring to extinguish the flames, and for a time it looked as though another terrible conflagration was inevitable.

When a well directed shell would drop in, and explode where the firemen were at work and scatter them, we would send up a cheer that must have been heard where the flames were raging.

Citizens gathered upon the flat roofs of their dwellings and watched the conflict, between the Charleston firemen on one side, and the crackling flames and General Gilmore's batteries on Morris Island, on the other.

I saw a man and woman upon their roof near the burning building, and when the shells began to drop in pretty thick and fast, and some of them most uncomfortably near to where they stood, the gentleman seemed to suddenly think of some duty he was obliged to attend to below, while the lady pluckily staid it out. The wonderful accuracy with which General Gilmore sent those immense projectiles into any part of the city, from his batteries on Morris Island, five miles away, was simply astonishing. He seemed to be able to drop them just where he pleased and there was no time, day or night, when the citizens of that doomed city had not good reason to expect that they might receive one of Gilmore's compliments, as we used to call them. While we were waiting in the Broad Street House for the order to start for Columbia, after we had got all packed up, the officers commenced writing their names on the wall near where they had slept, and being in rather a poetical mood just then, I took my pencil and wrote on the wall in the corner where my quarters had been, the following:

> I have slept in this corner for many a night,
> A prisoner of war in a pitiful plight,
> I have ate my corn dodger, my bacon and rice,
> And have skirmished my shirt and my drawers for lice.
>
> Here's health to Jeff Davis and bad may it be,
> May mercy and pardon afar from him flee,
> May he find, when too late, to his sorrow and cost,
> That not only the Confederacy, but Heaven he's lost.

Chapter XXIX.

exchange on the brain.

Many of the prisoners were afflicted to a greater or less extent, with what was termed exchange on the brain.

This disease would manifest itself in various ways, and different persons would be differently affected by it.

I remember numerous cases of this malady, (for it really was a malady) in the different prisons. Persons thus afflicted, would improve every opportunity to inform themselves of the prospects of there being an exchange of prisoners, and every paper they got hold of would be carefully scanned for exchange news, and whenever they came across an article on this subject ever so vague and unsatisfactory, they would pore over it, and try to construe it as an evidence that an exchange would soon take place.

If papers were not to be had they would stroll around the camp, stopping to talk with any one that could be induced to listen to them, about what they had heard on this subject, and try to hear something that they could console themselves with, and in their perambulations about the grounds, their whole and only theme was "Exchange." Should those they met commence talking upon any other subject, they were uninterested and would, as soon as possible, change the subject to the prospects for exchange.

The first question they would ask upon meeting an acquaintance would be, "Do you hear anything about exchange?" Should they find two or three officers talking together, especially if they seemed to be talking rather earnestly, they would get up near enough to find out whether the subject under discussion was exchange.

It was the subject of all their thoughts and conversation by day, and of their dreams by night.

The most improbable rumors would be started in camp in regard to exchange, just to play upon the credulity of those who were afflicted with exchange on the brain, and they would believe them too, and would excitedly circulate the rumors.

One officer in Savannah, Captain Johnson, was afflicted badly with this malady, and could never see two or three officers together talking, without trying to ascertain if there was anything being said about exchange. We used to play upon his credulity to an extent that was really cruel.

While at Savannah, Col. F. C. Miller, 147th N. Y., was detailed as senior officer of the camp, and all communications to the commandant of the prison had to be forwarded through him, and all orders from the commandant to us were received through him.

Being very intimate with Col. Miller, I was supposed, next to him, to be the most probable one to know what was going on. The Colonel had made a backgammon board, and we used to sit in his tent and play a good deal of the time.

Captain Johnson and I both belonged to the same squad, which was designated as No. 9. One evening, I had been up to Colonel Miller's tent until quite late, and when I returned, the squad had all retired. As I came to my tent, which was just opposite Capt. Johnson's, I said to my tent-mates somewhat excitedly, and in a tone loud enough for Johnson to hear: "Well, boys, I have now got some news that is reliable. I just came from Col. Miller's tent, and the Colonel told me that Col. Smith told him — " here I dropped my voice so that Johnson could not hear. In a second Johnson jumped out of bed and came across the street, minus everything but his night clothes, and asked excitedly: "What did Col. Miller tell you?" "Well," said I, "Col. Miller told me that No. 9 squad would be detailed to police the camp to-morrow."

Johnson, without saying a word, returned to his bunk amid the roars of laughter from the whole squad. I know it was cruel, to laugh at, and play jokes upon men who were half insane upon the subject. There were those who were clearly insane upon the subject of exchange, and were really to be pitied.

A Captain, whose name I have forgotten, became perfectly insane while we were at Savannah, and I think he died while in prison. At first those who noticed his peculiar actions thought he was playing a dodge to get paroled and sent North, but we were all soon convinced that the poor fellow had brooded over his imprisonment until his mind had completely lost its balance.

His mind seemed to be continually dwelling upon exchange, and for days and weeks he could not be induced to talk upon another subject. He would tell the most improbable stories, that no one else had heard, about a general exchange of prisoners that was soon to take place, but as such stories were continually floating around the camp, not much attention was paid to him, and if anyone thought upon them at all, they looked upon his stories as silly canards, gotten up to fool someone with.

His mind finally seemed to run to sumptuous dinners, and he would invite eight or ten of his prison companions to dine with him at a certain hour, and upon their arrival, they would find perhaps a half baked corn meal pome, that had been cooked in a dirty old wash basin, over a smoky fire, having been mixed up without salt or rising of any kind, to be the princely spread he had invited them to.

He would do the honors in a courteous and dignified manner and seem to think he was at home entertaining some distinguished guests in a royal manner, to a regal feast.

Of course his comrades would excuse themselves on one pretext and another, and would leave him to enjoy his dinner alone.

He would eat his pome with all the apparent relish, with which he would have partaken of a dinner such as he seemed to imagine he was indulging in.

Of course, in its half-cooked condition, it would be not only perfectly unpalatable, but injurious to the health as well. When it is remembered that rumors of exchange were being almost weekly circulated through our camp, sometimes by the reb authorities in order to keep us from trying to escape, and sometimes I believe for very cussedness, the only wonder is that the majority of the prisoners were not driven to insanity. I have seen men sit moping for hours with a look of utter dejection, their elbow upon their knee, and their chin resting upon their hand, their eyes having a vacant far-away look, brooding over the cruel fate that placed them in the prison pen, and wondering why an exchange of prisoners was not made, and whether they would ever be released.

On the 21st of June, 1864, a Catholic priest came into the prison at Macon, and gave us such a harrowing picture of Andersonville, which place he had visited the day before, that it made our own sufferings seem insignificant.

He said that he passed up between two lines of Union dead, who had been laid there that morning by their comrades to be carted off to the burying ground, that must have numbered at least a hundred, and that he saw thousands there that were scarcely able to walk, or in many cases even to sit up.

Some to whom he administered the last rites of the Catholic church, showed by the glassy expression of their lusterless eyes, that the grim visitor already held them within his grasp.

The picture he drew of the sufferings, starvation and death he had witnessed there, sent a chill of horror to the heart of his listeners, and created a feeling of indignation that could scarcely find expression in words.

The next day, upon the advice and recommendation of the Confederate authorities, two from each squad met in the large hall that was used for the field officers, and also as a sort of hospital, and drew up a petition to the Rebel Secretary of War, for permission for Majors Marshal, Beatie and Owen of the army, and Lieutenant Alexander, of the navy, to go to Andersonville and examine into the condition of the enlisted men and then proceed to Washington and urge upon the United States government a speedy exchange of prisoners.

When it became known throughout the camp that such a scheme was on foot and that the petition had been signed by this self-constituted delegation and was about to be forwarded to Richmond, an indignation meeting was held from the steps of this building, and was addressed by Captain Ives and others, and the action of the Committee was denounced, as not being in accordance with the sentiment of the prison camp.

The almost unanimous sense of the meeting was, that we had faith in our government and believed it was doing all it could do, consistent with its dignity to relieve and release us, and that we would rather suffer the tortures of prison life, than to harass our government and thereby give aid and comfort to their enemy. The meeting closed by our asserting our confidence in the wisdom and ability of our friends at the North, to do what was for the best interests of the country, and that if we could do more or better service for the country in prison than in the field, as good soldiers and true patriots it was our duty to submit to all the indignities that were being heaped upon us, rather than even impliedly stigmatize the U. S. government as being unmindful of our sufferings, and screen the fiendish brutes who were heaping all of this suffering upon us.

While the meeting was in progress the petition was secretly taken out of camp by a rebel officer, who had instigated their preparation, and as we supposed, forwarded through to rebel Capt. Gibbs to Richmond. We never heard anything from the petition, and the belief was that the rebel authorities, seeing the indignation they had caused, concluded their interests would not be advanced by complying with its provisions.

To show how the large majority of officers confined in Macon felt about how the affairs of the government had been conducted under the administration of President Lincoln, I quote from my diary of June 7th, 1864:

"This being the day upon which the Convention is to meet at Baltimore to nominate a candidate for President, our camp went into convention and nominated Abraham Lincoln by a vote of 533 out of a total vote cast of 625."

This was considered not only an endorsement of the policy pursued by the President in the prosecution of the war, but also our approval of his exchange policy.

We well understood that the cartel was suspended, because the South refused to exchange the negroes taken in arms, but proposed to return such soldiers to servitude, and we believed that as they were taken while bearing arms in defense of the government, that government was in duty bound to protect them in their rights and it was our duty as good soldiers to suffer and even die, if need be, in prison or in field, to maintain the dignity of the nation.

This is why such indignation was manifested when we were asked to lend ourselves to the scheme of Jeff. Davis, to even impliedly stigmatize the authorities at Washington, as being derelict in their duties towards us, by demanding an immediate resumption of the exchange cartel, unless all who wore the blue could be classed in the category of United States soldiers. We believed that all whose loyalty to the flag, had led them to risk their lives in its defense, whether their skin was white or black, were entitled to protection beneath its folds.

While on the tramp with Captain Alban through the Confederacy, after our escape, he told me an amusing story about his capture at Chicamauga. He belonged to the 21st Ohio, and that regiment was armed with the Henry rifle.

The portion of the line occupied by the 21st Ohio, was assaulted with determined gallantry six or seven times, and was every time repulsed with heavy loss.

The Johnnies would charge with an impetuosity that was wonderful, and would advance until they received the sixth or seventh discharge from those repeating rifles, which shoot sixteen times without reloading, when they would break and fly in disorder; receiving as they went back two or three more shots, before they would be out of range. They would again be re-formed and make another gallant assault, only to again be broken and driven back with fearful slaughter.

After having charged, as I have said, six or seven times, and each time been repulsed with great loss, Captain Alban was taken prisoner and hurried to the Confederate rear. One of the privates was taken at the same time, and his rifle which he had just emptied, was examined with much curiosity by the reb who had taken him, who, after looking it over thoroughly, turned to Alban and said, "What kind of guns do youens use! You load up Saturday night and shoot all the week, don't you?" After having learned how to handle it he thought it would be a good one for him, but as the soldier had exhausted his supply of ammunition, the piece would be useless until they could get some to fit it.

Chapter XXX.

scouting in north carolina — sergeant c——— in a well — the accident prevents a fight with our own troops — a fight with north carolina troops — mrs. modlin turns a back somersault — our irish lieutenant.

hile at Plymouth on detached service, with "I" and "F" troops, we were in the habit of scouting ten to fifteen miles once or twice a week, sometimes in one direction and sometimes in another. We were seldom ordered out on a scout by General Wessels, but all that was necessary for us to do when going out on one of these scouts, was to notify the General of the fact that we were going out on a certain road, ten or fifteen miles, at a certain time, and would be back about such a time.

I have frequently taken twenty-five or thirty men for a scout into the country, to capture parties with loads of provisions for the Confederates, or to bring in some prisoners.

I have mentioned two guides, Modlin and Wynn, who were in the habit of going with me on these raids, and who were both taken prisoners at Plymouth, and escaped into the woods while on the march, after being spotted by some of the North Carolina troops as "Buffaloes."

These two guides, who were natives of North Carolina, and who knew every turpentine path through those immense pine forests, and who had friends outside our lines who kept them well posted on what was going on outside, while they in turn kept me posted as to the movements of the rebs.

One day Wynn came to me and said that he had positive information that five or six loads of bacon, for the Confederate army, would stop over night at a certain house about fifteen miles south of Plymouth, on the Washington road, and that the guard would consist of ten men besides the teamsters. I immediately rode up to General Wessel's headquarters and told him that I was going to take thirty men and go out on the Washington road at five o'clock that afternoon, and would return the next morning. I, as usual, procured the countersign for that night, so as to be able to get inside the picket post if I should come back in the night, and selecting thirty men, started at five p. m., guided by Wynn for the South.

After getting out about five miles, we left the road and followed one of the turpentine paths through the woods in a parallel direction.

It had become quite dark by this time and we proceeded in single file, Wynn and myself riding at the head of the column.

Among the men under my command that night was Sergeant C ——— , a tall, powerful man, and an excellent soldier, whose pluck could always be relied upon, but who had a great weakness for following up any noise on the march, especially if it sounded anything like the crowing of a cock, and was therefore not always in the line while on the march.

We had proceeded about five miles through the woods when our path crossed a road at right angles, just at a school house.

As we crossed the road the guide said to me, there is a well on our left, keep to the right a little. We turned a little to the right and at the same time I ordered the word passed down to the rear that there was a well on the left, keep to the right. This word was passed from one to another until it had reached the rear of the column.

Now Sergeant C ——— had stopped a little way back on some important business, probably connected with a chicken roost, and of course did not hear the cautionary word and after we had passed on about two hundred yards a cry came from the rear of the column, C ——— is in the well.

I halted the column, and going back found, by the aid of a lantern we carried, that both C ——— and his horse were in a dry well about ten or twelve feet deep, and about as wide as it was deep. There was nothing to do but to buckle our saddle straps together, which C ——— placed under his horse, and lift it out bodily and then pull C ——— out.

This took us half an hour, and I was fearful that we would not reach the house before the teams had got started, and we would be unable to capture the guard. It was just daylight when we came out on the road, about six hundred yards from the house, and I at once charged down and surrounded it.

I secured six yoke of oxen and six loads of bacon, but could find no guard or teamsters. After placing my pickets I had some of the boys bring in a ham, and that, with some eggs and sweet potatoes, and a hoe cake that the woman cooked for us, together with some coffee, which we always carried with us, made us a good breakfast.

To our enquiries about the teamsters and guard, the woman told us that about half an hour before we came a company of Cavalry came from the opposite direction and passed on towards Plymouth, and that at their approach, the guard and teamsters fled to the woods.

I took the teams and loads of bacon and, throwing out an advance and rear guard, proceeded back to Plymouth, not knowing what moment I might run onto this Cavalry troop, which I thought must be rebel Cavalry, as there were no Union Cavalry between Plymouth and Little Washington, which were about eighty miles apart, and knowing that no other troop had left Plymouth, and none would leave until my return.

I reached Plymouth without opposition and then learned that the troop that had passed the house just before we got there, was thirty of our Cavalry from Little Washington, with dispatches for Plymouth, and had already arrived.

When I learned this I was very thankful that C —— had got into the well, for otherwise, we would have reached the road half an hour sooner and would in all probability have met this troop, and mistaken them for the reb guard, have charged them; and as they were not expecting to meet any one but enemies, they would very likely have attempted to break through and a fight would have taken place between us, which must have resulted in loss of life before the mistake was found out.

Shortly after this, Modlin, our other guide, wanted to move his wife and household effects into Plymouth and asked Captain Roache, who was then in command of the detachment of Cavalry, to accompany him to his farm, which was about fourteen miles from our lines, as a protection against a company of rebs that were sometimes in the neighborhood.

Captain Roache took eighty-five men of Companies "A" and "F," and with Captain Hock, Lieutenant Russel and myself, accompanied him home.

I had command of the advance going out, and after we reached the house, was sent with twenty-five men across a piece of woods to another road, and about a mile out on that road, to a house where he thought I might capture some prisoners. Modlin went along as my guide, and as we emerged from the woods, and came out on the road near a school house, I dismounted and went into the school house to see if there was anyone there. I found on the hearth the dying embers of a fire and quite a number of egg shells, showing that the school house had been occupied the previous night and assuring me that there were rebs in the vicinity.

I did not delay, but moved rapidly down upon the farm house and surrounded it, but after a thorough search of the premises failed to reveal the rebs I was in search of, I mounted again and returned to Modlin's house, and found two carts loaded with his furniture, &c., and ready to start for Plymouth.

On our return trip Lieutenant Russel was placed in command of the advance, and I was given command of the rear guard of twelve men to protect the carts. The mule in the head cart was driven by one of my guards, who led his horse behind, and the other was driven by a darkey boy, and upon this cart was seated Mrs. Modlin, upon the top of a load of bedding, etc.

We had proceeded perhaps a mile, when we came to a small stream or run, where we stopped to water the horses. We were passing through a swampy piece of woods, called cedar swamp, and just up the road, perhaps six hundred yards from the stream, was a small wood-colored meeting house.

The advance and the main column had watered and started on, and I was watering the horses of the rear guard, when a brisk fire of musketry was opened upon the column now four hundred yards ahead, from the woods on our right.

The column pushed by, and then halted and dismounted, while I told the mule-driver to drive up past before they had time to reload; but the mules were frightened at the firing and were hard to manage, and while I was assuring Mrs. Modlin that she had nothing to fear, as they would not fire at a woman, my guard galloped past the firing up to the column, the one who was driving the mule deserting it, and mounting his horse, going with the rest. The mule thus left without a driver, ran away up towards the company, scattering the goods along the road. The darkey jumped off the other cart and ran into the woods, and as this mule started to run, Mrs. Modlin, turned a back somersault off the back end of the cart and followed the darkey; the mule running against a tree beside the road, demolished the cart and spilled the goods in a most promiscuous manner. My position behind them all, enabled me to take in the whole of this ludicrous scene and I should have laughed if they had all been killed.

Being deserted by my guard and left alone, I started towards the column, firing a small pistol that had been presented to me, into the woods, the rebs being within five or six rods of the road, but a cap got foul and it would not revolve, so I returned it to my belt and drew my navy revolver. As I passed them they gave me a volley, but all fired over my head, and neither myself or horse were touched.

As I rode up towards the column, I saw Captain Hock out in front five or six rods, firing his pistol into the woods, and everyone seemed to be fighting on his own hook.

I called out and asked where Captain Roache was, and someone said he was hurt. I then called to the men to come out, where I was still sitting on my horse, and form, which they did with alacrity. Capt. Roache, soon recovering from a stun he had received in dismounting, took command and we soon had the Johnnies driven back. Our men were all dismounted and followed the rebs a short distance, but as they were in the swamp we remounted and started on towards Plymouth without further molestation, except that they came out into the road again, after we had gone eight hundred or a thousand yards, and fired one volley at my rear guard.

We had five horses wounded, but lost no men either in killed or wounded. Five or six months after, when I was taken prisoner at Plymouth, I saw the Lieutenant, who was in command of the ambushing party, and in talking about that skirmish he said, that when that volley was fired at me at such close quarters (not over fifteen rods) and I being such a splendid mark sitting on my horse, he thought I was gone sure.

Mrs. Modlin, the next day having recovered her mules, and picked up her household goods, came into Plymouth alone.

We had an Irish Lieutenant in the 12th Cavalry, whose quaint expressions gave us much merriment. When we first went to Camp Palmer, we had daily drills; he being 1st Lieutenant, drilled the first platoon of the company, and I the second. We used to take them out separately, and I used to be greatly amused at the orders he would give. We commenced by drilling the men in the saber exercise, and I was watching him the first day. When he got his men into line, and after having them take the proper distance, he gave the command something like this: "Attention, min! Now I am going to larn yees how to draw saber. Whin I say 'draw!' don't you draw; but whin I say 'saber!' out wid it." Now those who do not understand the saber drill may want a little explanation as to how this was to be done. At the command "draw" the saber is loosened from the scabbard and drawn about six inches; and at the command "saber" it is drawn out and describing a half circle to the front, carried to the shoulder.

Another favorite order of his when he wished to give the order, "fours right" and then form the squad on right into line, was this: "On ladin set of fours, form line of battle, faced to the rare, march!" Turning to the Major, who was watching him drill one day, after executing this maneuver he said, "Major this is a bully movement on a retreat." While we were near Camp Palmer, our advance picket post was about five miles from camp, at a place called Deep Gully; and it was usual for the officer of the day after guard mount, to march his guard under command of the Sergeant, to Deep Gully, in columns of fours. This Irish Lieutenant, being officer of the day one time, after the inspection of the guard was completed and the Adjutant had turned them over to him with the usual instructions, rode out in front and gave his orders thus: "Attention guard, draw saber! carry, saber! be twos or be fours, whichever yees like. Deep Gully, to the front! Away wid yees."

While at Plymouth, the two Captains and four Lieutenants, of our two Cavalry companies, formed a mess, each officer contributing his share towards the expenses. After a while, however, one of the Captains offered to run the mess, for so much a head per week, agreeing to give us good board. Well, for a week or two, everything went smoothly and all seemed satisfied with the fare. One day we had chicken for dinner, made up into a sort of soup, or more properly speaking, gruel. This, by breaking some hardtack into it, though rather thin, was rendered quite palatable by judicious seasoning, and there being plenty left it was warmed up for dinner again. The third day as we sat down to dinner, we found another dish of this gruel on our plates, somewhat diluted, and looking rather feeble.

When this Irish Lieutenant sat down to dinner he took a look at the soup, and recognizing in it some infinitesimal portions of the old friend of the two previous days, shoved back his plate and with flushed face ejaculated: "Be jabers I like soup; I'm fond of soup, I like soup for forty or fifty meals, but by jabers as a gineral diet I don't think much of it."

We had good quarters in Plymouth. Our quarters were in a two-story white house, built as most of the houses in the South are, with a wide hall running through the centre and instead of a cellar, the house was set upon posts, so as to give free access to the air underneath. Our Irish Lieutenant occupied one large room upstairs, and I occupied one just across the hall from him. One Sunday morning I heard a noise in his room, and stepping across the hall, opened his door, and at first thought by his language that he was engaged in his Sunday morning devotions, as he was a strict Catholic. When I opened the door and took a look at him, I was startled at the sight which met my gaze. He was standing in the middle of the room, with a new white flannel shirt about half on, his head protruding, and his face of apoplectic hue, his arms extending upward, and he seemed incapable of either getting out of or into the shirt. It was one of those heavy white flannel shirts such as we all took with us at the commencement of the service, which would shrink in washing to about one-half their original size.

As I entered the room there was a look of discouragement upon his face, which from a liberal use of commissary and natural swarthiness, was always somewhat flushed, and now looked like a boiled lobster, which gave it a frightful appearance. The first sentence I heard sounded like a prayer; he said, "Oh! may the Lord take particular pains to damn the nagur that washed this shurret." Taking in the situation at a glance, I discreetly withdrew and allowed him to conclude his devotions.

Making Yankees out of the Contrabands, was a pleasing pastime for our boys after the war had ended; and hundreds of these dusky "innocent causes" flocked into Tarboro, N. C., after we occupied that Secesh town, to be transformed into "Lincum Yankees." Instead of going to headquarters, they would generally go directly to the company quarters, where the boys would heartily welcome them. To the question, "well boy, do you want to be made a Yankee?" They would say "yes massa, I spects I does." A good strong blanket would be brought out and six stalwart fellows would hold it on either side and the candidate would be gently placed upon it.

The question would then be asked, "Do you promise to support the Constitution of the United States?" to which they would usually respond, "I 'spects I does, massa." The order would then be given, attention! one, two, three, go; and he would go. At first they would toss him gently, but at every successive toss he would go higher and higher, until he could almost, as one expressed it, see the "gates ajar;" some would almost turn white when they were tossed up to such a fearful height, but as soon as one was pronounced reconstructed and entitled as such to all the rights and privileges of an American citizen, another would step forward and signify his desire to become a Yankee. There was very seldom any accident in these initiating exercises, but I remember of one, in which some of the boys became too weak, from excessive laughter, to hold onto the blanket, and a strapping young negro came near being killed; as I think he surely would have been, had he not fortunately struck the ground head first.

Conclusion

Reader, while I do not claim for this volume any rare literary merit, I trust a perusal of its pages may have afforded you some little pleasure, and instruction. I can cheerfully place it in the hands of my old prison associates, confident that they will testify to its truthfulness and fairness.

While the language is my own, I can confidently claim that it conveys no imaginary sufferings and privations. I have endeavored to speak of the Southern prisons and of the treatment meted out to those whom the fortunes of war compelled to endure and suffer the hardships, tortures and privations of a lingering confinement in those loathsome pens of starvation, provided by the self-styled Southern Confederacy, as a punishment for loyalty to country and the flag, just as I found them. Not to the *people of the South* do I lay the blame of the frightful mortality among prisoners, in those pens of starvation, but to Jeff. Davis and the infamous Winder; who boasted that they were doing more execution among the prisoners, than Lee's whole army was doing in the field; to them I say that the blood of thirty-five thousand loyal hearted patriots, cry from the ground of Andersonville, Salisbury, Florence and Belle Island, unto a just God, for vengeance upon those who so cruelly, heartlessly and fiendishly *murdered them*.

To them I say that should they flee to the uttermost parts of the earth, they cannot escape the contempt of an outraged world, nor the curse of the thousands of mothers, widows, and fatherless children, whom they have in their fiendish hatred, robbed of their beloved sons, husbands and fathers.

Appendix

The author of this volume, Alonzo Cooper, was born in the town of Victory, Cayuga Co., N. Y., April 30th, 1830. His father John Cooper, who was born August 15th, A. D. 1794, enlisted from Scoharie County in the war of 1812-13-14, and during his term of service, was for a time employed on the construction of the famous 110 Gun, line of battle ship "NEW ORLEANS" at Sackets Harbor, which was built and all ready for caulking in six weeks from the time the first tree was felled. Abraham Cooper, an older brother of John, was also in the service during the war of 1812, serving as Captain in a Militia company.

The mother of the author, Amanda Cochran, was a daughter of John Cochran, a Revolutionary soldier. John Cochran was an Irishman by birth and as such was claimed as a British subject, and was arrested by the "press gang" as they were then called, and taken on board an English man-of-war to be impressed into the service of Great Britain.

The vessel was anchored about one and a half miles from shore, the better to prevent the escape of the impressed seamen; but, notwithstanding the strict surveillance under which they were placed, John Cochrane and a comrade one dark night, tied their clothing into a bundle, which they fastened on their heads and dropped into the water from the fore chains of the vessel where they were stationed, and swam to the shore and made good their escape. The story as frequently told me by my mother, is a long one and filled with thrilling incidents, as was also the military life of my father, John Cooper. My father died October 23d, 1831, when I was only eighteen months old, leaving my mother with a family of nine children, one of whom was a babe only a few weeks old. Her only income was the products of a farm of 25 acres, and the trifling wages as a carpenter's apprentice of my eldest brother, Lorenzo.

In the spring of 1836, my mother having sold her farm in Victory and bought fifty acres in Sterling, we moved into a new log house that my brother had built during the winter and early spring, and around which he had made a clearing of sufficient dimensions to avert the danger of the house being crushed by falling trees. This clearing was extended during the summer to ten or fifteen acres by cutting off the timber, and afforded us youngsters plenty of work, piling brush and burning them, and the log heaps which a bee of neighbors had constructed.

The house had not been chinked, and the floor was made of split basswood slabs, hewn smooth and nicely fitted together, which if not as elegant as the more modern floors, at least possessed the elements of strength and durability. A large Dutch fire place, and a wide chimney built of sticks and mud, took up nearly half of the north side of the house, while at the right of the fire place was constructed a rude pair of stairs leading to the upper rooms. The lower part of the house consisted of this one room, about 16x18, which served as parlor, dining room and kitchen, and a bedroom and recess occupied the south side.

The upper rooms were two in number and were supplied with rough board floors, and with a window in each room. A cellar was dug under the front room for the storage of apples and vegetables during the winter, and was entered by a trap door near the center of the floor.

The district school was about half a mile north and was kept in what was called the VanPetten school house. Here it was that the author first attended school, which was taught that summer by Miss Rachel Lester — now Mrs. McFadden. For seven seasons I attended school there under the instruction of different teachers, among whom were, Miss Sarah J. McCrea, now Mrs. George Turner, Mr. Emerson Crane, Mr. Mathew B. VanPetten, Obediah Cooper, Dennis Cooper, John B. VanPetten, and others. Up to the time of my mother's death, which occurred January 17, 1845, just before I was fifteen years old, I had attended school summer and winter, with the exception of part of the last two summers, when I was obliged to stay at home to assist in the farm work, and being easy to learn, had acquired a fair education in the primary branches for a boy of my age — 14 years.

At the death of my mother the only legacy I inherited was a robust constitution, a cheerful and happy disposition, and the faculty of always looking upon the bright side of life. These characteristics were clearly inherited from my mother, to whom obstacles that would have seemed insurmountable to most women seemed only an incentive to more determined efforts.

To her household duties were added the work of the loom and the spinning wheel, and up to the time of her death there were very few clothes worn by the family that she did not weave and afterwards make up into garments.

The linen trousers and shirts that were bleached to snowy whiteness for our summer wear, and the full suits of comfortable sheeps-gray for winter, were alike the production of her own toil. The dresses worn by the girls, especially those for Sunday wear, were also the production of her loom, and were dyed and pressed by herself. Besides all this, all the time that could be spared from the duties of her own household was employed in weaving for others.

Both she and my father were members of the old Reformed Dutch Church at Cato — now Meridian — that was at that time under the pastorage of the good old dominie Houghman, and her well worn Bible bore testimony to her faithfulness in her Christian duties. She was faithful in instilling into the hearts of her children the religion she practiced, but rather appealed to their sense of duty than to the fear of punishment.

After the death of my mother I followed the pursuit of a farmer, attending the district school during the winter, until I was 19 years of age, when I entered the employ of Mr. Charles Burnett, of Skaneateles, N. Y., in his dry goods and grocery store. I remained with Mr. Burnett one year and then, as he retired from business, I came to Oswego and entered the drug store of the late James Bickford, jr.

Not liking the drug business, I at the end of the first year entered into the employment of the late Worden Newkirk, as a dry goods clerk, with whom I remained three years, and was afterwards for a short time in the large dry goods house of Downs & VanWick, of Chicago.

Thrown out of employment in Chicago by the panic of 1856, and being fond of adventure, when the great "Lager Beer Riot," as it was called, broke out in that city in the spring of that year, I went to the city hall in response to a call for three hundred special police and was sworn in as a special to serve during the riot. The riot lasted three days and was a lively skirmish.

We took three hundred prisoners in the first three hours and there were a number killed and wounded.

The rioters marched across Clark street bridge in good order, armed with shot guns, pistols, hatchets and clubs, and were met by the police at the corner of Clark and Lake streets, where the first conflict took place.

Almost the first shot fired by the rioters wounded the man next to me in the arm near the shoulder, and he fell as though he had been knocked down by a powerful blow. I was too closely engaged to pay any attention to him and for a time it was pretty lively work for all of us.

I commenced business for myself in the spring or summer of 1857, by starting a fruit, confectionery and oyster store on West First street, about where the middle of the Lake Shore Hotel now is. I moved around on Utica street while the "Revenue Block" (now the Lake Shore block) was under process of construction, and upon its completion, took the store in the north end of that block, which I kept until after the war of the Rebellion broke out. Having served six years in the Old Oswego Guards, and become somewhat proficient in the drill, I was anxious to join one of the regiments then being raised. But the store could not be disposed of, and needed, at that time, my individual attention. Finally, without disposing of my store, I enlisted in the 12th N. Y. Cavalry, which was then being recruited in Oswego, by Major Ward Gasper; who intended at first to raise two companies of Cavalry for the "Harris Light," but subsequently went on and made the two companies, then raised a nucleus, from which the 12th was finally formed.

The two companies were taken to Albany, where we were again examined by a surgeon as to our fitness to perform military duty, and from there went to Staten Island.

Authorization papers having been procured for me I was sent on recruiting service, and was subsequently mustered as 1st Lieutenant of company "I" Sept. 1st 1862.

We remained on Staten Island all winter perfecting ourselves in the Cavalry tactics and drill; but before spring the men had become so dissatisfied with the inactivity on the Island, that by desertions, our eight companies were reduced to four, and by order of General John E. Wool, the eight companies were consolidated into four, thus rendering four Captains and eight Lieutenants supernumerary, who were ordered mustered out of the service as such. I was among the number so mustered out, but went to work immediately recruiting more men and was in due time again mustered in, this time as 2nd Lieutenant of Company "I." With this Company I joined the regiment at Camp Palmer near Newbern, N. C.

I was soon sent to Plymouth, N. C., on detached service, under General W. H. Wessels.

On January 25th, 1864, I was promoted to 1st Lieutenant of Co. "F," but was not able to get to the mustering office, and was therefore not mustered as such until after my return from prison in 1865, and consequently could not be promoted to a Captain, as I otherwise should have been, when a vacancy occurred.

During my service I never lost a day's duty, except once, when I was disabled by having two of my ribs broken, and my back severely injured, and never applied for leave of absence, except as a paroled prisoner, as before stated.

The detachment to which I was assigned were never defeated in any of the numerous skirmishes while at Plymouth, until the battle of Plymouth, which lasted four days and in which the enemy acknowledged a loss nearly equal to the whole number engaged on our side, and in which battle the enemies force amounted to 8000 and the Ram Albemarle, and ours less than 2000.

List Of Officers Confined In Macon, GA.

The following is a list of officers who were confined as prisoners of war at Macon, Ga., in 1864. I do not claim the list to be complete, but as nearly so as I can make it at this time:

BRIGADIER-GENERALS.

Wessels,

Shaler,

Hickman.

Seymour,

Scammon,

COLONELS.

Grove,

Harrison,

LaGrange,

White,

Brown,

F. A. Bartleson, 100 Ill.

C. H. Carlton, 89 O.

P. D. Cesnola, 4 N. Y. C.

Wm. G. Ely, 18 Conn.

W. P. Kindrick, 3 W. T. C.

O. A. Lawson, 3 O.

H. LeFavour, 22 Mich.

J. H. Ashworth, 1 Ga. U. V.

T. H. Butler, 5 Ind. C.

S. J. Crooks, 22 N. Y. C.

J. Frasier, 140 Pa.

Hawkins,

Lehman,

Lee,

Bollinger,

Dana,

R. W. McClain, 51 O.

W. H. Powell, 2 Va. C.

Tho. E. Rose, 77 Pa.

A. D. Streight, 51 Ind.

Chas. W. Tilden, 16 Me.

A. H. Tippin, 58 Pa.

W. T. Wilson, 123 O.

Pennock, Huey, 6 Pa. C.

F. C. Miller, 147 N. Y.

W. Shedd, 13 Ill.

Daniel White, 31 Me.

C. W. Fardella, 85 N. Y.

LIEUT. COLONELS.

Burnham,	Baldwin,
Bartholomew,	Cook,
Dickinson,	Fellows,
Fairbanks,	Glenn,
Higginbotham,	Mills,
Maxwell,	Moffit,
Alcott,	Postley,
Rogers,	Hepford,
Stewart,	Swift,
S. M. Archer, 17 Ia.	W. P. Lasselle, 9 Md.
I. F. Boyd, 20 A. C.	W. E. McMackin, 21 Ill.
T. F. Cavada, 114 Pa.	D. A. McHolland, 51 Ind.
C. Farnsworth, 1 Conn.	C. C. H. Mortin, 84 Ill.
W. A. Glenn, 86 O.	J. D. Mayhew, 8 Ky.
H. P. Hunter, 123 O.	D. Miles, 79 Pa.
A. P. Henry, 15 Ky. C.	W. B. McCreary, 21 Mich.
E. L. Hays, 100 O.	R. S. Northcott, 12 Va.
H. C. Hobert, 21 Wis.	M. Nichols, 18 Conn.
O. C. Johnson, 15 Wis.	Wm. Price, 139 Va. M.
G. C. Joslin, 15 Mass.	P. S. Piver, 77 Penn.
I. J. Polsley, 8 Va. V. I.	A. Van Schrader, A. I. G.
A. F. Rogers, 80 Ill.	I. H. Wing, 3 O.
J. P. Spofford, 79 N. Y.	J. N. Walker, 73 Ind.
J. M. Sanderson, S. O.	J. Williams, 25 O.
G. Von Helmrich, 4 Mo. C.	T. S. West, 24 Wis.
M. B. Buffum, 4 I. R.	Benj. B. Morgan, 75 O.
J. B. Conyngham, 52 Pa.	H. R. Stoughton, 2 U.S.S.S.
C. W. Clancy, 52 O.	A. H. Sanders, 16 Iowa.
M. A. Leeds, 153 O.	T. J. Thorp, 1 N. Y. Drag.
C. C. Matson, 6 Ind. C.	G. Von Helmrick, 4 Mo. C.
D. B. McCreary, 145 Pa.	G. Wallace, 47 O.
O. Moulton, 25 Mass.	Taylor.

MAJORS.

Beeres,	Baker,
Bates,	Clark,
Carpenter,	Crandall,
Grant,	Hall,

E. N. Bates, 80 Ill.

W. T. Beatly, 2 O.

C. H. Beers, 16 Ill. C.

J. P. Collins, 29 Ind.

M. E. Clarke, 5 Mich.

D. A. Carpenter, 2 Tenn.

J. J. Edwards, 32 Mass.

G. W. Fitzsimmons, 30 Ind.

N. Goff, jr., 4 W. Va. C.

J. H. Hooper, 15 Mass.

J. Hall, 1 Va. C.

Jno. Henry, 5 O. C.

J. B. Hill, 17 Mass.

I. H. Johnson, 11 Tenn.

S. Kovax, 54 N. Y. C.

W. D. Morton, 14 N. Y. C.

S. McIrvin, 2 N. Y. C.

B. B. McDonald, 101 O.

J. H. Dewees, 14 Pa. C.

M. Dunn, 19 Mass.

W. N. Denny, 51 Ind.

D. English, 11 Ky. C.

C. K. Fleming, 11 Vt.

G. B. Fox, 75 O.

W. H. Forbes, 2 Mass. C.

J. H. Filer, 55 Pa.

T. J. Hasley, 11 N. Y.

W. P. Hall, 6 N. Y. C.

E. H. Smith, 2 Pa. C.

L. B. Speece, 7 Pa. V. R. Cps.

T. A. Smith, 7 Tenn C.

M. H. Soper, 5 Ind. C.

A. McMahan, 21 O.

D. M. Kercher, 10 Wis.

M. Moore, 29 Ind.

W. S. Marshall, 5 Ia.

S. Marsh, 5 Md.

J. R. Muhlman, A. A. G.

W. P. Nieper, 57 Pa.

W. N. Ovens, 1 Ky. C.

E. M. Pope, 8 N. Y. C.

L. N. Phelps, 5 Va.

A. Phillips, 77 Pa.

T. B. Rodgers, 140 Pa.

W. I. Russell, A. A. G.

I. C. Vananda, 3 O.

A. Von Mitzel, 74 Pa.

H. A. White, 13 Pa C.

J. B. Wade, 73 Ind.

Harry White, 67 Pa.

J. H. Isett, 8 Ind. C.

C. M. Lynch, 145 Pa.

P. McLernan, 22 N. Y. C.

C. P. Mattock, 17 Me.

P. Nelson, 66 N. Y.

J. E. Pratt, 4 Vt.

W. L. Parsons, 2 Wis.

D. Quigg, 14 Ill. C.

W. H. Reynolds, 14 N. Y. A.

J. Steele, 2 Pa. C.

D. Thomas, 135 O.

D. Vickers, 4 N. J.

G. G. Wanzer, 24 N. Y. C.

J. W. Young, 76 N. Y.

Johnson.

CHAPLAINS.

White,

Dixon.

CAPTAINS.

R. B. Hock, 12ᵗʰ N. Y. C.

— Cady, 24 N. Y. Ind. Bat.

— Sampson, 2 Mass. H. A.

W. F. Armstrong, 74 O.

S. C. Arthurs, 67 Pa.

W. Airey, 15 Pa. C.

E. C. Alexander, 1 Del.

W. B. Avery, 132 N. Y.

I. A. Arthur, 8 Ky. C.

H. H. Alban, 21 O.

W. R Adams, 89 O.

C. A. Adams, 1 Verm.

Jno. Albright, 87 Pa.

E. W. Atwood, 16 Me.

M. Boyd, 73 Ind.

Chas. Byron, 3 O.

E. Baas, 20 Ill.

L. T. Borgers, 67 Pa.

H. P. Barker, 1 R. I. C.

W. K. Boltz, 181 Pa.

W. J. Barnes, 83 N. Y.

A. Carley, 73 Ind.

H. Casker, 1 N. Y. C.

W. F. Conrad, 25 Ia.

J. W. Chamberlain, 123 O.

D. S. Caldwell, 123 O.

J. Carroll, 5 Md.

J. C. Carpenter, 67 Pa.

B. G. Casler, 154 N. Y.

C. C. Comee, 94 N. Y.

E. Charleer, 157 N. Y.

Jno. Cutler, 34 O.

R. T. Cornwall, 57 Pa.

Jno. Craig, 1 Va. Cav.

Jno. Christopher, 16 U. S.

J. P. Cummins, 9 Md.

M. A. Cochran, 16 U. S.

T. Clarke, 79 Ill.

J. Cusac, 21 O.

W. A. Collins, 10 Wis.

B. F. Campbell, 36 Ill.

— Geere.

H. R. Bending, 61 O.

M. R. Baldwin, 2 Wis.

C. D. Brown, 18 Conn.

W. P. Bender, 123 O.

John Bird, 14 Pa. C.

L. B. Blinn, 100 O.

D. E. Bohannon, 3 T. C.

Dav. I. Bailey, 99 N. Y.

A. J. Bigelow, 79 Ill.

Jno. Birch, 42 Ind.

D. M. Barrett, 89 O.

W. M. Beeman, 1 Va. C.

F. Barton, 10 Mass.

J. H. Barton, 1 Ky. C.

E. B. Bascom, 5 Ia.

B. V. Banks, 13 Ky.

John G. Bush, 16 Ill. C.

G. C. Davis, 4 Me.

R. H. Day, 56 Pa.

E. Day, Jr., 80 O.

R. Dinsmore, 5 Pa.

E. J. Dunn, 1 Tenn. C.

E. Dillingham, 10 Va.

F. C. Dirks, 1 Tenn.

H. H. Eberhardt, 120 O.

B. F. Evers, 100 O.

S. H. Ewing, 26 O.

M. Ewen, 21 Wis.

A. Eglin, 45 O.

Jno. M. Flinn, 51 Ind.

E. A. Fobes, C. S.

B. F. Fischer, S. O.

A. Field, 94 N. Y.

J. B. Fay, 154 N. Y.

E. Frey, 82 Ill.

W. Forrester, 24 O.

J. W. Foster, 42 Ill.

D. Getman, 10 N. Y. C.

S. S. Canfield, 21 O.

T. Cummins, 19 U. S.

Miles Caton, 21 O.

D. S. Cannover, 125 Ill.

G. A. Crocker, 6 N. Y. C.

W. N. Cochran, 42 Ill.

M. Callahan, 9 Md.

W. E. Conway, 9 Md.

J. P. Cummins, 9 Md.

M. C. Carns, 3 Tenn.

J. R. Copeland, 7 O. C.

A. R. Calhoun, 1 Ky.

R. S. Curd, 11 Ky. C.

E. M. Driscoll, 3 O.

W. N. Deung, 51 Ind.

B. Domschke, 26 Wis.

F. B. Doten, 14 Conn.

F. W. Dillion, 1 Ky. C.

H. C. Davis, 18 Conn.

Jno. Dunce, A. D. C.

W. H. Douglas, C. S.

K. S. Dygert, 16 Mich.

H. Dietz, 45 N. Y. C.

J. M. Dushane, 142 N. Y.

S. G. Hamlin, 134 N. Y.

W. L. Hubbell, 17 Conn.

P. H. Hart, 19 Ind.

A. Heffley, 142 Pa.

W. W. Hant, 100 O.

Chas. Hasty, 2 N. Y. C.

A. G. Hamilton, 12 Ky.

T. Handy, 79 Ill.

V. K. Hart, 19 U. S.

H. Hescock, 1 Mo. A.

R. Harkness, 10 Wis.

H. E. Hawkins, 78 Ill.

C. C. Huntley, 16 Ill.

J. B. Herold, 9 Md.

S. C. Honeycutt, 2 E. T.

G. C. Gordon, 24 Mich.

G. W. Green, 19 Ind.

H. W. Gimber, 150 Pa.

W. L. Gray, 151 Pa.

J. H. Green, 100 O.

Chas. Gustaveson, 15 Wis.

J. F. Gallaher, 2 O.

J. Goetz, 22 Mich.

A. G. Galbraith, 21 Mich.

J. Gates, 33 O.

O. C. Gatch, 89 O.

S. A. Glenn, 89 O.

J. W. Grose, 18 Ky.

B. Grafton, 64 O.

H. H. Gregg, 13 Pa. C.

Jas. Galt, A. Q. M.

M. Gallagher, 2 N. Y. C.

Dan'l Hay, 80 Ill.

A. Hodge, 80 Ill.

J. G. Hagler, 5 Tenn.

A. M. Heyer, 10 Va. C.

J. Hendricks, 1 N. Y. C.

John Heil, 45 N. Y.

A. Haack, 18 N. Y.

D. H. Mull, 73 Ind.

D. A. McHolland, 51 Ind.

J. B. McRoberts, 3 O.

McMoore, 29 Ind.

W. M. Morris, 93 Ill.

H. C. McGuiddy, 1 T. C.

F. Mennert, 5 Md.

E. J. Matthewson, 18 Conn.

W. F. Martins, 14 Mass. A.

P. Marsh, 67 Pa.

D. B. Meany, 13 Pa. C.

C. C. Moses, 58 Pa.

C. A. Mann, 5 Ill. C.

S. Marsh, 5 Md.

J. McMahon, 94 N. Y.

S. Irvin, 3 Iowa.

S. F. Jones, 80 Ill.

J. M. Imbrie, 3 O.

R. Johnson, 6 N. Y. C.

F. Irsh, 45 N. Y.

J. C. Johnson, 149 Pa.

F. R. Josselyn, 11 Mass.

R. O. Ivro, 10 Mass.

D. I. Jones, 1 Ky. C.

J. S. Jackson, 22 Ill.

J. M. Johnson, 6 Ky.

J. A. Johnson, 11 Ky. C.

J. T. Jennings, 45 O.

W. M. Kendall, 73 Ind.

E. M. Koch, 5 Md.

S. B. King, 12 Pa. C.

A. M. Keeler, 22 Mich.

D. A. Kelly, 1 Ky. C.

J. Kelly, 73 Pa.

D. F. Kelly, 73 Pa.

J. Kennedy, 73 Pa.

W. D. Lucas, 5 N. Y. C.

R. F. Lownsberry, 10 N. Y. C.

L. P. Lovett, 5 Ky.

John Lucas, 5 Ky.

J. W. Lewis, 4 Ky. C.

E. M. Lee, 5 Mich. C.

J. E. Love, 8 Ks.

J. R. Land, 66 Ind.

S. McKee, 14 Ky. C.

F. W. Perry, 10 Wis.

E. J. Pennypacker, 18 Pa. C.

W. F. Pickerill, 5 Ia.

J. E. Page, 5 Ia.

J. A. Richley, 73 Ind.

M. Russell, 51 Ind.

P. C. Reed, 3 O.

W. C. Rossman, 3 O.

J. F. Randolph, 123 O.

E. A. Mass, 88 Pa.

A. J. Makepeace, 19 Ind.

H. H. Mason, 2 N. Y. C.

C. W. Medcalf, 42 Ind.

J. S. McDowell, 77 Pa.

J. G. Williams, 51 Ill.

J. Meagher, 40 O.

W. McGinnis, 74 Ill.

J. M. McComas, 9 Md.

A. W. Metcalf, 14 N. Y. C.

M. R. Milsaps, 2 E. T.

A. Marney, 2 E. T.

W. M. Murray, 2 E. T.

J. C. Martin, 1 Tenn. A.

S. Meade, 11 N. Y.

W. A. Noel, 5 Md.

H. Noble, 9 Md.

T. W. Olcott, 134 N. Y.

E. O'Brien, 29 Mo.

N. C. Pace, 80 Ill.

J. D. Phelps, 73 Ind.

F. A. Patterson, 3 Va. C.

J. F. Porter, 14 N. Y. C.

J. A. Pennfield, 5 N. Y. C.

E. Porter, 154 N. Y.

S. V. Pool, 154 N. Y.

F. Place, 157 N. Y.

S. H. Pillsbury, 5 Me.

R. Pollock, 14 Pa. C.

G. S. Pierce, 19 U. S.

A. H. Stanton, 16 U. S.

R. H. Spencer, 10 Wis.

S. A. Spencer, 82 O.

E. L. Smith, 19 U. S.

J. P. Singer, 33 O.

A. P. Seuter, 2 E. Tenn.

P. S. Scott, 85 Ill.

T. Thornton, 161 N. Y.

John Teed, 116 Pa.

A. Robbins, 123 O.

C. H. Riggs, 123 O.

O. H. Rosenbaum, 123 O.

W. Rowan, Indp. C.

M. Rollins, 2 Wis.

J. C. Rose, 4 Mo. C.

Thos. Reed, 1 Va.

W. A. Robinson, 77 Ia.

B. F. Riggs, 18 Ky.

N. S. Randall, 2 O.

J. A. Rice, 73 Ill.

W. J. Robb, 1 Va.

A. Rodgers, 4 Ky. C.

C. Rowan, 96 Ill.

S. B. Ryder, 5 N. Y. C.

C. Reynolds, 8 Tenn.

W. H. Robbins, 2 E. Tenn.

J. A. Russell, 93 Ill.

W. W. Searce, 51 Ind.

W. A. Swayze, 3 O.

D. D. Smith, 1 Tenn. C.

E. Szabad, A. D. C.

H. W. Sawyer, 1 N. J. C.

E. A. Shepherd, 110 O.

D. Schirtz, 12 Pa. C.

Geo. L. Schell, 88 Pa.

S. A. Urquhard, C. S.

G. H. Starr, 88 Pa.

J. R. Stone, 157 N. Y.

Wm. Syring, 45 N. Y.

R. Scofield, 1 Va. C.

T. M. Shoemaker, 100 O.

J. A. Scammerhorn, 112 Ind.

J. C. Shroad, 77 Pa.

J. B. Alters, 75 O.

W. N. Algbaugh, 51 Pa.

H. B. Andrews, 17 Mich.

John Aigan, 5 R. I. Art.

M. A. Auer, 15 N. Y. C.

O. Templeton, 107 Pa.

H. D. Taylor, 100 O.

B. E. Thomson, A. D. C.

T. Ten Eyck, 18 U. S.

A. Tubbs, 9 Ky. C.

T. Thornton, 5 U. S.

G. C. Urwiler, 67 Pa.

J. D. Underdown, 2 E. D.

J. W. Vanderhoef, 45 N. Y.

G. M. Van Buren, 6 N. Y. C.

A. Wilson, 80 Ill.

W. R. Wright, 80 Ill.

J. A. Wistlake, 73 Ind.

Wm. Walleck, 51 Ind.

G. W. Warner, 18 Conn.

C. W. White, 3 Va. C.

W. Willets, 7 Mich.

J. C. Whiteside, 94 N. Y.

T. E. Wentworth, 16 Me.

W. C. Wilson, 104 N. Y.

H. C. White, 94 N. Y.

C. C. Widdis, 150 Pa.

Geo. M. White, 1 Va.

W. H. Williams, 4 N. Y. C.

P. Wellsheimer, 21 Ill.

H. P. Wands, 22 Mich.

W. B. Wicker, 21 O.

J. E. Wilkens, 112 Ill.

J. G. Wild, 9 N. Y. C.

J. H. Whelan, A. Q. M.

E. A. Wolcott, 16 Ill.

M. G. Whitney, 29 Mo.

H. Zeis, 80 Ill.

J. C. Slover, 3 E. T.

L. S. Clark, 62 N. Y.

H. C. Chapin, 4 Vt.

F. S. Case, 2 O. C.

T. Coglin, 14 N. Y. H. Art.

J. W. Colville, 5 Mich.

C. D. Amory, A. A. Gen.

James Belger, 1 R. I. Art.

C. H. Burdick, 1 Tenn.

G. Bradley, 2 N. J.

C. W. Boutin, 4 Vt.

C. D. Bowen, 18 Conn.

B. Bennett, 22 N. Y. C.

N. Bostwick, 20 O.

J. F. Benson, 120 Ill.

B. C. Beebee, 13 Ind.

A. N. Benson, 1 D. C. C.

E. A. Burpee, 19 Me.

J. W. Bryant, 5 N. Y. C.

H. Biebel, 6 Conn.

J. A. Barrett, 7 Pa. R. C.

G. A. Bayard, 148 Pa.

Geo. A. Blanchard, 85 Ill.

S. Bremen, 3 Mich.

A. D. Bliss, 10 N. Y. C.

H. D. Baker, 120 Ill.

W. F. Bennett, 39 Ia.

J. H. Brown, 17 Iowa.

S. D. Barnum, 23 U. S. C. T.

W. F. Baker, 87 Pa.

H. H. Burbank, 32 Me.

O. E. Bartlett, 31 Me.

J. T. Chalfant, 11 Pa.

C. H. Call, 29 Ill.

J. D. Clyde, 76 N. Y.

C. R. Chauncey, 34 Mass.

A. F. Cole, 59 N. Y.

J. P. Carr, 93 Ind.

H. P. Cooke, A. A. Gen.

T. B. Camp, 52 Pa.

E. Grant, 9 U. C.

E. H. Green, 107 Pa.

A. Grant, 19 Wis.

A. L. Goodrich, 8 N. Y. C.

J. L. Galloway, A. A. G.

L. M. Carperts, 18 Wis.

E. N. Carpenter, 6 Pa. C.

M. W. Clark, 11 Iowa C.

E. S. Daniels, 35 U. S. C. T.

C. C. Dodge, 20 Mich.

O. J. Downing, 2 N. Y. C.

J. G. Derrickson, 66 N. Y.

J. B. Dennis, 7 Conn.

T. F. Davenport, 75 O.

C. L. Dirlan, 12 O.

W. Dusbrow, 40 N. Y.

A. Duzenburgh, 35 N. Y.

E. B. Doane, 8 Ia. C.

W. H. Davis, 4 Md.

G. B. Donohey, 7 Pa. Res.

L. B. Davis, 93 Ind.

E. C. Dicey, 1 Mich. S. S.

J. B. Dibeler, 45 Pa.

S. S. Elder, 1 U. S. Art.

B. W. Evans, 4 O. C.

M. Eagan, 15 W. Va.

N. C. Evans, 184 Pa.

W. W. Farr, 106 Pa.

E. W. Ford, 9 Minnesota.

F. W. Funk, 39 N. Y.

W. M. Fisk, 73 N. Y.

J. L. Francis, 135 Ohio.

D. Flamsburg, 4 Ind. Bat'y.

J. Fiedler, Eng. R.C. U. S. A.

J. P. Fall, 32 Me.

W. W. Fay, 56 Mass.

J. B. Gillespie, 120 Ill.

E. C. Gilbert, 152 N. Y.

A. W. H. Gill, 14 N. Y.

W. W. McCarty, 18 Ohio.

J. W. Morton, 4 Mass. C.

J. McHugh, 69 Pa.

W. M. McFadden, 59 N. Y.

H. McCray, 115 Pa.

J. L. Green, A. A. G. U. S. A.

C. Gutajahr, 16 Ill.

P. Grayham, 54 Pa.

H. B. Huff, 184 Pa.

W. R. Hitt, 113 Ill. C.

W. Harris, 24 Mo. C.

C. A. Hobbie, 17 Conn. C.

T. A. Heer, 28 O.

G. D. Hart, 5 Pa. C.

H. B. Hoyt, 40 N. Y. C.

D. J. Hume, 19 Mass.

R. C. Hutchison, 8 Mich.

C. W. Hastings, 12 Mass.

E. Haynes, 95 N. Y.

M. C. Hobart, 7 Wis.

J. A. Hayden, 11

W. L. Hodge, 120 Ill.

H. A. Haines, 184 Pa.

J. B. Heltemus, 18 Ky.

S. Hymer, 115 Ill.

P. Hienrod, 105 Ohio.

F. W. Heck, 2 Md.

T. H. Hill, 2 Md.

A. J. Holmes, 37 Wis.

L. Ingledew, 7 Mich.

B. A. Jobe, 11 Pa. R. V. C.

D. Jones, 14 N. Y. Art.

S. C. Judson, 106 N. Y.

H. Jenkins, 40 Mass.

C. G. Jackson, 85 Pa.

J. D. Johnson, 10 N. J.

J. G. Kessler, 2 Ind. C.

G. E. King, 103 Ill.

P. D. Kenyon, 15 Ill. Bat.

F. Kenfield, 17 Vt.

W. S. Logan, 7 Mich.

J. S. Little, 143 Pa.

C. W. Lyttle, 145 Pa.

G. Law, 6 W. Va. C.

J. May, 15 Mass. Art.

N. H. Moore, 7 N. Y. Art.

S. F. Murray, 2 U. S. S. S.

L. Marsh, 87 Pa.

A. C. Mattison, 12 N. J.

J. Metzger, 55 Pa.

LeRoy Moore, 72 Pa.

S. M. Morgan, A. A. Gen.

M. McGraylis, 93 Ind.

H. P. Merrill, 4 Ky.

H. J. McDonald, 11 Conn.

M. Melkorn, 135 O.

J. A. Manley, 64 N. Y.

A. G. Mudgett, 11 Me.

B. J. McNitt, 1 Pa. C.

L. McIntyre, 15 Wis.

L. Moore, 72 O.

R. J. Millard, 2 Pa. Art.

J. H. Nutting, 27 Mass.

L. Nolan, 2 Del.

C. H. Nichols, 7 Conn.

E. E. Norton, 24 Mich.

W. H. Nash, 1 U. S. S. S.

E. Newson, 81 Ill.

A. Nuhfer, 72 Ohio.

C. Newlin, 7 Pa. C.

J. Norris, 2 Pa. Art.

C. S. Noyse, 31 Me.

H. W. Ogan, 14 Ohio.

H. V. Pemberton, 14 N. Y. A.

J. Parker, 1 N. J.

J. P. Powell, 146 N. Y.

L. B. Paine, 121 N. Y.

J. T. Piggott, Jr., 8 Pa. C.

W. B. Place, 87 U. S.

D. H. Powers, 6 Mich C.

A. C. Paul, A. A. Gen.

G. Pettit, 120 M. Y.

D. B. Pendleton, 5 Mich C.

E. C. Latimer, 27 U. S. C. T.

S. C. Pierce, 3 N. Y. C.

B. B. Porter, 10 N. Y. Art.

J. A. Paine, 2 Ind. C.

T. Ping, 17 Iowa.

J. Rourke, 1 Ill Art.

H. Ritter, 52 N. Y.

W. J. Reynolds, 75 Ohio.

A. C. Rosencranz, 4 Ind. C.

— Reed, 107 N. Y.

R. C. Richards, 45 Pa.

W. J. Reynolds, 4 R. I.

Geo. W. Reir, 107 N. Y.

C. Robinson, 31 U. S. C. T.

J. Snyder, 14 N. Y.

G. F. C. Smart, 145 Pa.

H. J. Smith, 53 Pa.

D. Schooley, 2 Pa. Art.

H. W. Strang, 30 Ill.

J. H. Smith, 16 Iowa.

A. S. Skilton, 57 Ohio.

W. Shittz, 37 Ohio.

A. B. Smith, 48 Ill.

R. R. Swift, 27 Mass.

S. A. Spencer, 82 Ind.

J. R. Stevens, 40 N. Y.

E. J. Swan, 76 N. Y.

E. Schofield, 11 Pa. V.R.C.

C. B. Sutcher, 16 Ill.

E. Shurtz, 8 Iowa C.

M. L. Stansbury, 95 Ohio.

J. G. Snodgrass, 110 Ohio.

H. R. Sargant, 32 Me.

S. U. Sherman, 4 R. I.

D. M. Porter, 120 Ill.

B. T. Stewart, 138 Pa.

D. W. Scott, 23 U. S. C. T.

L. D. C. Taylor, 106 Pa.

S. C. Timpson, 95 N. Y.

H. Tilbrand, 4 N. H.

J. H. Turner, 15 Iowa.

H. G. Tibbles, 12 Ohio.

J. Thompson, 4 Ohio C.

C. L. Unthank, 11 Ky. C.

H. A. Ulffar, A. A. Gen.

J. Wuderwood, 57 Ohio.

A. Von Keiser, 30 N. Y. Bat.

Z. Vaughn, 1 Me. C.

A. Von Haack, 68 N. Y.

J. H. West, 11 Ky.

E. F. Wyman, ——

W. Washburn, 35 Mass.

A. R. Willis, 8 Me.

U. S. Westbrook, 135 Ohio.

B. F. Wright, 146 N. Y.

W. M. Wilson, Jr., 122 Ohio.

H. B. Wakefield, 55 Ind.

G. W. Webb, 2 Pa. Art.

J. Wilson, 57 Ohio.

R. Williams, 12 Ohio.

M. Wiley, 1 Tenn.

E. B. Whittaker, 72 Pa.

R. J. Wright, 6 Ohio.

H. H. Walpole, 122 N. Y.

M. W. Wall, 69 N. Y.

D. G. Young, 81 Ill.

E. K. Zarracher, 18 Pa. C.

LIEUTENANTS.

H. H. Lyman, 147 N. Y.

M. Ahern, 10 Va.

C. L. Alstead, 54 N. Y.

H. Lee Clark, 2 Mass. H. A.

L. C. Bisby, 16 Me.

M. Beedle, 123 N. Y.

S. A. Albro, 80 Ill.

Jas. Adams, 80 Ill.

W. D. Adair, 51 Ind.

H. Appel, 1 Md. C.

R. W. Anderson, 122 O.

H. F. Anshutz, 12 Va.

 F. S. Armstrong, 122 O.

H. M. Anderson, 3 Me.

J. H. Ahlert, 45 N. Y.

C. L. Anderson, 3 Ia.

G. D. Acker, 123 O.

H. W. Adams, 37 Ill.

E. E. Andrews, 22 Mich.

A. Allee, 16 Ill. C.

H. S. Alban, 79 Ill.

R. J. Allen, 2 E. Tenn.

P. Atkin, 2 E. Tenn.

A. B. Alger, 22 O. B.

J. W. Austin, 5 Ia.

Michael Ahern, 10 Va.

H. C. Abernathy, 16 Ill. C.

T. I. Brownell, 51 Ind.

J. W. Barlow, 51 Ind.

J. G. Blue, 3 O.

O. P. Barnes, 3 O.

G. W. Bailey, 3 O.

J. L. Brown, 73 Ind.

A. H. Booher, 73 Ind.

J. F. Bedwell, 80 O.

W. Blanchard, 2 U. S. C.

B. F. Blair, 123 O.

H. S. Bevington, 123 O.

F. W. Boyd, 123 O.

F. A. Breckenridge, 123 O.

Jno. D. Babb, 5 Md.

J. G. W. Brueting, 5 Md.

T. J. Borchers, 67 Pa.

W. Bierbower, 87 Pa.

G. C. Bleak, 3 Me.

C. T. Barclay, 149 Pa.

J. D. Bisby, 16 Me.

S. G. Boone, 88 Pa.

D. S. Bartram, 17 Conn.

Jas. Burns, 57 Pa.

S. H. Ballard, 6 Mich. C.

S. T. Boughton, 71 Pa.

M. M. Bassett, 53 Ill.

R. Y. Bradford, 2 W. T.

W. Bricker, 3 Pa. C.

J. T. Brush, 100 O.

O. G. Ballow, 100 O.

J. F. Baird, 1 Va.

E. G. Birun, 3 Mass.

G. E. Blaire, 17 O.

Jas. Biggs, 123 Ill.

Y. Bickham, 19 U. S.

J. P. Brown, 15 U. S.

M. C. Bryant, 42 Ill.

O. B. Brandt, 17 O.

G. W. Button, 22 Mich.

C. A. Burdick, 10 Wis.

J. L. Brown, 73 Ind.

F. T. Bennett, 18 U. S.

Jno. Baird, 89 O.

W. O. Butler, 10 Wis.

D. A. Bannister, 59 O.

Jno. Bradford, C. S.

G. R. Barse, 5 Mich C.

C. P. Butler, 29 Ind.

E. P. Brooks, 6 Wis.

W. L. Brown, R. O.

G. W. Buffun, 1 Wis.

Guy Bryan, 18 Pa. C.

S. S. Baker, 6 Mo.

H. Bader, 29 Mo.

S. H. Byers, 5 Ia.

W. L. Bath, 132 N. Y.

Geo. M. Bush, U. S. T.

W. H. Berry, 5 Ill. C.

H. Bath, 45 N. Y.

Jno. H. Conn, 1 Va. C.

S. Carpenter, 3 O.

W. A. Curry, 3 O.

R. J. Connelly, 73 Ind.

A. M'Callahan, 73 Ind.

J. W. Custed, 23 Ind.

J. D. Cook, 6 Ia.

J. Carothers, 78 O.

S. R. Colloday, 6 Pa. C.

T. B. Calver, 123 O.

L. B. Comins, 17 Mass.

J. H. Cook, 5 Md.

J. H. Chandler, 5 Md.

E. D. Carpenter, 18 Conn.

H. F. Cowles, 18 Conn.

W. Christopher, 2 Va. C.

J. Q. Carpenter, 150 Pa.

H. B. Chamberlain, 97 N. Y.

T. J. Crossley, 57 Pa.

J. A. Carman, 107 Pa.

J. A. Coffin, 157 N. Y.

D. J. Connelly, 63 N. Y.

J. U. Childs, 16 Me.

D. B. Caldwell, 75 O.

W. B. Cook, 140 Pa.

J. W. Chandler, 1 Va. C.

H. A. Curtiss, 157 N. Y.

J. Chatborn, 150 Pa.

S. E. Cary, 13 Mass.

A. Cloadt, 119 N. Y.

J. Clement, 15 Ky. C.

G. A. Chandler, 15 Mo.

J. H. Cain, 104 N. Y.

B. Coles, 2 N. Y. C.

J. B. Carlisle, 2 Va.

G. B. Coleman, 1 Mass. C.

G. A. Coffin, 29 Ind.

A. H. Bassett, 79 Ill.

J. C. Colwell, 16 Ill. C.

O. L. Cole, 51 Ill.

Rudolph Curtis, 4 Ky. C.

M. C. Causton, 19 U. S.

E. Cottingham, 35 O.

W. Clifford, 16 U. S.

M. Cohen, 4 Ky. C.

A. S. Cooper, 9 Md.

J. F. Carter, 9 Md.

W. A. Crawford, 2 E. T.

C. W. Catlett, 2 E. T.

C. J. Carlin, 151 N. Y.

H. Cuniffe, 13 Ill.

C. H. Coasdorph, 8 V. C.

G. W. Carey, 65 Ind.

J. G. Dougherty, 51 Ind.

J. A. Dilan, 51 Ind.

A. F. Dooley, 51 Ind.

T. B. Dewies, 2 U. S.

M. Diemer, 10 Mo.

V. R. Davis, 123 O.

C. G. Davis, 1 Mass. C.

L. N. Dueherney, 1 Mass. C.

J. R. Day, 3 Me.

J. S. Devine, 71 Pa.

Geo. A. Deering, 16 Me.

A. Dixon, 104 N. Y.

Jno. Daily, 104 N. Y.

C. H. Drake, 142 Pa.

B. Davis, 71 Pa.

A. K. Dunkle, 114 Pa.

F. Donyley, 27 R. I.

J. W. Drake, 136 N. Y.

C. D. Dillard, 7 Ia.

J. W. Day, 17 Mass.

J. M. Dushane, 142 Pa.

O. G. Deugton, 100 O.

T. G. Darnin, 16 U. S.

J. L. Cox, 21 Ill.

W. N. Culbertson, 30 Ind.

F. G. Cochran, 77 Pa.

Geo. Cleghorn, 21 O.

W. W. Calkins, 104 Ill.

G. Celly, 4 O. C.

H. B. Crawford, 2 Ill.

T. S. Coleman, 12 Ky.

W. A. Daily, 8 Pa. C.

E. H. Duncan, 2 E. T.

A. Dieffenbach, 73 Pa.

C. L. Edmunds, 67 Pa.

D. C. Edwards, 2 Md.

J. Egan, 69 Pa.

S. Edmiston, 89 O.

W. H. Ellenwood, 10 Wis.

C. W. Earle, 96 Ill.

G. H. Erickson, 57 N. Y.

Geo. W. Fish, 3 O.

A. Frey, 73 Ind.

J. A. Francis, 18 Conn.

W. Flick, 67 Pa.

J. M. Fales, 1 R. I. C.

L. P. Fortescue, 29 Pa.

M. Fellows, 149 Pa.

W. Fenner, 2 R. I. C.

G. D. Forsyth, 100 O.

G. H. Fowler, 100 O.

J. C. Fishler, 7 Ind. B.

T. C. Freeman, 18 U. S.

R. J. Fisher, 17 Mo.

Chas. Fritze, 24 Ill.

J. A. Flemming, 90 N. Y.

E. F. Foster, 30 Ind.

H. Fairchild, 10 Wis.

O. P. Fairchild, 89 O.

W. H. Follette, Mass. A.

A. W. Fritchie, 26 Mo.

I. Fontaine, 73 Pa.

H. C. Dunn, 10 Ky.

W. G. Dutton, 67 Pa.

L. Drake, 22 Mich.

E. J. Davis, 44 Ill.

M. V. Dickey, 94 O.

Jno. Dugan, 35 Ind.

Thos. J. Dean, 5 Mich.

Jno. Davidson, 6 N. Y. A.

J. Gilmore, 79 N. Y.

S. P. Gamble, 63 Pa.

G. L. Garrett, 4 Mo. C.

F. M. Gilleland, 15 Ky.

Geo. H. Gamble, 8 Ill. C.

D. Garlet, 77 Pa.

T. Gross, 21 Ill.

H. Gerhardt, 24 Ill.

R. H. Gray, 15 U. S.

J. M. Goff, 10 Wis.

W. G. Galloway, 15 U. S.

J. H. Gageby, 19 U. S.

R. C. Gates, 18 U. S.

C. W. Green, 44 Ind.

J. B. Gore, 15 Ill.

J. A. Green, 13 Pa. C.

W. W. Glazier, 2 N. Y. C.

E. Gordon, 81 Ind.

A. L. Gates, 10 Wis.

M. Gray, 13 N. Y.

W. G. Griffin, 112 Ill.

C. Greble, 8 Mich. C.

Geo. Good, 84 Pa.

M. E. Green, 5 Md. C.

J. B. Holmes, 6 O.

Jno. Hood, 80 Ill.

R. J. Harmer, 80 Ill.

W. H. Harvey, 51 Ind.

G. D. Hand, 51 Ind.

D. H. Harns, 3 O.

Jno. Haideman, 129 Ill.

E. H. Fobes, 131 N. Y.

D. D. Fox, 16 Ill. C.

A. Gude, 51 Ind.

H. Gamble, 73 Ind.

Jno. A. Garces, 1 Md. C.

Th. G. Good, 1 Md. C.

C. M. Gross, 100 O.

S. L. Gilman, 3 M.

G. W. Grant, 88 Pa.

A. Goodwin, 82 O.

O. Grierson 45 N. Y.

F. C. Gay, 11 Pa.

C. F. Gutland, 134 N. Y.

E. G. Gorgus, 90 Pa.

H. H. Hinds, 57 Pa.

Thos. Huggins, 2 N. Y.

Eug. Hepp, 82 Ill.

C. P. Heffley, 142 Pa.

J. M. Henry, 154 N. Y.

G. Halpin, 116 Pa.

E. H. Harkness, 6 Pa. C.

J. D. Hatfield, 53 Ill.

A. W. Hayes, 34 O.

J. F. Hammond, R. B.

H. Hubbard, 12 N. Y.

W. S. Hatcher, 30 O.

Jno. Hine, 100 O.

M. B. Helmes, 1 Va. C.

C. B. Hall, 1 Va. C.

Eli Holden, 1 Va. C.

B. Howe, 21 Ill.

P. W. Houlchen, 16 U. S.

C. D. Henry, 4 O. C.

J. Hanon, 115 Ill.

C. E. Harrison, 89 O.

Geo. Harris, 79 Ind.

W. B. Hamilton, 22 Mich.

S. S. Holbruck, 15 U. S.

L. D. Henkley, 10 Wis.

H. S. Horton, 101 Pa.

W. E. Hodge, 5 Md.

W. Hawkins, 5 Md.

D. W. Hakes, 18 Conn.

J. D. Higgins, 18 Conn.

W. Heffner, 67 Pa.

F. A. Hubble, 67 Pa.

J. C. Hagenbach, 67 Pa.

J. Hersh, 87 Pa.

J. Hall, 87 Pa.

P. Horney, 110 O.

T. J. Higginson, M. C.

J. G. Hallenberg, 1 O.

A. Hauf, 54 N. Y.

C. W. Jones, 16 Pa. C.

P. O. Jones, adj't, 2 N. Y. C.

J. A. Jones, 21 Ill.

J. H. Jenkins, 21 Wis.

R. W. Jackson, 21 Wis.

T. W. Johnson, 10 N. Y. C.

H. P. Jordan, 9 Md.

H. Jones, 5 U. S. C.

R. B. Jones, 2 E. T.

H. H. James, 6 Ind. C.

John King, 5 Ill. C.

M. D. King, 3 O.

A. J. Kuhn, 5 Md.

H. V. Knight, 20 Mich.

J. S. Kephart, 5 Md. C.

Jas. Kerin, 6 U. S. C.

J. B. King, 10 N. Y. C.

G. Keyes, 18 Conn.

J. N. Kibbee, 18 Conn.

A. Kresge, 67 Pa.

R. O. Knowles, 110 O.

H. Kendler, 45 N. Y.

M. Kupp, 167 Pa.

Jas. Kane, 13 Pa. C.

R. C. Knaggs, A. D. C.

E. G. Higby, 33 O.

W. M. Hudson, 92 O.

H. Horway, 78 Ill.

C. F. Hall, 13 Mich.

G. C. Houston, 2 N. Y. C.

P. A. Hagen, 7 Md.

J. R. Hutchinson, 2 Va. C.

G. W. Hale, 101 O.

R. Huey, 2 E. T.

W. P. Hodge, 2 E. T.

E. Harbour, 2 E. T.

B. F. Herrington, 18 Pa. C.

Jas. Heslit, 3 Pa. C.

Jno. Hoffman, 5 Ia.

T. W. Hayes, 5 Ia.

M. Hoffman, 5 Ia.

J. M. Holloway, 6 Ind.

C. M. Hart, 45 Pa.

J. P. Jones, 55 O.

C. L. Irwin, 78 Ill.

A. H. Lindsay, 18 Conn.

L. Lapton, 116 O.

W. H. Locke, 18 Conn.

J. Leydecker, 45 N. Y.

L. Lindemeyer, 45 N. Y.

H. G. Lombard, 4 Mich.

W. L. Laws, 18 Pa. C.

A. T. Lamson, 104 N. Y.

A. W. Locklin, 94 N. Y.

G. R. Lodge, 53 Ill.

T. Lloyd, 6 Ind. C.

C. H. Livingston, 1 Va. C.

J. L. Leslie, 18 Pa. C.

D. R. Locke, 8 Ky. C.

J. Ludlow, 5 U. S. A.

A. Leonard, 71 N. Y.

W. J. Lintz, 8 Tenn.

Jno. McAdams, 10 Va.

L. Markbreit, A. D. C.

J. Kunkel, 45 N. Y.

J. W. Kennedy, 134 N. Y.

J. C. Kellogg, 6 Mich.

D. O. Kelly, 100 O.

J. D. Kautz, 1 Ky. C.

T. A. Krocks, 77 Pa.

T. D. Kimball, 88 Ind.

Wm. Krueger, 2 Mo.

E. E. Knoble, 21 Ky.

E. M. Knowler, 42 Ind.

J. Keniston, 100 Ill.

S. Koach, 100 Ill.

C. E. Keath, 19 Ill.

Theo. Kendall, 15 U. S.

H. B. Kelly, 6 Ky. C.

D. F. Kittrell, 3 E. T.

W. S. Lyon, 23 O.

T. Lennig, 6 Pa. C.

F. A. Leyton, 18 Ind.

A. W. Loomis, 18 Conn.

B. N. Mann, 17 Mass.

J. A. Mitchell, 82 O.

A. McDade, 154 N. Y.

J. A. Mendenhall, 75 O.

J. R. Mell, 82 Ill.

V. Mylieus, 68 N. Y.

F. Moran, 73 N. Y.

J. Mooney, 107 Pa.

F. Murphy, 97 N. Y.

G. H. Morisey, 12 Ia. Q. M.

H. E. Mosher, 12 N. Y. C.

S. T. Merwin, 18 Conn.

Thos. Mayer, 100 O.

T. H. McKee, 21 Ill.

J. W. Messick, 42 Ind.

D. F. McKay, 18 Pa.

R. G. McKay, 1 Mich.

Wm. McEboy, 3 Ill.

N. S. McKee, 21 Ill.

J. McKinstry, 16 Ill. C.

T. Milward, 31 O.

W. H. McDill, 80 Ill.

W. S. Marshall, 51 Ind.

J. H. Murdock, 3 O.

C. A. Maxwell, 3 O.

H. S. Murdock, 73 Ind.

J. D. Munday, 73 Ind.

J. S. Mettee, 5 Md.

Jno. McCumas, 5 Md.

W. J. Morris, 5 Md.

T. F. McGinnes, 18 Conn.

F. McKeag, 18 Conn.

H. Morningstar, 87 Pa.

J. S. Manning, 100 O.

Thos. Mosbey, 12 Pa. C.

D. McNiel, 13 Pa. C.

W. A. Murray, 106 N. Y.

H. Moultin, 1 U. S.

L. Mayer, 12 Pa. C.

W. J. McConnelee, 4 Ia.

D. McCully, 75 O.

O. Mussehl, 68 N. Y.

H. H. Moseley, 25 O.

Thos. Myers, 107 Pa.

C. Murry, 15 Mo.

J. McBeth, 45 O.

R. H. Montgomery, 5 U. S. C.

F. Moore, 73 Pa.

J. McGovern, 73 Pa.

A. McNiece, 73 Pa.

G. Maw, 80 G.

J. F. Morgan, 17 Mich.

C. Miller, 14 Ill. C.

W. J. Nowlan, 14 N. Y.

A. N. Norris, 107 Pa.

Wm. Nelson, 13 U. S.

J. C. Norcross, 2 Mass. C.

J. F. Newbrandt, 4 Mo. C.

J. Mitchell, 79 Ill.

J. McGowan, 29 Ind.

M. Mahon, 16 U. S.

J. F. Mackey, 16 U. S.

C. H. Morgan, 21 Wis.

A. S. Mathews, 22 Mich.

J. S. Mahony, 15 U. S.

S. McNeal, 51 O.

L. C. Mead, 22 Mich.

A. U. McCane, 2 O.

M. V. Morrison, 32 O.

A. H. Makinson, 10 Wis.

W. H. Mead, 6 Ky. C.

A. Morse, 78 Ill.

A. Morris, 4 Ky. C.

J. McKinley, 28 O.

H. Morey, 10 N. Y. C.

G. W. Moore, 9 Md.

H. F. Meyer, 9 Md.

R. A. Moon, 6 Mich. C.

M. M. Moore, 6 Mich. C.

John Millis, 66 Ind.

J. McDonald, 2 E. T.

J. McColgen, 7 O. C.

D. T. Moore, 2 E. T.

J. H. Mason, 21 O.

L. D. Phelps, 8 Pa. C.

C. M. Brutzman, 7 Wis.

A. E. Patelin, 10 Wis.

M. B. Pulliam, 11 Ky. C.

R. M. Pond, 12 U. S.

W. P. Pierce, 11 Ky. C.

S. B. Petrie, 126 O.

Wm. Randall, 80 Ill.

E. W. Pelton, 2 Md.

Jno. Ritchie, 3 O.

J. C. Roney, 3 O.

Wm. Reynolds, 73 Ind.

A. C. Roach, 51 Ind.

Wm. Nyce, 2 N. Y. C.

B. H. Niemeger, 11 Ky. C.

O. P. Norris, 111 O.

Jno. O'Connor, 59 O.

O. C. Oug, 2 Va. C.

E. W. Pelton, 2 Md.

E. W. Parcey, 80 Ill.

S. B. Piper, 3 O.

G. A. Pottee, 2 Ky.

J. B. Pumphrey, 123 O.

W. G. Purnell, 6 Md.

C. G. A. Peterson, 1 R. I. C.

E. B. Parker, 1 R. I. C.

Henry S. Platt, 11 Mich.

E. C. Parker, 94 N. Y.

H. C. Potter, 18 Pa. C.

T. Paulding, 6 U. S. C.

J. F. Poole, 1 Va. C.

J. L. Powers, 107 N. Y.

D. B. Pettijohn, 2 U. S.

G. H. Potts, 74 O.

C. P. Potts, 151 Pa.

E. Potter, 6 Mich.

E. L. Palmer, 57 N. Y.

J. S. Paul, 122 O.

Z. R. Prather, 116 Ill.

G. Pentzel, 11 N. Y.

Jas. Perley, 13 Mich.

H. Perleen, 2 O.

J. V. Patterson, 1 O. C.

W. N. Paxton, 140 Pa.

C. Powell, 42 O.

J. G. Spalding, 2 U. S. C.

A. Stole, 6 U. S.

D. M. V. Stuart, 10 Mo.

M. H. Smith, 123 O.

T. H. Stewart, 5 Md.

John Sachs, 5 Md.

Jno. Sweadner, 5 Md.

E. Reynolds, 1 Tenn. C.

E. Reed, 3 O.

J. M. Rothrock, 5 Mo.

J. P. Rockwell, 18 Conn.

J. Ruff, 67 Pa.

J. F. Robinson, 67 Pa.

W. F. Randolph, 5 U. S. A.

John Ryan, 69 Pa.

W. E. Rockwell, 134 N. Y.

J. H. Russel, 12 Mass.

J. O. Rockwell, 97 N. Y.

J. A. Richardson, 2 N. Y. C.

N. A. Robinson, 4 Me.

H. E. Rulon 114 Pa.

H. Richardson, 19 Ind.

J. Remie, 11 Mass.

Geo. Ring, 100 O.

D. P. Rennie, 73 O.

T. J. Ray, 49 O.

W. L. Retilley, 51 O.

G. W. Robertson, 22 Mich.

J. M. Rader, 8 Tenn.

S. H. Reynolds, 42 O.

E. W. Rubbs, 1 E. T.

G. F. Robinson, 80 O.

L. S. Smith, 14 N. Y.

D. J. Shepherd, 5 Ky. C.

H. Silver, 16 Ill. C.

G. Scuttermore, 80 Ill.

Th. Segar, 80 Ill.

D. B. Stevenson, 3 O.

E. E. Sharp, 51 Ind.

G. L. Sollers, 9 Md.

L. L. Stone, Q. M.

R. F. Scott, 11 Ky. C.

J. C. Shaw, 7 O. C.

L. W. Sutherland, 126 O.

T. B. String, 11 Ky. C.

Chas. Sutler, 39 N. Y.

J. F. Shuylar, 123 O.

C. H. Sowro, 123 O.

E. L. Schroeder, 5 Md.

G. W. Simpson, 67 Pa.

A. G. Scranton, 18 Conn.

J. Smith, 67 Pa.

C. P. Stroman, 87 Pa.

A. M. Stark, 110 O.

H. L. Sibley, 116 O.

S. Stearns, 4 Md.

G. L. Snyder, 104 N. Y.

A. W. Sprague, 24 Mich.

Geo. Schuele, 45 N. Y.

H. B. Seeley, 86 N. Y.

W. S. Stevens, 104 N. Y.

E. Schroeders, 74 Pa.

G. C. Stevens, 154 N. Y.

D. C. Sears, 96 N. Y.

H. Schroeder, 82 Ill.

J. B. Samson, 2 Mass. H. A.

Jno. Sullivan, 7 R. I.

M. R. Small, 6 Md.

E. Shepard, 6 O. C.

J. M. Steele, 1 Va.

C. Smith, 4 N. Y. C.

Jno. Sterling, 3 Ind.

F. Spencer, 17 O.

A. W. Songer, 21 Ill.

Wm. Stewart, 16 U. S.

W. H. Smith, 16 U. S.

J. D. Simpson, 10 Ind.

F. Schweinfurth, 24 Ill.

A. C. Spafford, 21 O.

E. G. Spalding, 22 Mich.

E. S. Scott, 89 O.

A. C. Shaeffer, 2 N. Y. C.

H. C. Smith, 2 Del.

Jno. Spindler, 73 Ill.

R. P. Wallace, 120 O.

Jno. H. Stevens, 5 Me.

Chas. Trommel, 3 O.

H. H. Tillotson, 73 Ind.

A. N. Thomas, 73 Ind.

D. Turner, 118 Ill.

Ira Tyler, 118 Ill.

M. Tiffany, 18 Conn.

H. O. Thayer, 67 Pa.

A. A. Taylor, 122 Pa.

R. Tyler, 6 Md.

R. Thompson, 67 Pa.

L. Thompson, 2 U. S. C.

M. Tower, 13 Mas.

E. A. Tuthill, 104 N. Y.

J. R. Titus, 3 U. S. C.

H. Temple, 2 N. Y. C.

E. M. B. Timoney, 15 U. S.

G. W. Thomas, 10 Wis.

H. C. Taylor, 21 Wis.

A. J. Tuter, 2 O.

R. F. Thorn, 5 Ky. C.

S. H. Tresoutheck, 18 Pa. C.

J. Turner, Q. M.

H. Taylor, 65 Ind.

A. J. W. Ullen, 3 O.

T. R. Uptigrove, 73 Ind.

M. Undutch, 9 Md.

G. A. Vanness, 73 Ind.

Geo. Veltford, 54 N. Y.

R. N. Vannetter, 1 Mich. C.

D. Vansbury, 4 Md. B.

D. L. Wright, 51 Ind.

A. H. Wonder, 51 Ind.

Wm. Willis, 51 Ind.

I. D. Whiting, 3 O.

A. K. Wolbach, 3 O.

J. C. Woodrow, 73 Ind.

C. P. Williams, 73 Ind.

C. N. Winner, 1 O.

Thos. Worthen, 118 Ill.

L. Weiser, 1 Md. C.

Wm. A. Williams, 123 O.

J. W. Wooth, 5 Md.

J. B. Wilson, 5 Md.

J. E. Woodard, 18 Conn.

P. A. White, 83 Pa.

E. J. Weeks, 67 Pa.

T. J. Weakley, 110 O.

W. H. Welsh, 78 Pa.

A. Wallber, 26 Wis.

A. H. White, 27 Pa.

D. Whitson, 13 Mass.

T. Wuschow, 54 N. Y.

M. Wadsworth, 16 Me.

J. N. Whitney, 2 R. I. C.

M. F. Williams, 15 Ky.

M. Wilson, 14 Pa. C.

J. Woods, 82 Ind.

J. R. Charnel, 1 Ill. Art.

W. S. Damrell, 13 Mass.

W. G. Davis, 27 Mass.

S. V. Dean, 145 Pa.

J. S. Drennan, 1 Vt. Art.

J. Dunn, 64 N. Y.

A. J. Dunning, 7 N. Y. Art.

J. Donovan, 2 N. J.

E. B. Dyre, 1 Conn. C.

W. C. Dorris, 111 Ill.

H. G. Dodge, 2 Pa. C.

C. Downs, 33 N. J.

J. Duven, 5 N. H.

W. H. Dorfee, 5 R. I.

G. Dorbine, 66 N. Y.

W. H. Dieffenbach, 7 Pa. Res.

R. De Lay, 3 Iowa C.

O. W. Demmick, 11 N. H.

L. Dick, 72 O.

E. Dickerson, 44 Wis.

W. L. Watson, 21 Wis.

Wm. Willots, 22 Mich.

J. Weatherbee, 51 O.

J. M. Wasson, 40 O.

Jas. Wells, 8 Mich. C.

H. Wilson, 18 Pa. C.

J. R. Weaver, 18 Pa. C.

W. H. H. Wilcox, 10 N. Y.

A. B. White, 4 Pa. C.

C. F. Weston, 21 Wis.

W. F. Wheeler, 9 Md.

N. L. Wood, Jr., 9 Md.

E. Wilhort, 2 E. Tenn.

J. W. Wilshire, 45 O.

J. W. Wright, 10 Ia.

Hyde Crocker, 1 N. Y. C.

J. B. Williamson, 14 W. Va.

C. H. Gates, 96 Ill.

Sam Leith, 132 N. Y.

S. Fatzer, 108 N. Y.

E. Fontaine, 7 Pa. R. C.

D. Forney, 30 O.

S. Fisher, 93 Ind.

D. S. Finney, 14 and 15 Ill. V.

L. Fitzpatrick, 146 N. Y.

L. D. C. Fales, ——— .

H. C. Foster, 23 Ind.

John Foley, 59 Mass.

Louis Faass, 14 N. Y. Art.

R. J. Frost, 9 Mich. C.

G. J. George, 40 Ill.

T. M. Gunn, 21 Ky.

J. Gottshell, 55 Pa.

J. M. Godown, 12 Ind.

H. D. Grant, 117 N. Y.

J. A. Goodwin, 1 Mass. C.

C. V. Granger, 88 N. Y.

C. O. Gordon, 1 Me. C.

J. W. Goss, 1 Mass. Art.

D. Driscoll, 24 Mo.

H. G. Dorr, 4 Mass. C.

J. M. Drake, 9 N. J.

H. A. Downing, 31 U. S. C. T.

J. W. Davison, 95 O.

G. H. Drew, 9 N. H.

Chas. Everrett, 70 Ohio.

F. R. Eastman, 2 Pa. C.

J. L. F. Elkin, 1 N. J.

T. E. Evans, 52 Pa.

J. W. Eyestone, 13 Ind.

T. K. Eckings, 3 N. J.

John Eagan, 1 U. S. A.

John Elder, 8 Ind.

J. Fairbanks, 72 Ohio.

G. E. Finney, 19 Ind.

J. M. Ferris, 3 Mich.

E. M. Faye, 42 N. Y.

J. Furgeson, 1 N. J.

D. Flannery, 4 N. J.

H. M. Fowler, 15 N. J.

G. W. Flager, 11 Pa. R. C.

C. A. Fagan, 11 Pa. R. C.

H. French, 3 Vt.

L. W. Fisher, 4 Vt.

H. N. Hamilton, 59 N. Y.

E. S. Huntington, 11 U. S.

W. H. Hoyt, 16 Iowa.

R. M. Hughes, 14 Ill. C.

J. Hewitt, 105 Pa.

J. Heston, 4 N. J.

J. Heffelfinger, 7 Pa. R. V.

J. L. Harvey, 2 Pa. Art.

H. V. Hadley, 7 Ind.

M. V. B. Hallett, 2 Pa. C.

A. J. Henry, 120 Ill.

V. G. Hoalladay, 2 Ind. C.

D. Havens, 85 Ill.

C. A. Hays, 11 Pa.

H. M. Gordon, 143 Pa.

J. Gallagher, 4 Ohio Vet.

E. A. Green, 81 Ill.

T. Griffen, 55 U. S. C. T.

M. L. Godley, 17 Ohio.

Philip Grey, 72 Pa.

A. M. Hall, 9 Minn.

E. R. Hart, 1 Vt. Art.

J. F. Hodge, 55 Pa.

R. F. Hall, 75 Ohio.

J. T. Haight, 8 Iowa C.

G. W. Hill, 7 Mich. C.

E. J. Hazel, 6 Pa. C.

R. Herbert, 50 Pa.

S. H. Horton, 101 Pa.

W. B. Hurd, 17 Mich C.

E. Holden, 1 Vt. C.

S. P. Hedges, 112 N. Y. C.

H. C. Hinds, 102 N. Y.

J. Hopper, 2 N. Y. C.

C. O. Hunt, 5 Me. Bat.

W. R. Hulland, 5 Md. C.

G. W. Hull, 135 Ohio.

D. W. Hazelton, 22 N. Y. C.

C. P. Holaham, 19 Pa. C.

J. F. Kempton, 75 Ohio.

J. H. Kidd, 1 Md. Art.

R. H. Kendrick, 25 Wis.

G. C. Kenyon, 17 Ill.

G. C. Kidder, 113 Pa.

G. Knox, 109 Pa.

J. M. Kelly, 4 Tenn.

F. H. Kempton, 58 Mass. Art.

J. R. Kelly 1 Pa. C.

J. C. Knox, 4 Ind. C.

Ade King, 12 Ohio.

J. Kepheart, 13 Ohio.

J. Kellow, 2 Pa. Art.

G. L. Kibby, 4 R. I.

J. L. Hastings, 7 Pa. R. V. C.

J. W. Harris, 2 Ind. C.

F. Herzbery, 66 N. Y.

J. T. Haight, 8 Iowa C.

E. H. Higley, 1 Vt. C.

W. H. Hendryks, 11 Mich. B.

J. Huston, 95 Ohio.

R. Henderson, 1 Mass. Art.

A. N. Hackett, 110 O.

S. P. Hand, 43 U. S. C. T.

T. B. Hurst, 7 Pa. Res. V. C.

Geo. Hopf, 2 Md.

O. M. Hill, 1 Mo. Art.

J. B. Hogue, 4 Pa. C.

L. E. Haywood, 58 Mass.

A. B. Isham, 7 Mich. C.

H. A. Johnson, 3 Me.

C. K. Johnson, 1 Me. C.

G. W. Jenkins, 9 W. Va.

J. C. Justus, 2 Pa. R. V. C.

S. E. Jones, 7 N. Y. Art.

J. W. Johnson, 1 Mass. Art.

Alfred Jones, 50 Pa. Vet.

J. Jacks, 15 W. Va.

P. Krohn, 5 N. Y. C.

E. Kendrick, 10 N. J.

S. C. Kerr, 126 Ohio.

H. T. Kendall, 50 Pa.

A. Kelly, 126 Ohio.

J. Keen, 7 Pa. V. R. C.

J. D. Kennuly, 8 Ohio C.

J. G. B. Adams, 19 Mass.

E. P. Alexander, 26 Mich.

H. M. Anderson, 3 Me.

J. F. Anderson, 2 Pa. Art.

A. L. Abbey, 8 Mich. C.

A. O. Abbott, 1 N. Y. Drag.

A. S. Appelget, 2 N. J. C.

Robert Allen, 2 N. J. Drag.

C. E. Lewis, 1 N. Y. Drag.

J. B. Laycock, 7 Pa. R. V. C.

H. H. Lyman, 147 N. Y.

W. H. Larrabee, 7 Me.

A. Lee, 152 N. Y.

J. L. Lynn, 145 Pa.

E. De C. Loud, 2 Pa. Art.

M. S. Ludwig, 53 Pa.

D. W. Lewry, 2 Pa. Art.

J. Lyman, 27 Mass.

J. O. Laird, 35 U. S.

M. Laird, 16 Iowa.

J. C. Luther, Pa. V. R. C.

M. W. Lemon, 14 N. Y. Art.

L. M. Lane, 9 Minn.

T. D. Lamson, 3 Ind. C.

A. Limbard, McLau's S. Q. M.

G. H. Lawrence, 2 N. Y. M. R.

C. H. Lang, 59 Mass.

J. Monaghan, 62 Pa.

J. C. McIntosh, 145 Pa.

F. W. Mather, 7 N. Y. Art.

P. B. Mockrie, 7 N. Y. Art.

E. T. McCutcheon, 64 N. Y.

E. J. McWain, 1 N. Y. Art.

J. McKage, 184 Pa.

S. F. Muffley, 184 Pa.

H. F. Mangus, 53 Pa.

J. McLaughlin, 53 Pa.

W. A. McGinnes, 19 Mass.

A. D. Mathews, 1 Vt. Art.

W. C. Adams, 2 Ky. C.

E. T. Effleck, 170 O. Nat. G.

E. A. Abbott, 23 O. Vet. Vol.

Count S. Brady, 2 N. J. C.

A. Bulow, 3 N. J. C.

J. H. Bryan, 184 Pa.

C. W. Baldwin, 2 N. J.

H. E. Barker, 22 N. Y. C.

G. A. Austin, 14 Ill. Bat.

G. C. Alden, 112 Ill.

C. A. Brown, 1 N. Y. Art.

W. R. Bospord, 1 N. Y.

J. L. Barton, 49 Pa.

W. Buchanan, 76 N. Y.

W. Blane, 43 N. Y.

J. H. Bristol, 1 Conn. C.

H. H. Dixby, 9 Me.

D. W. Burkholder, 7 Pa. V.

S. Brum, 81 Ill.

W. H. Brady, 2 Del.

J. Breon, 148 Pa.

G. N. Burnett, 4 Ind. C.

W. J. Boyd, 5 Mich. C.

S. W. Burrows, 1 N. Y. Vet. C.

M. Brickenhoff, 42 N. Y.

H. Buckley, 4 N. H. Vol.

A. T. Barnes, Ill. Vet. Batt.

J. L. Beasley, 81 Ill.

A. Barringer, 44 N. Y.

F. P. Bishop, 4 Tenn. C.

C. T. Bowen, 4 R. I.

Wm. Bateman, 9 Mich. C.

Wm. Baird, 23 U. S. C. T.

J. N. Biller, 2 Pa. Art.

F. S. Bowley, 30 U. S. C. T.

C. Boettger, 2 Md.

W. A. Barnard, 20 Mich.

Wm. Blasse, 43 N. Y.

C. O. Brown, 31 Me.

R. K. Beechan, 23 U. S. C. T.

A. N. Briscol, Cole's Md. C.

H. M. Bearce, 32 Me.

A. J. Braidy, 54 Pa.

C. A. Bell, A. D. C.

R. Burton, 9 N. Y. Art.

H. E. Beebee, 22 N. Y. C.

V. L. Coffin, 31 Me.

C. H. Bigley, 82 N. Y.

M. Burns, 13 N. Y. C.

C. H. Cutter, 95 Ill.

G. W. Creacy, 35 Mass.

R. H. Chute, 59 Mass.

H. M. Cross, 59 Mass.

H. A. Chapin, 95 N. Y.

W. Cahill, 76 N. Y.

J. L. Castler, 76 N. Y.

H. Chisman, 7 Ind.

H. Cribben, 140 N. Y.

G. M. Curtis, 140 N. Y.

J. S. Calwell, 16 Ill. C.

S. Crossley, 118 Pa.

L. B. Carlise, 145 Pa.

J. P. Codington, 8 Iowa C.

W. H. Curtis, 19 Mass.

J. W. Clark, 59 N. Y.

J. H. Clark, 1 Mass. Art.

D. L. Case, Jr., 102 N. Y.

J. D. Cope, 116 Pa.

J. W. Core, 6 W. Va. C.

W. J. Colter, 15 Mass.

J. Casey, 45 N. Y.

W. H. Carter, 5 Pa. R. C.

J. L. Chittendon, 5 Ind. C.

W. H. Canney, 69 N. Y.

W. F. Campbell, 51 Pa.

J. F. Cameron, 5 Pa. C.

M. Clegg, 5 Ind. C.

H. R. Chase, 1 Vt. H. Art.

W. H. Conover, 22 N. Y. C.

D. F. Califf, 2 W. S. S. S.

D. B. Chubbuck, 19 Mass.

M. Cunningham, 42 N. Y.

A. M. Charters, 17 Iowa.

W. A. Copeland, 10 Mich.

T. Clemons, 13 Ill.

W. C. Cook, 9 Mich. C.

L. A. Campbell, 152 N. Y.

C. W. Carr, 4 Vt.

J. Cunningham, 7 Pa. R. C.

C. Coslett, 115 Pa.

R. Cooper, 7 N. J.

C. H. Crawford, 183 Pa.

S. O. Cromack, 77 N. Y.

H. Correll, 2 Vt.

A. Morse, 1 Vt. Art.

J. H. Morris, 4 Ky.

W. H. Myers, 76 N. Y.

J. McGeehan, 146 N. Y.

H. W. Mitchell, 14 N. Y.

J. C. McCain, 9 Minn.

T. McGuire, 7 Ill.

J. W. Miller, 14 Ill. C.

J. Murphy, 69 N. Y.

J. Mallison, 94 N. Y.

J. A. Mullegan, 4 Mass. C.

W. F. Mathews, 1 Md.

N. J. Menier, 93 Ind.

H. Miller, 17 Mich.

P. W. McMannus, 27 Mass.

E. McMahon, 72 Ohio.

G. C. Morton, 4 Pa. C.

E. Mather, 1 Vt. C.

C. McDonald, 2 Ill. Art.

G. W. Mayer, 37 Ind.

J. McCormick, 21 N. Y. C.

A. J. Mashland, 2 Pa. Art.

W. H. Mix, 19 U. S. C. T.

T. J. Munger, 37 Wis.

A. McNure, 73 Pa.

H. G. Mitchell, 32 Me.

J. D. Marshall, 57 O.

McLane, 9 Minn.

C. Niedenhoffen, 9 Minn.

A. Nelson, 66 N. Y.

J. B. Meedham, 4 Vt.

C. P. Cramer, 21 N. Y. C.

Geo. Corum, 2 Ky. C.

M. B. Case, 23 U. S. C. T.

D. J. Kline, 75 O. V. M. I.

C. G. Conn, 1 M. S. S.

M. Cunningham, 1 Vt. H. A.

C. D. Copeland, 58 Pa.

C. P. Cashell, 12 Pa. C.

R. O'Connell, 55 Pa.

J. Ogden, 1 Wis. C.

G. C. Olden, 112 Ill.

A. C. Pickenpaugh, 6 W. Va.

H. Picquet, 32 Ill.

J. T. Parker, 13 Iowa.

A. Phinney, 90 Ill.

W. M. Provine, 84 Ill.

T. Purcell, 16 Iowa.

W. H. Powell, 2 Ill. L. Art.

G. M. Parker, 45 Ill.

J. S. Purveance, 130 Ind.

D. H. Piffard, 14 N. Y.

C. A. Price, 5 Mich.

E. B. Parker, 1 Vt. Art.

W. H. Patridge, 67 N. Y.

H. H. Pierce, 7 Conn.

G. W. Pitt, 85 N. Y. Vet.

L. S. Peake, 85 N. Y. Vet.

E. C. Pierson, 85 N. Y. Vet.

D. Pentzell, 4 N. Y. C.

J. G. Peetrey, 95 Ohio.

M. P. Pierson, 100 N. Y.

A. L. Preston, 8 Mich. C.

G. Peters, 9 N. J.

J. H. Pitt, 118 N. Y.

James Post, 149 ——— .

W. D. Peck, 2 N. J. C.

G. W. Paterson, 135 Ohio.

J. C. Price, 75 Ohio.

Z. Perrin, 72 Ohio.

C. L. Noggle, 2 U. S.

J. Norwood, 76 N. Y.

O. H. Nealy, 11 U. S.

W. McM. Nettervill, 12 U. S.

W. Neher, 7 Pa. R. V. C.

A. Neal, 5 Ind. C.

D. M. Niswander, 2 Pa. Art.

H. J. Nyman, 19 Mich.

W. R. Nulland, 5 Ind. C.

R. V. Outcolt, 135 O.

J. O. Harre, 7 N. Y. Art.

F. Osborne, 19 Mass.

D. Oliphant, 35 N. J.

E. O. Shea, 13 Pa. C.

J. R. Borsnels, 145 Pa.

G. Rieneckar, 5 Pa. C.

O. Rahu, 184 Pa.

G. A. Rowley, 2 U. S.

B. E. Robinson, 95 O.

W. E. Roach, 49 N. Y.

H. W. Raymond, 8 N. Y. Art.

J. E. Rose, 120 Ill.

E. R. Roberts, 7 Ill.

J. H. Reed, 120 Ill.

J. M. Richards, 1 W. Va.

H. Rothe, 15, N. Y. Art.

E. K. Ramsey, 1 N. J.

L. H. Riley, 7 Pa. R. V. C.

C. H. Ross, 13 Ind.

A. Ring, 12 Ohio.

T. Rathbone, 153 Ohio.

C. L. Rugg, 6 Ind. C.

J. S. Rice, 13 Ind.

J. Reade, 57 Mass.

A. J. Raynor, 19 U. S. C. T.

L. Rainer, 2 N. J. C.

J. S. Robeson, 7 Tenn. C.

W. L. Riley, 21 N. Y. C.

W. H. Randall, 1 Mich. S. S.

S. H. Platt, 35 Mass.

L. G. Porter, 81 Ill.

J. H. Palmer, 12 Ohio.

W. A. Pope, 18 Wis.

D. B. Pyne, 3 Mo.

Worthington Pierce, 17 Vt.

W. B. Phillips, 2 Pa. Art.

C. O. Poindexter, 31 Me.

A. P. Pierson, 9 Mich. C.

Chas. A. Price, 3 Mich.

M. Rees, 72 Ohio.

W. B. Rose, 73 Ill.

J. M. Ruger, 57 Pa.

L. S. Richards, 1 Vt. Art.

A. M. Smith, 1 Tenn. C.

J. C. Smith, 24 Ind. Bat.

J. B. Smith, 5 W. Va. C.

W. Sandon, 1 Wis. C.

J. P. Smith, 49 Pa.

J. G. Stevens, 52 Pa.

C. T. Swope, 4 Ky.

A. S. Stewart, 4 Ky.

E. P. Strickland, 114 Ill.

P. Smith, 4 Tenn. C.

J. W. Stanton, 5 Ind. C.

W. H. St. John, 5 Ind. C.

F. E. Scripture, R. Q. M.

A. B. Simmons, 5 Ind. C.

H. P. Starr, 22 N. Y. C.

B. Spring, 75 O.

A. C. Stover, 95 O.

C. P. Stone, 1 Vt. C.

J. Stebbins, 77 N. Y.

C. S. Schwartz, 2 N. J. C.

J. Sailor, 13 Pa. C.

H. C. Smyser, 2 Md.

R. R. Stewart, 2 N. Y. C.

M. W. Striblings, 61 Ohio.

J. Smith, 5 Pa. C.

W. B. Sturgeon, 107 Pa.

M. H. Stover, 184 Pa.

A. A. Sweetland, 2 Pa. C.

E. B. Smith, 1 Vt. Art.

C. Schurr, 7 N. Y. Art.

W. H. Shafer, 5 Pa. C.

M. G. Sargeant, 1 Vt. Art.

C. H. Stallman, 87 Pa. Art.

S. S. Smythe, 1 Ill. Art.

Geo. Scott, 10 Ind.

E. Swift, 74 Ill.

J. L. Skinner, 27 Mass.

F. Stevens, 190 Pa.

C. Stuart, 24 N. Y.

M. Shanan, 140 N. Y.

M. S. Smith, 16 Me.

E. Snowwhite, 7 Pa. V. R. C.

W. H. S. Sweet, 146 N. Y.

J. R. Sitler, 2 Pa. C.

A. L. Shannon, 3 Ind. C.

L. E. Tyler, 1 Conn. C.

A. Timm, 16 Iowa.

O. Todd, 18 Wis.

A. W. Tiffany, 9 Minn.

J. Taylor, 2 Pa. V. R. C.

D. W. Tower, 17 Iowa.

F. Tomson, 17 Iowa.

A. F. Tipton, 8 Iowa C.

David Turmer, 118 Ill.

C. Tobel, 15 N. Y. Art.

J. P. F. Toby, 31 Me.

S. H. Tinker, 73 Ind.

D. D. Von Valack, 12 U. S.

D. Van Doren, 72 Ohio.

C. Van Rensalaer, 148 N. Y.

W. C. Van Alin, 45 Pa.

A. Von Bulow, 3 N. J. C.

O. W. West, 1 N. Y. Drag.

J. O. Stout, McLaughlin's S. Ohio C.

M. N. Shepstrong, 60 Ohio.

J. W. Stanton, 5 Ind. C.

J. P. Sheehan, 31 Me.

J. F. Shull, 28 U. S. C. T.

S. B. Smith, 30 U. S. C. T.

B. F. Stauber, 20 Pa. C.

H. Schulter, 43 N. Y.

L. D. Seely, 45 Pa.

Frank Stevens, 12 Pa. V. R. C.

A. F. Septon, 8 Iowa C.

T. D. Scofield, 27 Mich.

C. B. Sanders, 30 U. S. C. T.

P. A. Simondson, 23 U. S. C. T.

N. W. Shaefer, 24 Ind. C.

H. S. Tainter, 82 N. Y.

D. Tanner, 118 Ill.

H. V. Tompkins, 59 N. Y.

B. W. Trout, 106 Pa.

J. S. Tompson, 10 Vt.

C. W. Wilcox, 9 N. H.

J. C. Watson, 126 Ohio.

F. M. Woodruff, 76 N. Y.

Geo. Weddle, 144 Ohio.

C. W. Woodrow, 19 Iowa.

H. H. Willis, 40 N. Y.

J. Winship, 88 Ill.

R. Wilson, 113 Ill.

B. F. Whitten, 9 Me.

J. W. Warren, 1 Wis. C.

W. Williams, 8 Mich. C.

T. H. Ward, 59 U. S. C. T.

J. Wheaton, 59 U. S. C. T.

B. W. Whittemore, 5 N. Y. C.

H. A. Wentworth, 14 N. Y. A.

W. H. Walker, 4 Ohio.

E. S. Wilson, 1 Mass. C.

D. H. Warren, A. Surg. 8 I. C.

J. B. Warner, 8 Mich. C.

G. Williams, 8 Mich. C.

J. Winters, 72 Ohio.

J. Warner, 33 N. J.

J. F. Wheeler, 149 N. Y.

F. Waidmann, 16 Iowa.

J. Walker, 8 Tenn.

T. A. Weesner, 14 & 15 Ill.

G. J. West, 6 Conn.

D. H. Wing, 14 N. Y. Art.

R. P. Wilson, 5 U. S. C.

E. C. Taw, 67 N. Y.

J. H. York, 63 Ind.

W. J. Young, 111 Ill.

A. Young, 4 Pa. C.

T. P. Young, 4 Ky.

Aaron Zeigler, 7 Pa. V. R. C.

A. Zimm, 15 Iowa.

C. Zobel, 15 N. Y. A.

G. H. Hastings, 24 N. Y. In. Bt.

NAVAL OFFICERS.

W. E. H. Fintress, A. V. Lt.

Edw. L. Haines, Act. M.

J. F. D. Robinson, Act. M.

E. H. Sears, Ast. P. M.

Robt. M. Clark, Act. Ensg.

Simon Strunk, Act. Ensg.

E. W. Dayton, Act. Ensg.

Thos. Brown, Act. M. M.

Wm. H. Fogg, Act. M. M.

Chas. A. Stewart, Act. M. M.

Dan'l Ward, Act. M. M.

B. Johnson, 2 Act. Eng.

Jas. McCaulley, 2 Act. Eng.

Jno. B. Dick, 2 Act. Eng.

A. D. Renshaw, 3 Act. Eng.

Jno. Mee, 3 Act. Eng.

Ch. McCormick, 3 Act. Eng.

Sam. B. Ellis, 3 Act. Eng.

Henry K. Stever, 3 Act. Eng.

E. J. Robinson, Pilot.

The End